# CHARMING

C000321299

# FRANCE

# CHARMING SMALL HOTEL GUIDES

# FRANCE

EDITED BY

Andrew Duncan

---

### ★ EXCLUSIVE READER OFFER ★

Hotels marked with an asterisk ★ have exclusive offers
for *Charming Small Hotel Guide* readers. These range
from free drinks on arrival or at meals to discounts at
certain times of the year. To find out more, contact the
hotel in advance. Be sure to take your copy of the guide
with you. Some proprietors may wish to endorse your
copy with an unobtrusive mark on the final page to
indicate that the offer has been redeemed.

---

DUNCAN PETERSEN

HUNTER
PUBLISHING

New edition, 2001

Copyright © Duncan Petersen Publishing Ltd 1988, 1989, 1990, 1991, 1992, 1994, 1997, 1998, 1999, 2001

Tenth edition

Conceived, designed and produced by
Duncan Petersen Publishing Ltd

**Editor** Andrew Duncan
**Revisions editor** Nicola Davies
**Art director** Mel Petersen
**Designers** Chris Foley and Beverley Stewart
**Editorial director** Andrew Duncan

This edition published in the UK and Commonwealth 2001 by
Duncan Petersen Publishing Ltd,
31 Ceylon Road, London W14 OPY

Sales representation and distribution in the U.K. and Ireland by
Portfolio Books Limited
Unit 5, Perivale Industrial Park
Horsenden Lane South
Greenford, UB6 7RL
Tel: 0208 997 9000 Fax: 0208 997 9097
E-mail: sales@portfoliobooks.com

ISBN 1-903301-13-0

A CIP catalogue record for this book is available
from the British Library

AND

Published in the USA 2001 by
Hunter Publishing Inc.,
130 Campus Drive, Edison, N.J. 08818
Tel (732) 225 1900 Fax (732) 417 0482

ISBN 1-58843-113-4

Typeset by Duncan Petersen Publishing Ltd
Printed by G. Canale & Co SpA, Turin

# Contents

# *Introduction*

**This new edition**
It's over twelve years now since we first set out to identify
the hotels that help to make travelling in France such a
special experience. Then, we were looking for the 300 most
captivating auberges, châteaux, moulins and chalets in the
land. After our recent major overhaul of the guide, we now
have an expanded coverage of over 360 hotels, with
photographs of more than 120. We've achieved this by
organising the book differently, as explained on page 8.

As usual, the guide has been updated for the new year,
but only a few hotels have had to be replaced because of
declining standards, poor readers' reports or closure,
although several hotels have undergone a change of owner.

**Charming and small**
There really are relatively few *genuine* charming small
hotels. Unlike other guides, we are particularly fussy about
size, rarely straying over 20 bedrooms. If a hotel has more
than that, it needs to have the *feel* of a much smaller place
to be in this guide.

We attach more importance to size than other guides
because we think that unless a hotel is small, it cannot give
a genuinely personal welcome, or make you feel like an
individual, rather than just a guest. For what we mean by a
personal welcome, see below.

Unlike other guides, we often rule out places that have
great qualities, but are nonetheless no more nor less than –
hotels. Our hotels are all special in some way.

We think that we have a much clearer idea than other
guides of what is special and what is not; and we think we
apply these criteria more consistently than other guides
because we are a small and personally managed company
rather than a bureaucracy. We have a small team of like-
minded inspectors, chosen by the editor and thoroughly
rehearsed in recognizing what we want. While we very
much appreciate readers' reports – see below – they are not
our main source of information.

Last but by no means least, we're independent – there's
no payment for inclusion.

**So what exactly do we look for?**
• An attractive, preferably peaceful setting.
• A building that is either handsome or interesting or historic, or at least with a distinct character.
• Ideally, we look for adequate space, but on a human
scale: we don't go for places that rely on grandeur, or that
have pretensions that could intimidate.
• Decoration must be harmonious and in good taste, and
the furnishings and facilities comfortable and well maintained. We like to see interesting antique furniture that is

there because it can be used, not simply revered.

• The proprietors and staff need to be dedicated and thoughtful, offering a personal welcome, *without being intrusive*. The guest needs to feel like an individual.

**Whole-page entries**
We rarely see all of these qualities together in one place; but our warmest recommendations – whole page, with photograph – usually lack only one or two of these qualities.

**Small entries**
Lack of space means that some hotel entries have shorter descriptions and no photograph. We consider all these hotels worthy to be in the guide.

**Pet hates**
We are, naturally, enthusiastic about French hotels in general. But we are not blind to their faults. Here is a list of our current pet hates.

**The 'confused' booking** You make a booking, even send a deposit, and on arrival find that you're not expected. If you can't be accommodated and are put up in some other house in the village, there is the teeniest suspicion that what is at work is not confusion but greed.

**The saggy bed** As we've observed in our British edition, it's the easiest thing in the world to fail to spot the gradual decay of a bed unless you take the precaution of occasionally testing every one in the house.

**The dreary breakfast** We know that the French aren't very keen on breakfast, but hoteliers ought to be aware that many other people are  – especially when travelling, and a good start to the day is important.

**The second-class pensionnaires' meals** If you're tempted to stay on pension or demi-pension terms, be sure you know what choice of dishes will be open. There may be none at all; or you may be confined to the cheapest menu.

**The windowless garden room** Quite a few French country hotels accommodate some or all of their guests in single-storey outbuildings with glazed doors opening on to the garden or the pool. And quite a few provide no ventilation other than those doors, which most travellers would naturally be reluctant to leave open at night.

**The rough deal for vegetarians** The acceptance of vegetarianism in France is still very limited, and progressing very slowly. Too many cooks, waiters and proprietors of small hotels find it hard to conceal the fact that they think vegetarians are mad, and a great nuisance.

**No fear or favour**
Unlike many guides, there is no payment for inclusion. The

selection is made *entirely* independently.

## Check the price first

See page 9 for the system we adopt in giving prices; to avoid unpleasant surprises, always double check the price at time of booking. Sometimes they go up after we've gone to press, sometimes there is a seasonal or other variation from the printed version.

## How to find an entry

In this guide, the entries are arranged in geographical groups. First, the whole country is divided into three major sections; we start with Northern France and proceed to Central and finally Southern France. Within these sections, the entries are dealt with in regions consisting of groups of départements. See page 5 for a list of the regions we have used.

Each regional section follows a set sequence:

> • First comes an Area introduction – an overview of that region, incorporating (if there's space) a summary of the tourist highlights. Under the heading 'Contenders', we list hotels that have failed to make an entry this year, but which we believe to be strong candidates for an entry in future. These listings may be useful if recommended hotels are full, or if there are no recommendations in a particular area. We particularly welcome reports on these hotels.

> • Then come the main, full-page entries for that region, arranged in alphabetical order by town. These are generally the hotels that we judge most

> • Finally come the shorter, quarter-page entries for that region, similarly arranged alphabetically by town. These are generally not as special as the hotels given a full-page entry; but don't disregard them – they are still hotels we would happily stay at, and many are clear candidates for 'promotion' in later editions.

To find a hotel in a particular area, simply browse through the headings at the top of the pages until you find that area – or use the maps following this introduction to locate the appropriate pages. The maps show not only the place-name under which each hotel appears, but also the page number of the entry.

# *Introduction*

To locate a specific hotel or a hotel in a specific place, use the indexes at the back, which list the entries alphabetically, first by name and then by place-name.

**How to read an entry**

At the top of each entry is a coloured bar highlighting the name of the town or village where the establishment is located, along with a categorization which gives some clue to its character.

**Fact boxes**

The fact box given for each hotel follows a standard pattern; the explanation that follows is for full entries – short, quarter-page entries have less detailed fact boxes.

Under **Tel** we give the full 10-digit telephone number. When dialling from outside France, begin with the international code 00 33, then dial the number given in the guide, remembering to drop the first zero.We also give **Fax** numbers, E-mail and website addresses where available.

Under **Location** we give information on the setting of the hotel and on its car parking arrangements, as well as pointers to help you find it. It is worth bearing in mind that many of our hotels are in remote spots where a large-scale road map is more-or-less essential for reliable route-finding.

Under **Meals** we list the meals available.

**Prices**

In this new edition of France we have coded the prices into bands. These prices range from the cheapest single room in low season to the most expensive double room in high season.

| | |
|---|---|
| **F** | under 600F |
| **FF** | 600F-1,000F |
| **FFF** | 1,000F-1,500F |
| **FFFF** | over 1,500F |

Do ask proprietors about special reductions for length of stay, for extra beds in the room or for children.

If the room price we give includes breakfast, we say so; otherwise, space permitting, we normally give the price band of breakfast separately; where it is not given, allow 40F to 80F, according to the room price. We then give the prices of other meals, concentrating on fixed-price menus, or of prices for a room plus meals – either for dinner, bed and breakfast (DB&B), or for full board (FB) – all meals included. All these meal-inclusive prices are **per person**. Prices includes tax and service.

Menus
**F**       under 100F
**FF**      100F-350F
**FFF**     over 350F

   Wherever possible we have given prices for 2001, but in some cases these were not available when the guide went to press. Bear in mind also that proprietors may change their prices from one year to another by more than the rate of inflation, particularly if the hotel has been upgraded in some important respect. Always check when booking.

   Under **Rooms** we summarize the number and style of bedrooms available. Our lists of facilities in bedrooms cover only mechanical gadgets, and not ornaments such as flowers or consumables such as toiletries or free drinks.

Under **Facilities** we list public rooms and then outdoor and sporting facilities which are either part of the hotel or immediately on hand; facilities in the vicinity of the hotel but not directly connected with it (for example, a nearby golf course) are not listed here, though they sometimes feature at the end of the main description in the **Nearby** section, which presents interesting things to see or do in the locality.

We use the following abbreviations for **Credit cards:**

   AE   American Express
   DC   Diners Club
   MC   MasterCard (Access/Eurocard)
   V    Visa (Barclaycard/Bank Americard/Carte Bleue etc)
Some hotels accept other credit cards as well as those listed in the guide.

**Pets**
Quite a few French hotels accept pets, especially small ones (with a charge), but always check with the hotel when booking.

The final entry in a fact box is normally the name of the proprietor(s); but where the hotel is run by a manager we give his or her name instead.

Please write and tell us about your experiences of small hotels, guest-houses and inns, whether good or bad, whether listed in this edition or not. As well as hotels in France, we are interested in hotels in Britain and Ireland, Italy, Spain, Austria, Germany, Switzerland and the USA. We assume that reporters have no objections to our publishing their views unpaid, either verbatim or in edited form.

Readers who report regularly and reliably may be invited to join our Travellers' Panel. Members give us notice of their own travel plans; we suggest hotels that they might inspect, and contribute to the cost of accommodation.

**The address to write to is:**

Duncan Petersen Publishing Ltd
31 Ceylon Road, London W14 0PY, England.

**Checklist**

Please use a separate sheet of paper for each report; include your name and address on each report.

Your reports will be received with particular pleasure if they are typed, and if they are organized under the following headings:

Name of establishment
Town or village it is in, or nearest
Full address, including post code
Date and duration of visit
The building and setting
The public rooms
The bedrooms and bathrooms
Comfort (chairs, beds, heat, light, hot water)
Standards of maintenance and housekeeping
Atmosphere, welcome and service
Food
Value for money

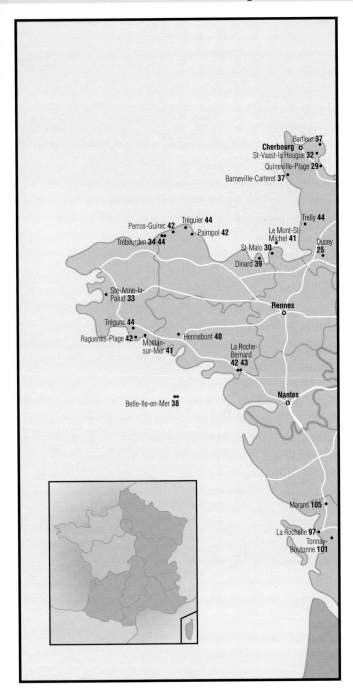

Barfleur **37**
**Cherbourg**
St-Vaast-la-Hougue **32**
Quineville-Plage **29**
Barneville-Carteret **37**

Trelly **44**

Perros-Guirec **42**    Tréguier **44**
                Paimpol **42**
Trébeurden **34 44**                Le Mont-St-
                                Michel **41**    Ducey
                            St-Malo **30**        **25**
                        Dinard **39**

Ste-Anne-la-
Palud **33**                            **Rennes**

Trégunc **44**
Raguenès-Plage **42**        Hennebont **40**
        Moëlan-
        sur-Mer **41**        La Roche-
                    Bernard
                    **42 43**

                            **Nantes**

Belle-Ile-en-Mer **38**

                        Marans **105**

                        La Rochelle **97**
                            Tonnay-
                        Boutonne **101**

# Hotel location maps

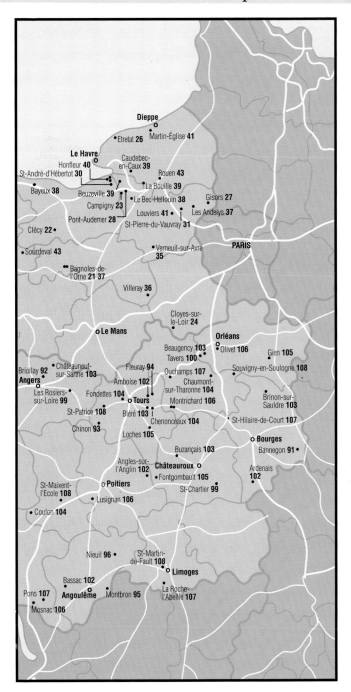

**Dieppe**

Martin-Église **41**

Etretat **26**

**Le Havre**

Honfleur **40**

Caudebec-en-Caux **39**

St-André-d'Hébertot **30**

Rouen **43**

La Bouille **39**

Bayeux **38**

Beuzeville **39**

Le Bec-Hellouin **38**

Gisors **27**

Campigny **23**

Louviers **41**

Les Andelys **37**

Pont-Audemer **28**

St-Pierre-du-Vauvray **31**

Clécy **22**

**PARIS**

Sourdeval **43**

Verneuil-sur-Avre **35**

Bagnoles-de-l'Orne **21 37**

Villeray **36**

Cloyes-sur-le-Loir **24**

**Le Mans**

**Orléans**

Beaugency **103**

Olivet **106**

Tavers **100**

Gien **105**

Briollay **92**

Châteauneuf-sur-Sarthe **103**

Fleuray **94**

Ouchamps **107**

Souvigny-en-Sologne **108**

**Angers**

Amboise **102**

Chaumont-sur-Tharonne **104**

Les Rosiers-sur-Loire **99**

Fondettes **104**

Brinon-sur-Sauldre **103**

St-Patrice **108**

**Tours**

Montrichard **106**

Bléré **103**

St-Hilaire-de-Court **107**

Chinon **93**

Chenonceaux **104**

Loches **105**

**Bourges**

Buzançais **103**

Bannegon **91**

Angles-sur-l'Anglin **102**

**Châteauroux**

Ardenais **102**

St-Maixent-l'Ecole **108**

Fontgombault **105**

**Poitiers**

St-Chartier **99**

Lusignan **106**

Coulon **104**

Nieuil **96**

St-Martin-du-Fault **108**

Bassac **102**

**Limoges**

Pons **107**

**Angoulême**

Montbron **95**

La Roche-l'Abeille **107**

Mosnac **106**

13

# *Hotel location maps*

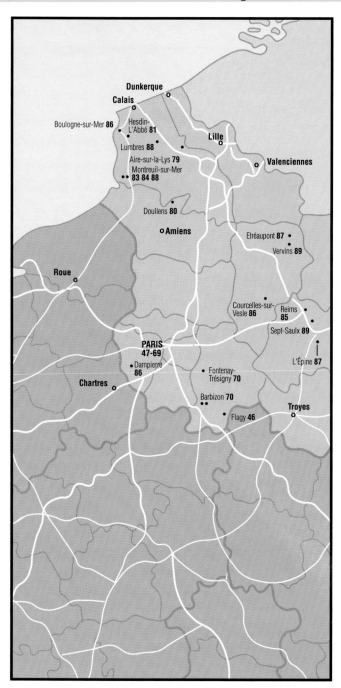

Dunkerque

Calais

Boulogne-sur-Mer **86**

Hesdin-
L'Abbé **81**

Lille

Lumbres **88**

Aire-sur-la-Lys **79**
Montreuil-sur-Mer
**83 84 88**

Valenciennes

Doullens **80**

Amiens

Etréaupont **87**

Vervins **89**

Roue

Courcelles-sur-
Vesle **86**

Reims
**85**

Sept-Saulx **89**

PARIS
**47-69**

L'Épine **87**

Dampierre
**86**

Fontenay-
Trésigny **70**

Chartres

Barbizon **70**

Troyes

Flagy **46**

14

# Hotel location maps

Futeau **87**

Metz

Marlenheim **82**

Nancy

Strasbourg

Ribeauvillé **88**

Lapoutroie **88**

Artzenheim **86**

Kaysersberg **87**

# *Hotel location maps*

**Dordogne**
Buisson-de-Cadouin **135**
Domme **150**
Eyzies-de-Tayac **138 151**
Floriment-Gaumier **139**
Lalinde **152**
Razac d'Eymet **153**
St-Cyprien **154**
Sarlat **155**
Trémolat **149**
Vézac **156**

Angoulême ○
St-Saud-Lacoussière **147**
Vieux-Mareuil **156**
Champagnac-de-Belair **136**
Brantôme **133 134**
Ribérac **154**
Périgueux ○
Coly **137**
Pauillac **143**
Bordeaux ○
St-Émilion **155**
Dégagnac **150**
Touzac **156**
Mauroux **141**
Mimizan **142**
Puymirol **153**
Sabres **154**
Poudenas **153**
Condom **150**
Soustons **156**
Hossegor **151**
Plaisance **153**
Montfort-en-Chalosse **152**
Auch ○
Escos **151**
St-Jean-de-Luz **155**
Pau ○
Sare **148**
Aïnhoa **132**
St-Etienne-de-Baïgorry **146**
Lestelle-Bétharram **152**

# Hotel location maps

St-Florentin **129**

Chatillon-sur-Seine **126**

La Celle-St-Cyr **124**

Chablis **124**

Tonnerre **130**

Auxerre **112**

Chassignelles **125**

Mailly-le-Château **117**

Vézelay **122**

Avallon **113 123**

**Côte d'Or**
Aloxe-Corton **110**
Arnay-le-Duc **123**
Châteauneuf **125**
Curtil-Vergy **127**
Gevrey-Chambertin **115**
Meursault **129**

Chagny **124**

Mercurey **120**

Givry **128**

Charolles **125**

Fleurville **127**

Poisson **121**

Cluny **126**

**Mâcon**

Igé **128**

Marcigny **119**

Bagnols **123**

**Clermont-Ferrand**

Chonas-l'Amballan **126**

Condrieu **127**

Valence **213**

Lamastre **206**

Rochegude **209**

St-Restitut **211**

Vallon-Pont-d'Arc **201**

Cornillon **176**

La Favède **205**

Villeneuve-lès-Avignon **213 214**

Madières **187**

Le Pontet **191**

Noves **207**

**Montpellier**

Olargues **208**

**Toulouse**

Carcassonne **203**

**Narbonne**

Les Stes-Maries-de-la-Mer **198**

Ornaisons **208**

**Perpignan**

St-Pierre-dels-Forcats **210**

Llo **186**

Céret **174 204**

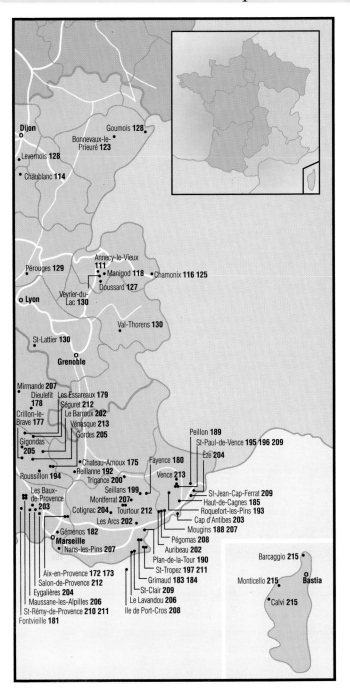

Dijon
Goumois **128**
Bonnevaux-le-
Prieuré **123**
Levernois **128**
Chaublanc **114**

Pérouges **129**
Annecy-le-Vieux **111**
Manigod **118**
Chamonix **116 125**
Veyrier-du-Lac **130**
Doussard **127**
Lyon
Val-Thorens **130**
St-Lattier **130**
Grenoble
Mirmande **207**
Dieulefit **178**
Les Essareaux **179**
Séguret **212**
Crillon-le-Brave **177**
Le Barroux **202**
Vénasque **213**
Gordes **205**
Peillon **189**
St-Paul-de-Vence **195 196 209**
Gigondas **205**
Èze **204**
Chateau-Arnoux **175**
Fayence **180**
Roussillon **194**
Reillanne **192**
Vence **213**
Trigance **200**
Seillans **199**
St-Jean-Cap-Ferrat **209**
Les Baux-de-Provence **203**
Montferrat **207**
Haut-de-Cagnes **185**
Cotignac **204**
Tourtour **212**
Roquefort-les-Pins **193**
Les Arcs **202**
Cap d'Antibes **203**
Gémenos **182**
Mougins **188 207**
Marseille
Pégomas **208**
Nans-les-Pins **207**
Auribeau **202**
Plan-de-la-Tour **190**
Barcaggio **215**
St-Tropez **197 211**
Aix-en-Provence **172 173**
Grimaud **183 184**
Monticello **215**
Bastia
Salon-de-Provence **212**
St-Clair **209**
Eygalières **204**
Calvi **215**
Maussane-les-Alpilles **206**
Le Lavandou **206**
St-Rémy-de-Provence **210 211**
Ile de Port-Cros **208**
Fontvieille **181**

19

# The North-West

## Area introduction

The North-west is familiar territory to many British visitors. Lush Normandy, full of apple orchards and contented cows, is close enough to be convenient for a weekend break, and many people who live in the west of Britain prefer to use the Normandy ports when aiming further south. Further to the west, Brittany is bucket-and-spade country, and has much in common with Cornwall – a dramatic coastline, and a vigorous climate. On the border between the two regions is the most popular tourist sight in France: Mont St Michel.

### Contenders in the North-west

**Agneaux, Château d'Agneaux** 02.33.57.65.88 Severe-looking little manor house, immaculately furnished.

**Balisne, Moulin de Balisne** 02.32.32.03.48 'Well-restored water mill' with good furnishings and extensive lawn.

**Bazouges, Hostellerie de Mirwault** 02.43.07.13.17 'Relaxing' English-run Logis with gardens overlooking the Mayenne.

**Bénouville, La Pommeraie** 02.31.44.62.43 Renowned restaurant with modern bedrooms in new building in grounds.

**Brélidy, Château de Brélidy** 02.96.95.69.38 Stern little stone manor house in peaceful setting.

**Concarneau, Le Galion** 02.98.97.30.16 Cosily beamed restaurant with rooms in old town, with neat modern rooms across the way.

**Creully, Hostellerie Saint Martin** 02.31.80.10.11 Shuttered Logis on village square with charming vaulted restaurant serving good-value menus.

**Honfleur, Hostellerie Lechat** 02.31.89.23.85 Smartly renovated inn, with bold colour schemes; central – parking not easy.

**Lisieux, La Ferme des Poiriers Roses** 02.31.64.72.14 Superbly furnished timbered house in a beautiful garden doing bed and wonderful breakfast.

**Mür-de-Bretagne, Auberge Grand'Maison** 02.96.28.51.10 One-star restaurant with rooms – some quite swish, though winning no prizes for taste.

**Percy, La Voisinière** 02.33.61.18.47 A pair of rustic cottages with prettily furnished rooms, in a beautiful flowery garden with pond.

**Pleugueneuc, Château de la Motte Beaumanoir** 02.99.69.46.01 Elegantly decorated 15thC château in ornamental grounds.

**Plouharnel, Les Ajoncs d'Or** 02.97.52.32.02 Cottagey stone-built Logis in shady, flowery garden.

**Plozevet, Moulin de Brenizenec** 02.98.91.30.33 Traditionally furnished old water mill in wooded grounds.

**Pluherlin, Château de Talhouet** 02.97.43.34.72 Slightly severe 16th/17thC château in grassy grounds, tastefully furnished and run as a B&B.

**Pornichet, Hôtel Sud Bretagne** 02.40.11.65.00 Smooth, luxurious seaside hotel (close to beach) with attractive garden.

**Roscoff, Le Brittany** 02.98.69.70.78 Neatly furnished stone manor house with particularly attractive restaurant, and indoor pool.

**St-Briac-sur-Mer, Manoir de la Duchée** 02.99.88.00.02 Little manor house B&B deep in countryside, handsomely furnished.

**St-Pierre-de-Plesguen, Le Petit Moulin du Rouvre** 02.99.73.85.84 Neatly restored 17thC water mill by a small lake.

# The North-West

**Country hotel, Bagnoles-de-l'Orne**

## Manoir du Lys

The addition of an outdoor swimming-pool has further enhanced this delightful, typically Norman half-timbered hunting lodge, with geraniums at its foot and dripping from its balconies. It was reopened as a hotel by the Quintons in 1985 after a long period of disuse, and many improvements have been introduced. The new building is harmonious, and bedrooms are very attractive – all spacious and well equipped, with stylish furnishings far removed from the French norm. The de-luxe rooms tend to be long and narrow. Most have balconies overlooking the gardens.

Marie-France oversees the smart dining-rooms (also overlooking the gardens, through floor-to-ceiling windows) where you can enjoy her son Franck's delicious Michelin starred cuisine, which is rooted in local tradition but acknowledges modern preferences. In good weather you can dine outside. There is also a polished little bar/sitting-room with a huge open fire and a grand piano (played on Friday nights). The Quintons are warm hosts and organise popular educational 'mushroom' weekends, during which up to 120 varieties may be picked in the surrounding woods; English-language tuition can be laid on.

**Nearby** Andaines forest – walking, riding, cycling.

La Croix Gauthier, Route de Juvigny, 61140 Bagnoles-de-l'Orne
**Tel** 02.33.37.80.69
**Fax** 02.33.30.05.80
**Location** in middle of countryside in forest of Andaines; with car parking
**Meals** breakfast, lunch, dinner
**Prices** rooms F-FF; menus FF
**Rooms** 25 double, 23 with bath, 2 with shower; 3 suites; all have phone, TV, minibar
**Facilities** dining-room, sitting-room/bar; billiards; tennis court, swimming-pool
**Credit cards** AE, DC, MC, V
**Children** welcome; special menu 80F
**Disabled** 1 bedroom
**Pets** dogs accepted in bedrooms only 35F
**Closed** 6 Jan to 14 Feb; Sun evening and Mon from Nov to Easter
**Proprietor** Marie-France and Paul Quinton

# The North-West

**Converted mill, Clécy**

# Hostellerie du Moulin du Vey

Just when we began to wonder about this old, creeper-clad water-mill, readers' reports arrived to reassure us about its continuing appeal. 'Bright, tastefully decorated rooms, excellent restaurant, friendly service.' 'Good for an overnight stop or short break.'

The Moulin is at the heart of some of the best scenery in the region, where the river Orne has carved a majestic valley between green, rolling hills. It is within easy driving distance of the ferry at Caen, and makes an attractive first- or last-night stop.

Both the buildings and the gardens are beautifully kept, and there is a pleasant waterside terrace for eating and drinking, with a garden beyond. Food in the half-timbered, rather barn-like restaurant, just across the courtyard from the main building, is carefully prepared and served, and the less expensive menus are sound value. Bedrooms are comfortable, furnished simply but with touches of style, and reasonably priced. Some rooms are in annexes: the Manoir de Placy, 400 metres away, and the Relais de Surosne, 3 km away on the other side of the village – a peaceful, small Gothic-style house with a lush garden.

**Nearby** Suisse Normande region; Thury-Harcourt (10 km) – ruined château; Falaise (30 km) – castle; Caen.

Le Vey 14570 Clécy
**Tel** 02.31.69.71.08
**Fax** 02.31.69.14.14
**Location** 2 km E of Clécy and 35 kms S of Caen; with river terrace and car parking
**Meals** breakfast, lunch, dinner
**Prices** rooms FF; menus FF-FFF
**Rooms** 17 double (7 twin) all with bath; 2 family rooms, one with bath, one with shower; all rooms have central heating, phone, colour TV

**Facilities** dining-room, banqueting-room, conference room
**Credit cards** AE, DC, MC, V
**Children** accepted
**Disabled** no special facilities
**Pets** accepted but not in dining-room
**Closed** Dec and Jan
**Proprietor** Denise Leduc

# The North-West

**Country hotel, Campigny**

## Le Petit Coq aux Champs

A thatched house with its own heliport – it sounds unlikely, but convention counts for little at this smart, secluded retreat, amid rolling meadows and sweeping forests in the Risle valley. Le Petit Coq offers an intriguing mixture of the rustic, the sophisticated and the downright idiosyncratic – a cocktail that may be too heady for some, to judge by our empty postbag.

The building, mostly 19th century, has two main wings with a spacious, airy, modern extension in between. The style varies considerably – modern cane furniture in the large sitting-room, while antiques predominate in the restaurant, which has a huge open fireplace at one end. An intimate piano bar has been squeezed into the new building. The bedrooms are all furnished and arranged in different ways, some brightly coloured, others more restrained; none is particularly large.

Jean-Marie Huard, who has returned to his Norman roots after some years in highly reputed restaurants in Paris, pays serious attention to detail, presentation and local tradition in his cooking – with impressive results.

**Nearby** fishing, golf; Pont-Audemer – half-timbered houses, church of Saint-Ouen; Honfleur (30 km) – old port.

Campigny 27500 Pont-Audemer
**Tel** 02.32.41.04.19
**Fax** 02.32.56.06.25
**Location** in countryside, 6 km S of Pont-Audemer; in gardens with ample car parking
**Meals** breakfast, lunch, dinner
**Prices** rooms F-FF; children under 12 sharing parents' room, free; breakfast F; menu FF
**Rooms** 12 double (4 twin), one family room, one suite, all with bath; all rooms have central heating, phone, TV, hairdrier
**Facilities** sitting-room, 4 dining-rooms, bar; swimming-pool **Credit cards** AE, DC, MC, V **Children** very welcome
**Disabled** dining-rooms and 8 bedrooms are on ground floor **Pets** welcome
**Closed** January
**Proprietors** Fabienne Desmonts and Jean-Marie Huard

# *The North-West*

# Le St-Jacques

An old coaching inn, with restaurant, 'Le P'tit Bistrot', below. Bedrooms (at the back and looking over the garden) have been smartly done out in designer fabrics and cherry-wood reproduction antiques.

The dining-room looks out over the garden and is pleasantly intimate. But in good weather meals are served in the shade of the trees in the garden, which is a lush expanse leading down to the banks of the little Loir.

Some readers record a poor reception, a mediocre bedroom, and disappointing food. But other reporters have been much happier, and we retain a soft spot for the place.

For the moment, look before you book – and let us know your conclusions.

**Nearby** Châteaudun (10 km) – feudal château; Vendôme – la Trinité, Porte St Georges; Beaugency (45 km) – bridge, keep.

Place du Marché aux Oeufs
28220 Cloyes-sur-le-Loir
**Tel** 02.37.98.40.08
**Fax** 02.37.98.32.63
**Location** in village, 28 km NE of Vendôme; with garden and car parking
**Meals** breakfast, lunch, dinner
**Prices** rooms F; breakfast F; menus FF
**Rooms** 22 double, 18 with bath, 4 with shower (5 twin); one family room; all rooms have central heating, phone,

TV
**Facilities** dining-room, sitting-room, bar
**Credit cards** MC, V
**Children** welcome
**Disabled** lift/elevator
**Pets** not accepted
**Closed** Nov to Mar
**Proprietor** Eric Thureau

# The North-West

**Village hotel, Ducey**

## Auberge de la Sélune

We revisited recently and found that extensive renovations have changed the character of this redoubtable small hotel. It used to be old fashioned in a conventional sort of way. Now the downstairs, at least, is modern in a somewhat soulless way. The new glass and metal lobby connecting the two old buildings might look better in an airport hotel, and the emerald green of the furnishings won't appeal to all our readers. Nonetheless, it's still highly recommendable, and we still get plenty of readers' letters saying just that. Of the two conventional dining-rooms, one is less formal than the other and gives on to a new terrace with tables and chairs, from which you can enjoy the garden with the river bubbling in the background.

Bedrooms are all different, with bright colour schemes and pleasant, but relatively simple furnishings. No 36 has a fine view over the garden. Bathrooms are dull, but practical. We can't fault this as a stopover, prices being particularly honest – if not good value – and staff – on our visit – dutiful and friendly. The food is well above average, with *pie au crabe* still a *piéce de résistance*. Breakfast is better than the norm. Ask about the salmon fishing.
**Nearby** Avranches (10 km) – museum; Le Mont-St-Michel.

2 Rue St-Germain 50220
Ducey
**Tel** 02.33.48.53.62
**Fax** 02.33.48.90.30
**E-mail** girres@club.internet.fr
**Location** by river in village, on N176 11 km SE of Avranches; with small garden and some car parking
**Meals** breakfast, lunch, dinner
**Prices** rooms F; breakfast F; menus F-FF
**Rooms** 19 double, all with bath (5 twin); one single; one family room with bath; all rooms have central heating, phone; TV on request
**Facilities** sitting-room, bar, conference room; salmon fishing
**Credit cards** DC, MC, V
**Children** accepted
**Disabled** no special facilities
**Pets** not accepted
**Closed** mid-Jan to mid-Feb
**Proprietor** Jean-Pierre Girres

# The North-West

**Seaside resort hotel, Etretat**

# Le Donjon

This extraordinary little hotel set on a steep hill used to be one of our favourite places for a short break (it's only half an hour from Le Havre). Recent reports suggest, however, that standards of service and food may no longer match the high prices charged.

It is a former hilltop castle, with venerable origins and a secret subterranean channel to the sea, now safely surrounded by the leafy suburbs of Etretat. Inside, all is bright and light, decorated with a Parisian sophistication by Madame Abo-Dib. The dining-room, candle-lit and mirrored, is wonderfully atmospheric; the cocktail bar overlooks Etretat's famous cliffs; and there is an impeccably kept small swimming pool surrounded by sunshades and loungers. But it is perhaps the eight bedrooms which best show off Madame Abo-Dib's creative skills: all are different, and immensely stylish. The largest, almost circular, has an Eastern theme, with black chintz drapes and gigantic mirror; another is in bright Impressionist hues, and one has a large fireplace for real log fires. Bathrooms, some in the turrets, are spacious and elegant in pure white; five have whirlpool baths.

The menu offers rather more possibilities for *pensionnaires*, with the option of choosing dishes from the *carte*, as well as the four-course *menu du Gentleman*. We welcome further reports.

**Nearby** Etretat – cliffs; Fécamp (17km) – Benedictine distillery.

Chemin de Saint Clair
76790 Etretat
**Tel** 02.35.27.08.23
**Fax** 02.35.29.92.24
**E-mail** ledonjon@wanadoo.fr
**Location** on hill behind resort, 28 km N of Le Havre; with garden and car parking
**Meals** breakfast, lunch, dinner
**Prices** DB&B FF; menus FF
**Rooms** 10 double, 9 with bath, one with shower (5 with whirlpool baths); all have central heating, phone, TV
**Facilities** dining-room, sitting-room; swimming-pool
**Credit cards** AE, V
**Children** accepted
**Pets** accepted
**Disabled** access difficult
**Closed** never
**Proprietor** Mme Abo-Dib

# *The North-West*

**Château hotel, Gisors**

## Château de la Râpée

'A comfortable stay, although we found the decoration, with carpets for wallcoverings, rather idiosyncratic,' commented one reporter on this 19th-century Gothic mansion. Well, yes: perhaps we should have warned about the carpet; but it is more-or-less confined (along with the antlers) to the reception area. The rest of this grandly conceived but small-scale period piece is less eccentric.

The château lies in a peaceful setting at the end of a long, rutted forest track from Bazincourt. Inside, original features have been carefully preserved and, although the public areas are rather dark in places, the house has been pleasantly furnished with antiques and reproductions. Some of the spacious, calm bedrooms are quite stately, with fine country views, plenty of antiques and creaky wooden floors; others verge on the eccentric (but are antler-free). Immediately next to the house is a small, pleasant flower-garden.

Pascal and Philippe Bergeron take their cooking seriously – classic dishes, with some regional influences and occasional original flourishes. Further reports would be welcome.

**Nearby** Gisors – castle; Jouy-sous-Thelle (25 km) – church.

Bazincourt-sur-Epte 27140 Gisors
**Tel** 02.32.55.11.61
**Fax** 02.32.55.95.65
**Location** in countryside 4 km NW of Gisors; in small park with ample car parking
**Meals** breakfast, lunch, dinner
**Prices** rooms F; apartment FF; menus FF
**Rooms** 20 double, 16 with bath, 4 with shower (5 twin); 2 rooms form an apartment; all rooms have central heating, phone
**Facilities** sitting-room, 2 dining-rooms, bar, banqueting-room; riding stables next door
**Credit cards** AE, DC, V
**Children** by arrangement
**Disabled** no special facilities
**Pets** small ones accepted
**Closed** Feb and mid to end Aug; restaurant Wed
**Proprietors** M. and Mme Bergeron

# *The North-West*

| Town inn, Pont-Audemer |
| --- |

# Auberge du Vieux Puits ★

Our latest report on this wonderful, half-timbered, 17thC building is short and to the point: 'Excellent.' It might equally well have said: 'Unchanging'.

Although war-damaged Pont-Audemer still has a charming historic centre, it is rather dwarfed by the nondescript suburbs which have grown up around it. The Vieux Puits shines out like a beacon – all crooked beams and leaded windows. The inside is a medievalist's dream, with its twisting wooden staircases and dark beams hung with shining copper and ancient pewter.

Jacques Foltz and his charming wife bring out the best in the building, by keeping the style simple and restrained. The small, intimate salon and dining-rooms are carefully furnished with antiques, and are decorated with fresh flowers. Three of the bedrooms in the old building have been converted into a family apartment; the other three are quite small but full of character. Across the peaceful, flowery courtyard a new wing provides six bedrooms – smarter and well equipped, but in keeping.

M. Foltz sees the *auberge* very much as a restaurant with rooms, and those who want to stay are encouraged to have dinner. To do so is hardly a penance, given the kitchen's high standards and the interesting dishes on the seasonal menus and *carte*.

**Nearby** Half-timbered houses, church of St-Ouen, the canalised Risle; Honfleur (25 km)

6 Rue Notre-Dame-du-Pré
27500 Pont-Audemer
**Tel** 02.32.41.01.48
**Fax** 02.32.42.37.28
**E-mail** vieux.puits@wanadoo.fr
**Location** near middle of town; with small garden and car parking
**Meals** breakfast, lunch, dinner
**Prices** rooms F; breakfast F; menus FF
**Rooms** 12 double (4 twin), 7 with bath, 4 with shower;

11 have phone
**Facilities** dining-rooms, bar/sitting-area
**Credit cards** MC, V
**Children** welome; special meals on request
**Disabled** 2 ground-floor rooms, specially equipped
**Pets** accepted in dining-room
**Closed** 20 Dec to 28 Jan; Mon and Tue, in low season
**Proprietors** Jacques and Hélène Foltz

# The North-West

**Château hotel, Quineville-Plage**

# Château de Quineville

In a drab seaside resort at the northern end of Utah Beach, this place has all the ingredients of a smart Relais et Château establishment: a fine, classically proportioned 18thC building (once inhabited by James Stuart), set in twelve hectares, with a tower dating back to the middle ages, an ice-house and *pigeonnier* in the grounds; an enticing swimming-pool; a moat with a Giverny-style bridge. But there's a difference: it's not been 'got at'.

Run by a simple family who speak no English, it's both sincere and endearing – if you appreciate the old style of French provincial hotel, warts and all: run-of-the-mill comfort, old fashioned wallpaper, unstinting puce velveteen in the bedrooms.

The graceful dining-rooms, straddling the width of the house, lit from tall windows on both sides, are airy and charming, with original panelling. Here you can savour traditional Normandy *cuisine* while admiring the murals and huge arrangements of artificial flowers.

Forgive the shortcomings in service and housekeeping and rejoice in the quaintness. A cockerel and geese roaming within yards of the house make for bright and early start to the day.

Golf, riding, tennis and sailing are all a short distance away.
**Nearby** Ile de Tatihou; Les Iles St-Marcouf; Barfleur; Normandy beaches, Musée de la Liberté.

50310 Quineville-Plage
**Tel** 02.33.21.42.67
**Fax** 02.33.21.05.79
**Location** 1 km from sea, in village, near church and town hall
**Meals** breakfast, lunch, dinner
**Prices** rooms F-FF; suite FF; breakfast F; menus FFF
**Rooms** 24 double, 19 with bath, 5 with shower; 2 suites; all rooms have phone

**Facilities** 2 sitting-rooms, dining-room, bar; billiards; heated swimming-pool (mid-May to mid-Sept); fishing lake
**Credit cards** AE, MC, V
**Children** accepted
**Disabled** 1 suitable bedroom
**Pets** accepted (F100)
**Closed** 5 Jan to 19 Mar
**Manager** Mme Ledanois

# The North-West

# Auberge du Prieuré

The Millets have extended their country home so vigorously over the last few years we can't help worrying that they might spoil their retreat simply by being too enterprising.

The former 13thC priory, built of pale stone beneath a steep slate roof, has made a delicious little hotel. Inside, it is all beams, stone walls, country antiques and earthy colours. There is a surprisingly big dining-room, with a black and white stone-flagged floor and heavy wood tables gleaming with polish. At one end, there are easy chairs before an open fire. On the first floor, a cosy sitting-room offers books and board games; next door is a billiard room. Bedrooms in the main house are full of character, and attic rooms are no less spacious than those on the first floor, although rather dark. An annexe accommodates about half the rooms (not sound-proofed), but was 'tired and run-down' according to a recent report. Outside, a lush garden is surrounded by Norman orchards and meadows, and features a neat heated pool. Traditional food is prepared by Madame Millet and offers one mid-priced menu and a more expansive *carte*. 'Good value accommodation; stiffly-priced dinner,' says a reporter.

**Nearby** Pont-l'Évêque; Honfleur (15 km); Deauville (20 km).

St-André-d'Hébertot 14130
Pont-l'Évêque
**Tel** 02.31.64.03.03
**Fax** 02.31.64.16.66
**Location** by church in village, S of N175 7 km E of Pont-l'Évêque; in gardens with some private car parking
**Meals** breakfast, lunch, dinner
**Prices** rooms F-FF; breakfast F, meals FF
**Rooms** 13 double (5 twin), 11 with bath; all rooms have central heating, phone, TV,
radio, hairdrier
**Facilities** billiard room, library; swimming-pool
**Credit cards** MC, V
**Children** welcome; special meals
**Disabled** ground-floor rooms
**Pets** 30F supplement
**Closed** restaurant only, Wed
**Proprietors** M. and Mme Millet

# *The North-West*

# Hostellerie St-Pierre

'Perfect for a short break,' says one report on this unusual hotel on the banks of the Seine. Could be; we've always seen it as an ideal stopover – reliably well run, and located only a short drive from the Paris-Rouen motorway. It is a bizarre concoction: a modern building, triangular in plan with a turret on one corner, half-timbered like a traditional Norman manor-house. It sounds naff, but don't dismiss it.

Not the least of the attractions is the cuisine – classical in style but inventive and light in approach, and of excellent quality, with the emphasis on fish and seafood – witness the enormous tank of langoustes and other consumables dominating the heavily decorated dining-room (which has big picture windows looking on to the river). The hotel's other public areas are limited, and solid rather than elegant – the baroque/rococo decoration does not suit all tastes – but the bedrooms are comfortable and well equipped, and many have balconies overlooking the river. (For the full flavour of this eccentric establishment, opt for the top room in the turret, with exposed beams and token four-poster.) The garden, which stretches down to the water's edge, is a relaxing place to sit. The hotel is family-run; service is friendly.

**Nearby** Louviers – church of Notre-Dame; Acquigny (10 km) – château; Gaillon (15 km) – château.; Giverny (30 km)

Chemin des Amoureux 27430 St-Pierre-du-Vauvray
**Tel** 02.32.59.93.29
**Fax** 02.32.59.41.93
**Location** on edge of village 8 km E of Louviers, beside Seine; with gardens and car parking
**Meals** breakfast, lunch, dinner
**Prices** DB&B F-FF; menus FF
**Rooms** 14 double (4 twin), all with bath; all rooms have central heating, phone, TV; most have minibar

**Facilities** dining-room, sitting-room
**Credit cards** V
**Children** accepted
**Disabled** lift/elevator
**Pets** accepted at extra charge
**Closed** 12 Nov to 20 Dec and 2 Jan to 13 Mar; restaurant only, Tue lunch
**Proprietors** Potier family

# The North-West

**Seaside town hotel, St-Vaast-la-Hougue**

# Hotel de France et des Fuchsias

'The garden is still in good order, as are the fuschias, and the conservatory where we ate a memorable, beautifully presented meal is very enticing; friendly and efficient staff.' So says a reporter, confirming that the essential attractions of this perennially popular halt for Cherbourg ferry passengers (French and British alike) are unchanged.

The emphasis is on the restaurant; and the expressions of delight at the superb seafood platters, or the wonderfully presented produce from the Brix family farm, prove that the customers are happy. The wine list offers plenty of half-bottles and good-value options, the service is friendly and efficient, the atmosphere warm – whether in the cosy dining-room or in the conservatory, recently redecorated by a local *décorateur anglais*.

At the far end of the delightful English-style garden, where free chamber music concerts are held on the last ten days of August, is the hotel's annexe. Here bedrooms are more spacious and decoration more sophisticated than in the fairly simple ones in the main part of the hotel. A suite sleeping two or three people and a ground-floor bedroom have been created.

**Nearby** museum, fortifications; Normandy beaches.

20 rue Marechal Foch
50550 Saint-Vaast-la-Hougue
**Tel** 02.33.54.42.26
**Fax** 02.33.43.46.79
**Website** france-fuschias.com
**Location** in quiet street near fishing port and marina; with garden
**Meals** breakfast, lunch, dinner
**Prices** rooms F; menus from F (weekdays only), F-FF
**Rooms** 33 double, 31 with bath or shower; all rooms have central heating, phone,
TV
**Facilities** dining-room, sitting-room
**Credit cards** AE, DC, MC, V
**Children** welcome; special menu available
**Disabled** access only to dining-room
**Pets** tolerated
**Closed** early Jan to late Feb; Mon, mid-May to mid-Sep
**Proprietor** Mme Brix

# *The North-West*

**Seaside hotel, Ste-Anne-la-Palud**

## Hôtel de la Plage

A seaside hotel indeed – yards from the shore, with a vast strand of pale sand just next door. But this is far from being a bucket-and-spade holiday hotel. Although prices are not high by the elevated standards of fellow Relais & Châteaux members, they are high by summer-fortnight-with-the-kids standards. And although children are welcome, as usual in France, there are no special facilities for them.

It's as a place for relaxing, pampering breaks with an outdoors element that the Plage wins a place here. The hotel combines its splendid, peaceful seaside setting – plus attractive pool and tennis court – with one of the best kitchens in Brittany (specialising, of course, in seafood), which earns a star from Michelin and two *toques* from Gault-Millau. Within the manicured grounds is a bar in a separate thatched cottage. Mme Le Coz and her staff generate a welcoming atmosphere; service is sometimes a little slow but always friendly, and details are not overlooked. Bedrooms are comfortable, even if they do tend towards traditional French styles of decoration, and some have stunning views (worth booking ahead).

**Nearby** Beach; Locronan (10 km) – town square; Quimper.

Ste-Anne-la-Palud 29127
Plonévez-Porzay
**Tel** 02.98.92.50.12
**Fax** 02.98.92.56.54
**E-mail** laplage@relaischateaux.fr
**Location** in countryside 4 km W of Plonévez and 25 km NW of Quimper; with garden and ample car parking
**Meals** breakfast, lunch, dinner
**Prices** rooms FF-FFF; breakfast F
**Rooms** 20 double (10 twin), 2 single, 4 family rooms, all with bath; all rooms have central heating, TV, phone, minibar
**Facilities** sitting-room, dining-room, bar, conference room
**Credit cards** AE, DC, MC, V
**Children** welcome
**Disabled** lift/elevator
**Pets** accepted but not in dining-room
**Closed** mid-Nov to Apr
**Proprietor** M. Le Coz

# The North-West

**Seaside hotel, Trébeurden**

# Ti Al-Lannec

Happy reports about this handsome house on the 'pink granite' coast of Brittany suggest that the hotel manages to pamper while at the same time coping with the families who are drawn to this seaside holiday area.

The house stands high above the sea with a path down to the beach; its south-facing terrace has a splendid view over the bay of Lannion. It is a supremely comfortable hotel, with that elusive private-house feel. Bedrooms are thoughtfully decorated, light and airy but cosy, with fresh flowers and books, small tables and table lamps liberally used. Some have terraces or verandas. The dining-room has the sea view, and is crisp and fresh with rich drapes and old stone walls. Antique and modern furnishings mix well in the comfortable sitting-room, dotted with pot plants.

The house was completely renovated and opened as a hotel in 1978 by Gérard and Danielle Jouanny, and is run by them with a convincing blend of charm, taste and efficiency. Danielle's food is 'consistently delicious', the service 'five-star' and the welcome for children genuine – witness the swing and seesaw on the lawn.

**Nearby** Perros-Guirec (15 km) – large resort; Tréguier (30 km

Allée de Mezo-Guen, BP 3
22560 Trébeurden
**Tel** 02.96.15.01.01
**Fax** 02.96.23.62.14
**E-mail** ti.al.lannec@wanadoo.fr
**Location** in wooded grounds above resort, 10 km NW of Lannion; with car parking
**Meals** breakfast, lunch, dinner
**Prices** rooms FF-FFF; lunch F-FF; menus FF-FFF, children's F
**Rooms** 20 double, 2 single, 7 family rooms, all with bath; all rooms have phone, TV

**Facilities** dining-room, 2 sitting-rooms, bar, billiards room, play room, beauty and fitness centre, sauna, jacuzzi
**Credit cards** AE, MC, V
**Children** welcome; early meals, baby-sitting available
**Disabled** lift/elevator; some bedrooms and WCs suitable
**Pets** accepted in bedrooms at extra charge
**Closed** mid-Nov to mid-Mar
**Proprietors** Danielle and Gérard Jouanny

# The North-West

**Manor house hotel, Verneuil-sur-Avre**

## Le Clos

Le Clos remains one of our favourite upmarket French hotels – partly because it remains just affordable by ordinary mortals, but also because it avoids the pretension and vulgarity that afflict so many château-style places. A recent report supports this view.

The hotel is on the edge of the pleasant little country town of Verneuil, in a quiet back street – though with a busy bypass visible (and just audible) in the background. It is a rather comical turn-of-the-century building of highly patterned brick-work, with a mock-medieval tower, set in well-kept leafy grounds with lawns and creeping willows that are overlooked by a large terrace. Inside, everything is of the highest quality: smart, antique-style cane chairs, heavy linen tablecloths and huge bunches of flowers in the dining-room, neat reproduction armchairs in the salon, chintzy drapes in the bedrooms, deep pile carpets everywhere – even in the luxurious bathrooms. The bedrooms are light and airy, and furnished in individual style. The kitchen wins no awards, but produces a range of classical dishes with absolute professionalism and finesse.

**Nearby** Church of la Madeleine (flamboyant tower); Château de Pin au Haras (40 km) – stud farm; Chartres – cathedral.

98 Rue de la Ferté-Vidame
27130 Verneuil-sur-Avre
**Tel** 02.32.32.21.81
**Fax** 02.32.32.21.36
**E-mail** leclos@relaischateaux.fr
**Location** on edge of town, 56 km NW of Chartres, 39 km SW of Evreux; gardens, parking
**Meals** breakfast, lunch, dinner
**Prices** rooms FF, suites FFF; apartments FFF; DB&B FF-FFF; breakfast F
**Rooms** 4 double, 2 suites, all with bath and shower; 3 ground-floor garden suites with Jacuzzi; 1 apartment; all rooms have central heating, phone, satellite TV
**Facilities** 2 dining-rooms, sitting-room, bar; tennis court
**Credit cards** AE, DC, MC, V
**Children** welcome
**Disabled** no special facilities
**Pets** accepted **Closed** mid-Dec to mid-Jan; restaurant Mon, except holiday periods
**Proprietors** Patrick and Colette Simon

# The North-West

## Converted mill, Villeray

# Moulin de Villeray ★

This grand old mill – restored from dereliction and gradually improved over a 20-year period (a smart outdoor swimming-pool, and most recently, 7 new bedrooms and an '*orangerie*' dining-room) – was taken over by the Eelsens in 1992. It remains one of our favourite ports of call in southern Normandy (despite showing some signs of wear and tear), and worth the detour from the A11 Nantes-Paris *autoroute*.

It is no longer what you would call a simple rustic retreat; but the mill-wheel is still there, and the setting is delectable – beside the rushing river Huisne, on the edge of a neat village of red-roofed stone houses, in rolling farmland on the fringe of the Perche region. Its membership of the Relais du Silence group is justified, even if prices are approaching Relais & Chateaux levels.

Much of the tall, white-painted mill has been rebuilt rather than restored, but its main focus, the restaurant, is thoroughly traditional, retaining old beams and a huge fireplace – and giving a view of the mill-wheel. The 'excellent' food is more than a match for the surroundings. Guests gather for drinks in the salon. Bedrooms are comfortable. Outside there is a pleasant terrace, a large, relaxing and informal garden bordering the river and, beyond that, countryside.

**Nearby** Nogent – Gothic and Renaissance buildings; Chartres (55 km) – cathedral; Alençon (55 km) – lace-making.

Villeray 61110 Condeau
**Tel** 02.33.73.30.22
**Fax** 02.33.73.38.28
**E-mail** moulin.de.villeray@wanadoo.fr
**Location** at foot of village, 10 km N of Nogent; with garden and car parking
**Meals** breakfast, lunch, dinner
**Prices** rooms F-FF, suite FFF; breakfast F; menus FF-FFF; DB&B F (obligatory between May and Sep); FB FF
**Rooms** 22 double, all with bath and shower (3 twin); 3 suites; all rooms have phone, minibar
**Facilities** sitting-room, dining-room, bar; helipad; heated outdoor swimming-pool
**Credit cards** AE, DC, V
**Children** accepted
**Disabled** 1 suitable bedroom; access to restaurant
**Pets** accepted (must be kept on lead) **Closed** never
**Proprietors** Christian and Muriel Eelsen

# The North-West

---

Riverside hotel, Les Andelys

## Hôtel de la Chaîne d'Or

This old inn, superbly set beside the Seine, has jumped upmarket since it was dropped from the guide some years ago. Bedrooms vary in size and style, but many share the restaurant's river views. Not the least of the improvements is in the food, which is now seriously good, as recent reports confirm.

■ 27 Rue Grande, 27700 Les Andelys (Eure) **Tel** 02.32.54.00.31 **Fax** 02.32.54.05.68 **Meals** breakfast, lunch, dinner **Prices** rooms F-FF; breakfast F; menus FF **Rooms** 10, all with bath, central heating, phone, TV **Credit cards** AE, MC, V **Closed** Jan; Sun eve and Mon

---

Spa hotel, Bagnoles-de-l'Orne

## Bois Joli

Past visitors to this 19thC Norman villa have praised 'pretty, airy, bedrooms; very good dinners; excellent service, excellent value'. Yvette and Daniel Mariette, who took over in 1999, are upholding the same standards, judging from a recent satisfied reporter. There is a pleasant garden, leading into the Andaine forest.

■ 12 Avenue Philippe du Rozier, 61140 Bagnoles-de-l'Orne (Orne) **Tel** 02.33.37.92.77 **Fax** 02.33 37.07.56 **E-mail** boisjoli@wanadoo.fr **Meals** breakfast, lunch, dinner **Prices** rooms F; breakfast F; menus F-FF **Rooms** 20, all with bath or shower, central heating, phone; TV on request **Credit cards** AE, DC, MC, V **Closed** Jan

---

Town hotel, Barfleur

## Le Conquérant

A shell's throw from the port, this fine grey-stone 17thC building offers a peaceful halt for travellers, and is inviting enough for a longer stay, with its spacious garden. Recent renovations have concentrated on making the bedrooms more comfortable. Delicious crêpes in the *salon de thé*.

■ 16-18 Rue St-Thomas Becket, 50760 Barfleur (Manche) **Tel** 02.33.54.00.82 **Fax** 02.33.54.65 .25 **Meals** breakfast, tea, light suppers **Prices** rooms F; breakfast F, supper F-FF **Rooms** 13, all with bath or shower, phone; some have satellite TV **Credit cards** MC, V **Closed** mid-Nov to mid-Mar

---

Seaside hotel, Barneville-Carteret

## La Marine

In a good situation near the head of a river estuary, with the open sea (wide, sandy beach) nearby; but the ambience would be even better if there wasn't a dilapidated, disused hotel alongside. Public rooms are attractively decorated with a marine theme, Bedrooms are spacious and light, conventional in decoration but smart and clean. There is a waterside terrace for drinks, and food is what one would expect from a Michelin star.

■ 11 rue de Paris, 50270 Barneville-Carteret (Manche) **Tel** 02.33.53. 83.31 **Fax** 02.33.53.39.60 **Meals** breakfast, lunch, dinner **Prices** rooms F-FF; breakfast F, menus FF-FFF **Rooms** 31, all with bath or shower, central heating, phone, TV **Credit cards** AE, DC, MC, V **Closed** 5 Nov to mid-Feb; restaurant only, Mon lunch (except Apr to Jun and Sept); Sun eve in Feb, Mar and Oct

# The North-West

---

Town mansion, Bayeux

# Hôtel d'Argouges

'Comfortable, quiet, helpful people'; 'atmosphere, welcome and service – impeccable,' run the latest reports on this 18thC house. There is a rather formal sitting-room and a small garden; bedrooms vary in size and are traditionally furnished; some are in an annexe across the courtyard. No restaurant. Car park.

■ 21 Rue St-Patrice, 14400 Bayeux (Calvados) **Tel** 02.31.92.88.86 **Fax** 02.31.92.69.16 **E-mail** dargouges@ad.com **Meals** breakfast **Prices** rooms F, suites F; breakfast F **Rooms** 25, all with bath or shower, central heating, phone, minibar **Credit cards** AE, DC, MC, V **Closed** never

---

Village inn, Le Bec-Hellouin

# Auberge de l'Abbaye

The archetypal atmospheric Norman inn, simple and welcoming, with tiled floors, rough stone walls and gleaming furniture. Bedrooms are cheerful and rustic, meals are typical of the region – with apples, cider and quantities of cream.

■ Le Bec-Hellouin, 27800 Brionne (Eure) **Tel** 02.32.44.86.02 **Fax** 02.32.46.32.23 **Meals** breakfast, lunch, dinner **Prices** rooms F; half-board F; breakfast F, menus FF **Rooms** 10, all with bath, central heating, phone **Credit cards** MC, V **Closed** restaurant only, Mon evening and Tue Nov to Apr

---

Seaside hotel, Belle-Ile-en-Mer

# Le Clos Fleuri

A new and stylishly simple hotel in grassy grounds 600m from the main port of Le Palais on Belle-Ile, 45 minutes by ferry from Quiberon. The catering is as fresh as the decoration, with meals tailored to guests' requirements, and the option of a substantial brunch instead of standard breakfast.

■ Bellevue, Route de Sauzon, Le Palais, 56360 Belle-Ile-en-Mer (Morbihan) **Tel** 02.97.31.45.45 **Fax** 02.97.31.45.57 **Meals** breakfast or brunch, lunch, dinner **Prices** rooms F; suites F; breakfast F, brunch F; menu around FF **Rooms** 20, all with bath, central heating, phone, cable TV **Credit cards** AE, DC, MC, V **Closed** never

---

Country hotel, Belle-Ile-en-Mer

# La Désirade

La Désirade, drawn to our attention by a satisfied reader, calls itself a 'hôtel-village'; it is an unusual creation – a grouping of new, traditional-style houses around a neat heated pool (beside which you can have breakfast in good weather). Stylishly simple furnishing in the rooms. Bikes and boats for hire.

■ 56360 Belle-Ile-en-Mer (Morbihan) **Tel** 02.97.31.70.70 **Fax** 02.97.31.89.63 **Meals** breakfast, dinner **Prices** rooms FF (with brunch); DB&B FF (obligatory in high season), menu FF **Rooms** 26, all with bath, central heating, phone, TV, hairdrier **Credit cards** AE, DC, MC, V **Closed** Jan, Feb

# The North-West

Town hotel, Beuzeville

## Cochon d'Or et Petit Castel

Two small hotels on opposite sides of the main street and under the same ownership. The Petit Castel offers simple, pleasant modern-style bedrooms; the Cochon d'Or has cheaper, rather more old-fashioned bedrooms with fewer facilities. The food is above average and excellent value.

■ Place du General-de-Gaulle, 27210 Beuzeville (Eure) **Tel** 02.32.57.70.46 (Cochon) 02.32.57.76.08.(Peti t Castel) **Fax** 02.32.42.25.70 **E-mail** auberge-du-cochon-dor@wanadoo.fr **Website** www.le-cochon-dor.fr **Meals** breakfast, lunch, dinner **Prices** rooms F; breakfast 38F; menus 82F-245F **Rooms** 20, all with bath or shower, central heating, phone; some have TV **Credit cards** MC, V **Closed** mid-Dec to mid-Jan

Restaurant with rooms, La Bouille

## Le Saint-Pierre

A clutch of satisfied readers' letters and an inspection visit confirms the attractions of this smart, thriving restaurant-with-rooms by the Seine, presided over by the charming Madame Huet. 'The food was first class, and thoroughly merits its rating – it was very special,' says one reporter of the inventive cooking, served in the airy, summery restaurant with riverside terrace; plainly decorated bedrooms mostly overlook the river.

■ La Bouille, 76530 Grand Couronne (Seine-Maritime) **Tel** 02.35.18.01.01 **Fax** 02.35.18.12.7 6 **Meals** breakfast, lunch, dinner **Prices** rooms F; menus FF **Rooms** 7, all with bath or shower, central heating, phone, TV **Credit cards** AE, DC, MC, V **Closed** Mon; Sun eve

Riverside hotel, Caudebec-en-Caux

## Le Normandie

A friendly and well-cared-for hotel, if uninspiring in style, in a good position on the Seine. Bedrooms are simple but comfortable, many with river views. Food is carefully prepared and sound value – typical of a two-fireplace Logis.

■ 19 Quai Guilbaud, 76490 Caudebec-en-Caux (Seine-Maritime) **Tel** 02.35.96.25.11 **Fax** 02.35 .96.68.15 **Meals** breakfast, lunch, dinner **Prices** rooms F; breakfast F; menus F-FF **Rooms** 16, all with bath or shower, central heating, phone, TV **Credit cards** AE, DC, MC, V **Closed** Feb

Seaside hotel, Dinard

## Roche Corneille

A tall château-style building in the middle of Dinard, renovated in a crisp and confident style by new owners, and run with clear attention to detail – fresh flowers, fluffy towels, impeccable housekeeping, reflected in the higher prices now charged. The gastronomic restaurant has weekly changing menus.

■ 4 Rue G Clemenceau, 35800 Dinard (Ille-et-Vilaine) **Tel** 02.99.46.14.47 **Fax** 02.99.46.40. 80 **Meals** breakfast **Prices** rooms F-FF; breakfast F; menus FF **Rooms** 28, all with bath, central heating, phone, TV **Credit cards** AE, MC, V **Closed** never

# *The North-West*

---

Château hotel, Hennebont

## Château de Locguénolé ★

A Dutch reader writes to recommend inclusion of this refined country house looking down on the estuary of Le Blavet. Splendid spacious bedrooms, plentiful sitting-rooms, very good (Michelin-starred) food. Lots of ways to mitigate the damage – walks, tennis, bikes, as well as a good-sized pool, sauna and turkish bath.

■ Route de Port-Louis en Kervignac, 56700 Hennebont (Morbihan) **Tel** 02.97.76.76.76 **Fax** 02.97.76.82.35 **Meals** breakfast, lunch, dinner **Prices** rooms FF-FFF, suites FFFF; breakfast F, menus FF-FFF **Rooms** 22, all with bath, central heating, phone, satellite TV; most have hairdriers **Credit cards** DC, MC, V **Closed** 1 Jan to 10 Feb

---

Country hotel, Honfleur

## La Chaumière

Set peacefully in an orchard garden with the sea in view (and direct access to the shore), this typically Norman timbered building offers deeply comfortable, relaxing accommodation. The bedrooms are decorated with flair and taste, and warmly furnished. Serious cooking of regionally-based dishes.

■ Route du Littoral, Vasouy, 14600 Honfleur (Calvados) **Tel** 02.31. 81.63.20 **Fax** 02.31.89.5 9.23 **Meals** breakfast, lunch, dinner **Prices** rooms FFF; breakfast F, menus FF-FFF **Rooms** 8, all with bath, central heating, phone, TV, minibar, hairdrier **Credit cards** AE, MC, V **Closed** never; restaurant only, Tue, and Wed lunch

---

Country hotel, Honfleur

## La Ferme Saint-Siméon

Owned by the Boellan family, as well as La Chaumière (see above), this fine old farmhouse used to be a favourite haunt of the Impressionist painters, and is still a tranquil spot. Cooking blends bold innovation with the traditional. Extensive wine list. Indoor heated swimming-pool, sauna, steam room and solarium.

■ Rue Adolphe-Marais, 14600 Honfleur (Calvados) **Tel** 02.31.31.81. 78.00 **Fax** 02.33.31.89.48.48 **Meals** breakfast, lunch, dinner **Prices** rooms FF-FFFF; apartments FFFF; menus FF-FFF **Rooms** 29, 4 apartments, all with bath or shower, central heating, phone **Credit cards** AE, MC, V **Closed** never

---

Country hotel, Honfleur

## Le Manoir du Butin

Situated 2 kilometres outside Honfleur, this typical !8thC Normandy manor house lies in a peaceful situation, overlooking the sea. Rustic beams, polished wood and huge open fireplaces create a welcoming atmosphere. Normandy cuisine in the attractive dining-room. Booking in advance is recommended.

■ Phare du Butin, 14600 Honfleur (Calvados) **Tel** 02.31.81.63.00 **Fax** 02.31.89.59.23 **Meals** breakfast, dinner **Prices** rooms 640F-1,970F; breakfast 65F; DB&B 570F-1,235; menus 128F-265F **Rooms** 9, all with bath or shower, central heating, phone, TV, minibar **Credit cards** AE, MC, V **Closed** restaurant only, Wed, and Thur, Fri lunch

# The North-West

---

Country hotel, Louviers

## La Haye-le-Comte

There's an energetic air about this pleasant little country house with *pétanque*, tennis, table-tennis, croquet, mountain bikes and local walks on offer. Bedrooms are neat and airy. Food is quite wide-ranging, with as much seafood as meat in evidence. Reports welcome.

■ 4 Route de la Haye-le-Comte, 27400 Louviers (Eure) **Tel** 02.32.40. 00.40 **Fax** 02.32.25.03. 85 **E-mail** hotel-la-haye-le-comte@wanadoo.fr **Meals** breakfast, lunch, dinner **Prices** rooms F; breakfast F, menus FF, children's F ; 10% reduction on DB&B for 3 nights **Rooms** 16, all with bath, central heating, phone, satellite TV **Credit cards** AE, DC, MC, V **Closed** restaurant only, Sun evenings out of season

---

Village inn, Martin-Église

## Auberge du Clos Normand

A delightfully simple old auberge built of patterned brick and timber with a flowery garden and stream behind. Bedrooms in a converted outbuilding are attractive and comfortable. Food is classically Norman, involving much cholesterol and alcohol.

■ 22 Rue Henri IV, Martin-Église, 76370 Neuville-les-Dieppe (Seine-Maritime) **Tel** 02.35.04.40.34 **Fax** 02.35.04.48.49 **Meals** breakfast, lunch, dinner **Prices** rooms F; breakfast F; DB&B F **Rooms** 8, all with bath or shower, central heating, phone, TV **Credit cards** AE, MC, V **Closed** mid-Nov to mid-Dec; Mon, Tue

---

Converted mill, Moëlan-sur-Mer

## Les Moulins du Duc

The main building of this unusual hotel is a former mill but the spacious and well equipped accommodation is in two-storey cottages scattered around the secluded grounds. Breakfast can be had on the terrace by the pond. Reporters rate the food 'totally delicious', and the 'delightful setting. Indoor swimming-pool.

■ 29350 Moëlan-sur-Mer (Finistère) **Tel** 02.98.96.52.52 **Fax** 02.98.96.52.53 **Meals** breakfast, lunch, dinner **Prices** rooms F-FF, suites FF; breakfast F, menus FF-FFF, children's F **Rooms** 27, all with bath or shower, phone, TV, minibar **Credit cards** AE, DC, MC, V **Closed** mid-Jan to Mar

---

Town hotel, Le Mont-St-Michel

## Auberge Saint-Pierre

The Saint-Pierre is the pick of the hostelries that line the main street at the foot of France's premier tourist attraction. Its dining-rooms are satisfyingly rustic, its bedrooms (half in an annexe up many steps) tastefully decorated and comfortable. Efficient service, good plain food.

■ BP16, 50116 Le Mont-St-Michel (Manche) **Tel** 02.33.60.14.03 **Fax** 02.33.48.59.82 **Meals** breakfast, lunch, dinner **Prices** rooms F-FF; breakfast F, dinner FF **Rooms** 20, all with bath or shower, central heating, phone, TV, hairdrier **Credit cards** AE, V **Closed** Dec to Feb

# *The North-West*

---

Quayside hotel, Paimpol

# Le Repaire de Kerroc'h

Set in an enviable position right on the quay, this handsome 18thC house has been beautifully restored. Bedrooms are well furnished and equipped. Excellent breakfasts. In the guide since our first edition, a new chef, Jann Trebuel, is now in charge of the cooking (one Michelin star). A recent reporter was well satisfied.

■ 29 Quai Morand, Port de Plaisance, 22500 Paimpol (Côtes-d'Armor) **Tel** 02.96.20.50.13 **Fax** 02.96.22.07.46 **Meals** breakfast, lunch, dinner **Prices** rooms F; DB&B FF ; breakfast F, menus FF-FFF **Rooms** 13, all with bath, phone, TV, minibar **Credit cards** MC, V **Closed** never

---

Seaside villa, Perros-Guirec

# Le Sphinx

There are splendid sea views from this tall house atop low cliffs on the 'pink granite coast' – both from the dining-room and the best of the spacious, tastefully decorated bedrooms. Service is friendly, food reliably good and night-time silence absolute.

■ Chemin de la Messe, 22700 Perros-Guirec (Côtes-d'Armor) **Tel** 02.96.23.25.42 **Fax** 02.96.9 1.26.13 **Meals** breakfast, lunch, dinner **Prices** rooms F-FF; breakfast F; menus FF **Rooms** 20, all with bath or shower, central heating, phone, alarm, TV **Credit cards** AE, MC, V **Closed** Jan to mid-Feb

---

Seaside hotel, Raguenès-Plage

# Chez Pierre

A family seaside Logis completely without pretension and offering reliably good, traditional, sea-based cooking. 'Superb' family rooms in the modern annexe (2 suitable for the disabled) next to the turn-of-the-century main house, have single beds upstairs and doubles downstairs. Big garden, early meals for kids.

■ Raguenès-Plage, 29920 Nevez (Finistère) **Tel** 02.98.06.81.06 **Fax** 02.98.06.62.09 **Meals** breakfast, lunch, dinner **Prices** rooms F; breakfast F, menus FF, children's F **Rooms** 28 (14 with bath, 14 with shower), 7 single, all with phone **Credit cards** MC, V **Closed** Oct to 7 Apr

---

Country inn, La Roche-Bernard

# Auberge Bretonne

Food takes pride of place at this small, welcoming auberge; people come from far afield for Jacques Thorel's cooking (two Michelin stars). There is a formidable cellar, too. Bedrooms are prettily furnished in rural Breton style; the rustic dining-room surrounds the vegetable garden.

■ 2 Place Duguesclin, 56130 La Roche-Bernard (Morbihan) **Tel** 02.99.90.60.28 **Fax** 02.99.90 .85.00 **Meals** breakfast, lunch, dinner **Prices** rooms F-FF; breakfast F, menus FF-FFF **Rooms** 8, all with central heating **Credit cards** AE, MC, V **Closed** mid-Nov to early Dec; 2 weeks in Jan

# *The North-West*

---

Town hotel, La Roche-Bernard

## Auberge des Deux Magots

A warm welcome awaits inside this prim-looking 17thC stone house. The furniture in the elegant dining-rooms and bedrooms may be reproduction, but it is all part of a careful, fresh decorative scheme. Good-value menus concentrate on traditional regional dishes.

■ 1 Place du Bouffay, 56130 La Roche-Bernard (Morbihan) **Tel** 02.99.90.60.75 **Fax** 02.99.90. 87.87 **Meals** breakfast, lunch, dinner **Prices** rooms F, family rooms F; breakfast F, menus F-FF, children's F **Rooms** 14, all with bath or shower, phone, satellite TV **Credit cards** MC, V **Closed** Sun eve and Mon, except long weekends; restaurant only Mon, except long weekends

---

Manor house hotel, La Roche-Bernard

## Manoir du Rodoir

This plain-looking house, recently taken over by a new owner, attracts golfing guests, who enjoy discounts at some of the excellent courses in southern Brittany. But with its peaceful wooded setting, relaxed ambience and tasteful decoration it also appeals to many others. Reports welcome.

■ Rte de Nantes, 56130 La Roche-Bernard (Morbihan) **Tel** 02.99.90.82.68 **Fax** 02.99.90.76.22 **Meals** breakfast, lunch, dinner **Prices** rooms F; suites FF; breakfast F; DB&B F; menus F-FF **Rooms** 26, all with bath, central heating, phone, TV **Credit cards** MC, V **Closed** never

---

Town hotel, Rouen

## Hôtel de la Cathédrale

This ancient, rambling, half-timbered hotel is tucked away down a pedestrian street, only yards from the cathedral. Most of the chintzy bedrooms have been renovated over recent years. Delightful courtyard with a mass of flowers. No restaurant but plenty of choice nearby. 'Friendly service'.

■ 12 Rue St-Romain, 76000 Rouen (Seine-Maritime) **Tel** 02.35.71.57.95 **Fax** 02.35.70.15.54 **E-mail** hotel-de-la-cathedrale.com **Meals** breakfast **Prices** rooms F; buffet breakfast F **Rooms** 24, all with bath or shower, central heating, phone, TV **Credit cards** MC, V **Closed** never

---

Bed and breakfast guest-house, Sourdeval

## La Maurandière

A chambres d'hôtes establishment, where you share the sitting and dining room of Mme Dupart. Her lovely stone farmhouse, in an idyllic setting, was beautifully restored about twelve years ago. The bedrooms are spacious and delightful. Breakfast can be served in the garden in summer.

■ 50150 Sourdeval (Manche) **Tel** 02.33.59.65.44 **Meals** breakfast **Prices** rooms F with breakfast **Rooms** 4, all with bath or shower, central heating **Credit cards** MC **Closed** never

# The North-West

---

Manor house hotel, Trébeurden

## Manoir de Lan-Kerellec

A member of the Relais & Châteaux group, but one of the least pretentious and most captivating, this handsome and unusual family house stands in trees high above the rocky shore, with splendid sea views from all rooms. Very relaxing and welcoming.

■ 22560 Trébeurden (Côtes-d'Armor) **Tel** 02.96.15.47.47 **Fax** 02.96.23.66.88 **Meals** breakfast, lunch, dinner **Prices** rooms FF-FFFF; breakfast F, menus FF **Rooms** 20, all with bath, central heating, phone, TV **Credit cards** AE, DC, MC, V **Closed** mid-Nov to mid-Mar; restaurant only, Mon (and Tue lunch in low season)

---

Manor house hotel, Tréguier

## Kastell Dinec'h

We have received enthusiastic reports in the past on this 'oasis' – a handsome old farmhouse, tucked away in lush wooded gardens. Bedrooms are small – beware the stable block – but comfortable and stylishly decorated. Food rated 'good' to 'excellent'. Neat heated pool.

■ Rte de Lannion, 22220 Tréguier (Côtes-d'Armor) **Tel** 02.96.92.49.39 **Fax** 02.96.92.34.02 **Meals** breakfast, dinner **Prices** rooms F; breakfast F, menus FF **Rooms** 14, all with central heating, phone **Credit cards** MC, V **Closed** Jan to mid-Mar, 2 weeks end of Oct; Tue evening and Wed out of season

---

Country hotel, Trégunc

## Les Grandes Roches

From the roadside this looks much like any other simple Logis, but in the extensive flowery grounds are charmingly restored farm buildings containing some of the bedrooms. 'Comfortable, peaceful, friendly, good value.' What more could you ask?

■ Route des Grandes Roches, 29910 Trégunc (Finistère) **Tel** 02.98.97.29.97 **Fax** 02.98.50.29.19 **Meals** breakfast, dinner (except Mon) **Prices** rooms F; breakfast F; DB&B F; menus F-FF **Rooms** 21, all with bath or shower, central heating, phone **Credit cards** MC **Closed** Nov to Easter

---

Country inn, Trelly

## La Verte Campagne

Pascal Bernou has won the Michelin star he set his sights on when he bought this 18thC farmhouse from his former employer. Reporters agree that the food is delicious: 'rich, intense flavours and truly imaginative dishes'. Bedrooms in the main building are delightful but vary widely in size. Some are in need of updating, but bear in mind the low prices.

■ Hameau Chevalier, 50660 Trelly (Manche) **Tel** 02.33.47.65.33 **Fax** 02.33.47.38.03 **Meals** breakfast, lunch, dinner **Prices** rooms F; menus FF **Rooms** 7, all with central heating, phone **Credit cards** MC, V **Closed** 1 week in Jan; restaurant Sun dinner and Mon out of season

# *Ile-de-France*

We've lumped together Paris and the surrounding *départements* of Ile de France because for many visitors they are sensible alternatives. If you're passing through the area and need a stopover, your instinct will probably be to stay out of the city; and if you're bent on a sightseeing holiday or a romantic break you'll probably want to be in the heart of things. But it's not necessarily so: an overnight stop in Paris can work perfectly well, and a rural base for city sightseeing can be very restful.

Paris is a compact city – much more so than London, for example – and for many visitors choice of location is not very important (from the convenience point of view) unless you intend to spend a lot of time in one place (the Louvre, say).

From the point of view of atmosphere and charm, location can make a deal of difference. It pays to know something about the districts (*arrondisements*) that make up the city. The one-digit or two-digit number at the end of Paris postcodes is the number of the *arrondisement*. Thus 75006 is the 6th, for example.

The *arrondisements* are numbered in a clockwise spiral starting in the centre on the Right Bank of the Seine (the northern bank). You'll mainly be interested in the first turn of the spiral.

The 1st is an upmarket area extending from the Place de la Concorde past the Louvre to Les Halles; we have a few entries here. We have none in the 2nd and only one in the 3rd (Pavillon de la Reine) to the east. But the spiral then turns back towards the Seine, and we have a number of entries in the 4th – in the revitalised Marais, east of the Pompidou centre, and around Notre Dame.

Across the river, the 5th, 6th and 7th make up the Left Bank, with the Boulevard St-Germain its main axis. Between the Jardin des Plantes in the east and the Eiffel Tower in the west, there are more Charming Small Hotels here than anywhere else. The spiral crosses the river again to the 8th, and the Champs Elysées area, where we have three entries. Outside this first central spiral, all our entries are to the north, in the 9th, 17th and 18th (Montmartre).

**Contenders in Paris**
**Paris, Hôtel Left Bank** (01) 43.54.01.70 Cosy, beamed, antique-filled place in excellent position.
**Paris, Hôtel Lido** (01) 42.66.27.37 Comfortable, richly decorated place near the Madeleine.
**Paris, Hôtel du Panthéon** (01) 43.54.32.95 Classical glossy lobby, vaulted breakfast room, neat bedrooms, some with beams.
**Paris, Hôtel Pergolèse** (01) 40.67.96.77 Ultra-modern designer interior behind an austere classical façade.

# Ile-de-France

**Converted mill, Flagy**

# Hostellerie du Moulin

Over the years since its inclusion in our first edition, we have received a steady flow of readers' reports approving of this imaginatively converted flour mill an hour from Paris.

The setting, with tables in the grassy garden beside the stream that still gently turns the mill wheel, is idyllic. Beyond the neat gardens you look out on to cultivated fields which until the 1950s supplied the grain that was milled here. The heavy beams, wheels and pulleys of the mill dominate the cosy sitting-room, and the bedrooms, named after cereals, are as quirkily captivating as you would hope in a building of this character; space is at a premium, and low beams lead some guests to move about with a permanent stoop.

A new chef at the Moulin (reports please) specializes mainly in traditional dishes – the menu and *carte* have English translations, underlining the Moulin's popularity with British travellers. Claude Scheidecker is a charming and friendly host who gives his little hotel, which he has been running for over twenty years, an exceptionally welcoming atmosphere. And he still manages to keep his prices admirably low.

**Nearby** Fontainebleau Château; Sens (40 km) – cathedral.

2 Rue du Moulin 77940 Flagy
**Tel** 01 60.96.67.89
**Fax** 01.60.96.69.51
**Location** in village, 23 km SE of Fontainebleau, 10 km W of Montereau; with car parking
**Meals** breakfast, lunch, dinner
**Prices** rooms F; breakfast F; menus FF and *à la carte*
**Rooms** 7 double, 3 family rooms, all with bath; all rooms have phone
**Facilities** dining-room, bar, sitting-room; fishing
**Credit cards** AE, DC, MC, V
**Children** accepted
**Disabled** access to dining-room, not to bedrooms
**Pets** accepted
**Closed** mid- to end Sep, mid-Dec to mid Jan; Sun evening and Mon (except public holidays at Easter and Whitsun, 1 and 8 May; closed Mon evening and Tue)
**Proprietor** Claude Scheidecker

# *Ile-de-France*

**Town hotel, Paris**

## Hôtel de l'Abbaye

If we gave awards, this gorgeous hotel would be a very strong contender on all counts. Indeed, we find it hard to fault at all, save to say that the standard bedrooms are fairly small (and feel even smaller compared to the spaciousness of the public rooms); you would do well to upgrade to a larger room if you can afford it. One on the ground floor has its own terrace, as do the four duplex apartments. Take note that you should book well in advance, as the hotel is usually full.

The moment we walked in to this skilfully converted former abbey we felt calmed and cossetted. The hotel has a reputation for attentive yet unobtrusive service which it justly deserves: the courteous staff seem genuinely eager to be of help. The public rooms are inviting yet chic, with several sitting areas, the sofas and armchairs attractively upholstered in floral or striped fabrics, warmly lit by huge table lamps and filled with fresh flowers; in cool weather there's an open fire. The breakfast room/bar must be one of the most alluring in Paris, conservatory style, with walls covered in trellis and pretty leaf print curtains surrounding French doors which overlook a large courtyard garden complete with fountain. Here you can take breakfast or a drink in warm weather. Worth every penny.

**Nearby** Jardin de Luxembourg; blvd Saint-Germain.

10 rue Cassette, 75006 Paris
**Tel** 01.45.44.38.11
**Fax** 01.45.48.07.86
**E-mail** hotel.abbaye@wanadoo.fr
**Location** close to the junction with rue de Meziers; parking at Saint-Sulpice; metro Saint-Sulpice
**Meals** breakfast
**Prices** FFF; breakfast included
**Rooms** 42 double and twin, all with bath; 4 duplex apartments; all rooms have phone, satellite TV, air-conditioning, hairdryer
**Facilities** 2 sitting rooms, breakfast room/bar, courtyard garden **Credit cards** AE, MC, V **Children** accepted **Disabled** two rooms on ground floor **Pets** not accepted **Closed** never **Proprietors** M. & Mme Lafortune

# Ile-de-France

# Hôtel d'Angleterre

One of the most peaceful, comforting and gracious small hotels in Paris, the Angleterre has a faintly English air, befitting a building which was once the British Embassy. In 1783, Benjamin Franklin refused to enter it to sign the Treaty of Paris because he considered it to be British soil. Had he done so, he would have found well-proportioned rooms, fine mantlepieces, a beautiful staircase decorated with *trompe l'oeil* murals and a lovely courtyard garden, all of which are still in place.

The feeling of spacious calm in the public rooms is echoed in the bedrooms, all different but characteristically roomy, elegant and comfortable. One of our inspectors had a deluxe room with one of the largest hotel bathrooms he had seen, all marbled and mirrored glamour, based on a bathroom in the London Ritz. Another bathroom has a charming handpainted suite, with the basin set into a splendid wood and tiled washstand. A couple report that they stayed in the hotel's smallest room – normally let out as a single but with a double bed so that two can share if they wish. Their verdict? Despite the size, they were happy to enjoy the benefits and ambience of the Angleterre at a very modest price. Their only quibble was with the nose-in-air attitude of the receptionists, though not the manageress.

**Nearby** blvd Saint-Germain; Musée d'Orsay.

44 Rue Jacob 75006 Paris
**Tel** 01.42.60.34.72
**Fax** 01.42.60.16.93
**Location** in the stretch of rue Jacob between rues Bonaparte and Saints-Pères; parking at blvd Saint-Germain (rue du Dragon); metro Saint-Germain des-Près
**Meals** breakfast
**Prices** FF-FFF; suites FFFF; breakfast F

**Rooms** 24 double and twin, all with bath; 3 apartments; all rooms have phone, cable TV, hairdrier, safe **Facilities** sitting-room, breakfast room, bar, courtyard garden, lift/elevator to some rooms **Credit cards** AE, DC, MC, V **Children** accepted **Disabled** no special facilities **Pets** not accepted **Manager** Mme Michèle Blouin

# Ile-de-France

# Hôtel de Banville

This 1930s town house hotel offers an attractive combination of style, comfort and middle-of-the-road prices. Convenient, too, at least for motorists: finding your way from the Périphérique to boulevard Berthier is easy, and parking here does not pose an insoluble problem.

With its flower-filled window boxes, the airy art deco building – the work of a celebrated architect, we're told – looks promising, and does not disappoint. Inside, all is tastefully decorated and comfortable, bordering on the luxurious. There is an elegantly furnished sitting area/bar in reception, where a pianist often plays in the evenings. Another welcoming sitting-room (with antique pieces as well as comfy sofas), which can be closed off for meetings, puts the Banville comfortably ahead of the Parisian norm. Murals create a garden effect in the breakfast room. In the bedrooms, light furniture and wallpaper give a spacious feel; fabrics have been thoughtfully chosen, with antiques dotted throughout. Flower arrangements add a personal touch, as do such small details as having your bed turned down – a rare thing in the city nowadays. Peace is ensured by the efficient sound-proofing. Staff are extremely friendly, and we suspect that this hotel would be far more expensive if it were on the Left Bank.

**Nearby** Arc de Triomphe; Champs-Elysées; Palais des Congrès.

166 blvd Berthier, 75017 Paris
**Tel** 01.42.67.70.16
**Fax** 01.44.40.42.77
**E-mail** hotelbanville@wanadoo.fr
**Location** on service road off major boulevard, N of Arc de Triomphe; parking at blvd Berthier in street and garage metro Porte de Champerret;
**Meals** breakfast
**Prices** FFF; suite FFFF; breakfast F

**Rooms** 37 double, 1 suite, 2 triple, 1 family room; 36 with bath, 2 with shower; all rooms have phone, air-conditioning, satellite TV, hairdrier, safe
**Facilities** sitting area/bar, sitting-room, small dining-room, lift/elevator **Credit cards** AE, DC, MC, V **Children** accepted
**Disabled** no special facilities
**Pets** accepted **Closed** never
**Proprietor** Mme Moreau

# Ile-de-France

# Hôtel de la Bretonnerie

A distinctive 17thC townhouse, converted with sympathy and style, which, though conveniently placed in the middle of the picturesque and (now) fashionable Marais district, is – as a recent reporter points out – 'in a rather scruffy street' a little too close to the rowdy atmosphere of the Pompidou Centre for some tastes. The reporter continues, 'however once inside the hotel, all is calm and peaceful'.

The exposed beams in the public areas and the upper bedrooms are echoed throughout the house by the sturdy hardwood furniture (some antique, some reproduction). The small basement breakfast- and sitting-rooms attempt a medieval flavour, with pale stone vaulted ceilings, iron light fittings, richly coloured fabrics and polished tiled floors. Considering the apparent size of the hotel, the bedrooms are surprisingly roomy, also comfortable and pretty, and every one is different; some are arranged with the beds on a mezzanine gallery with the 'downstairs' used as a small sitting area. All have a glossy modern bathroom and guests will not find any lack of comfort.

Good-humoured staff extend a warm welcome, and cope admirably when all their guests arrive at the same time.

**Nearby** Hôtel de Ville; Pompidou Centre; Les Halles.

22 Rue Ste-Croix-de-la-Bretonnerie 75004 Paris
**Tel** 01.48.87.77.63
**Fax** 01.42.77.26.78
**Location** between rue des Archives and rue Vielle du Temple; parking at Hôtel de Ville; metro St Paul/Hôtel de Ville/Rambuteau
**Meals** breakfast
**Prices** FF-FFF; breakfast F
**Rooms** 27 double, 3 family rooms, all with bath; all rooms have phone, TV, minibar, hairdrier, safe
**Facilities** sitting area off lobby, cellar breakfast room, lift
**Credit cards** MC, V
**Children** accepted
**Disabled** no special facilities
**Pets** not accepted **Closed** 4 weeks 30 Jul to 27 Aug
**Proprietor** M. Sagot

# Ile-de-France

## Town hotel and restaurant, Paris

# Hôtel Degrés de Notre-Dame

Almost all the small hotels of Paris are without a dining room. Here, however, is an exception – the kind of family-run establishment well-known in the French countryside, but rarely found in the city: a restaurant with rooms. The restaurant has the feel of a simple *auberge*, and serves correspondingly rustic food. Guests also take breakfast here, which, assures the *patron*, (who does not speak English) features the freshest of bread, orange juice squeezed on the spot, and good coffee.

A steep wooden staircase, (staff carry your bags) decorated with charming murals leads to the bedrooms, which are good value: well equipped, with beamed ceilings and smart wooden furnishings including the bathroom mirrors. Some rooms have views over Notre-Dame; the ones at the front are the largest, with triple windows onto the street (with the exception of the first floor room). No. 24 is particularly handsome, with an expansive desk in the centre. In complete contrast is the attic conversion, very popular with Japanese guests, which swops Gallic character for modern decor, a private bar and a huge contoured bath. Rooms are spotlessly kept, and are often graced with that rare thing in Paris hotels – a vase of fresh flowers. Reports flow in proclaiming the Degrés de Notre Dame 'great value for money'.
**Nearby** Notre-Dame; Sainte-Chapelle; Musée de Cluny.

10 rue des Grands Degrés
75005 Paris
**Tel** 01.55.42.88.88
**Fax** 01.40.46.95.34
**Location** on a tiny square at junction with rue Fréderic-Sauton, close to quai de Montebello; parking at place Maubert; metro Saint-Michel; **Meals** breakfast, lunch, dinner
**Prices** FF; dinner: set menus

FF
**Rooms** 10 double, all with bath; all rooms have phone, fax/modem plug, TV, mini-bar, fridge, hairdrier
**Facilities** restaurant, bar
**Credit cards** V
**Children** accepted
**Disabled** not suitable (no lift)
**Pets** not accepted
**Closed** never
**Proprietor** M. Tahir

# Ile-de-France

**Town hotel, Paris**

# Hôtel Duc de St-Simon ★

A stylish hotel on a stylish street, just off the boulevard St-Germain. First glimpsed through two pairs of French windows which lie beyond a pretty courtyard, the interior of the Duc de St-Simon looks wonderfully inviting; and so it is – there is a warm, beautifully furnished salon with the distinctly private-house feel that the Swedish proprietor seeks to maintain, and elegant yet cosy bedrooms, all individually decorated with not a jarring note. The twin bedrooms are more spacious than those with double beds. Everywhere you look – both upstairs and downstairs – there are rich fabrics, gloriously overstuffed pieces of furniture, antique mirrors and cleverly conceived paint effects. The kilim-lined lift is a particularly original idea.

The white-painted 19thC house backs on to an 18thC building behind, also part of the hotel, with a tiny secret garden wedged in between. Breakfasts can be had in the courtyard or in the intimate cellar bar; service is smiling and courteous. But as the hotel's own brochure points out, there are two famous cafés (the Deux Magots and the Flore) only a few blocks away. Prices are high, but not unreasonable we felt, especially in comparison with other hotels in this category, and Gun Karin Lalisse, the manager, runs the hotel with great charm and efficiency.
**Nearby** Hôtel des Invalides; Musée d'Orsay; Rodin Museum.

14 rue de St-Simon, 75007 Paris
**Tel** 01.44.39.20.20/reservations 01.42.20.07.52
**Fax** 01.45.48.68.25
**Location** between blvd St-Germain and rue de Grenelle; parking at blvd Raspail; metro Rue du Bac/Solférino
**Meals** breakfast, light meals
**Prices** FFF-FFFF; breakfast F
**Rooms** 29 double, 28 with bath, one with shower; 5 suites; all rooms have phone, hairdrier, safe; TV on request; some rooms have air-conditioning
**Facilities** 2 sitting-rooms, bar, lift **Credit cards** AE, MC, V
**Children** accepted
**Disabled** no special facilities
**Pets** not accepted
**Closed** never
**Proprietor** M. Lindqvist

# Ile-de-France

## Hôtel Eber

Jean-Marc Eber remains as committed as ever to the little hotel he took over in the late 1980s after more than a decade practising his hotelkeeping in four-star Paris hotels.

The turn-of-the-century house, easily missed in a quiet residential street not far from the Champs Elysées and near the Parc Monceau, is well cared for and prettily furnished and decorated, and M. Eber's combination of warmth and professionalism makes sure that the hotel stays well out of the rut. The public areas are tiny, but inviting – there is a small beamed sitting area off the reception and a pretty little courtyard. Breakfast may be taken in either of these places, or in your bedroom. These vary in size and feel, priced accordingly – our inspector's had a little sitting-room and a shower room as well as a bathroom. Some have lofty ceilings, others are small-scale, all are attractive, using neutral colours with elegant flower-patterned curtains. Best of all is the top-floor apartment with its own private terrace, much favoured, says Monsieur Eber, by fashion directors during Parish Fashion Week. The house rule is to 'make yourself at home' – after a hard day's sightseeing, an inviting prospect.

**Nearby** Parc Monceau, Arc du Triomphe, Champs Elysées.

18 Rue Léon Jost 75017 Paris
**Tel** 01.46.22.60.70
**Fax** 01.47.63.01.01
**Location** in residential area, close to Champs Elysées; parking rue de Courcelles; metro Courcelles
**Meals** breakfast
**Prices** rooms FF, suites FFF-FFF; breakfast F
**Rooms** 18 double (3 twin), all with bath; all rooms have central heating, air-conditioning, cable TV, phone, minibar, hairdrier
**Facilities** some rooms have private sitting-area
**Credit cards** AE, DC, MC, V
**Children** accepted
**Disabled** no special facilities
**Pets** not accepted
**Closed** never
**Proprietor** Jean Marc Eber

# Ile-de-France

**Town hotel, Paris**

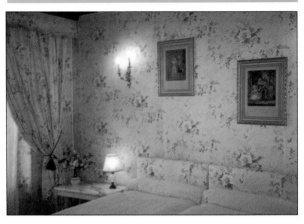

# Hôtel Ermitage

We were entranced when we found the Ermitage, a stone Baroque-style building tucked away behind Sacré Coeur. Only a sober wall plaque announces that this is a hotel, the door opening onto a smart little gold and cream lobby, followed by a dark blue hall with deep red carpet strewn with rugs. From the reception you can see a charming kitchen with its faïence stove from Lorraine (breakfast is prepared here and served in your room) and a little terrace beyond. Also on the ground floor: an old fashioned parlour, with green velvet hangings, filled with antiques and photographs. Par for the course so far, you may think, yet the Ermitage has a decorative surprise which starts in the hall and continues all the way up the stairs, on walls, doors, glass panels, skirtings: the charming, shadowy paint effects and murals of the artist Du Buc – those in the reception area, sketchy scenes of Montmartre, were done in 1986 when he was an old man.

Eclectic and friendly, the Ermitage is the creation of Maggie Canipel, its endearing *patronne*. Bedrooms are by and large light and spacious, with old fashioned charm: floral wallpapers, lace curtains, 'English fabrics', large *armoires*. Those on the ground floor benefit from the leafy terrace with views of eastern Paris. Bathrooms are tiny, many with mini baths, with showers above.
**Nearby** Sacré Coeur; Place du Tertre.

24 rue Lamarck, 75018 Paris
**Tel** 01.42.64.79.22
**Fax** 01.42.64.10.33
**Location** at eastern end of rue Lamarck, close to Sacré Coeur; parking in nearby private garage; metro Lamarck Caulaincourt
**Meals** breakfast
**Prices** F; breakfast included
**Rooms** 12 double; 3 family room; 11 rooms have bath or mini bath and shower; all rooms have phone, hairdrier
**Facilities** sitting-room
**Credit cards** not accepted
**Children** accepted
**Disabled** 2 rooms on ground floor
**Pets** accepted
**Closed** never
**Proprietor** Maggie Canipel

# Ile-de-France

**Town hotel, Paris**

# Hôtel de Fleurie ★

A model hotel, rightly very popular, where charm, efficiency and up-to-date comforts go hand-in-hand. Renovated in the 1980s by the Marolleau family, who used to own the well-known Latin Quarter brasserie, Balzar, it combines an immaculate appearance (not least the pretty façade, elegantly lit at night, complete with statues in the niches) with a cosy, intimate feel. The hands-on owners – parents and two sons – are determined to keep it so, and the place always feels fresh, clean and well cared for.

Instantly eye-catching in the terracotta-tiled reception is a delightful *faience* stove picked up by Madame Marolleau in the Saint Antoine flea market; the adjoining sitting room, with its exposed beams and section of ancient wall, has a discreet bar and little tables covered in Provençal cloths. The basement *cave*, where a generous breakfast is served, is equally cosy, cleverly lit by uplighters.

The spotless bedrooms do not disappoint. You will find pretty billowing curtains, walls of panelled wood and grasspaper, period style furniture, inviting beds and - a rare touch - fresh flowers. Bathrooms, all in pink-hued marble, are well equipped with thick towels on heated rails and towelling bath robes.

**Nearby** Saint-Sulpice; Jardin de Luxembourg.

32 rue Grégoire-de-Tours
75006 Paris
**Tel** 01.53.73.70.00
**Fax** 01.53.73.70.20
**E-mail** bonjour@hotel-de-fleurie.tm.fr
**Location** between blvd Saint-Germain and rue des Quatres-Vents; parking at rue de l'Ecole de Médecine; metro Mabillon, Odéon
**Meals** breakfast
**Prices** FF-FFF; family rooms

FFFF; breakfast F
**Rooms** 29 all with bath or shower; all rooms have phone, TV, fax/modem plug, air-conditioning, minibar, hairdryer, safe **Facilities** sitting room, bar, breakfast room, lift **Credit cards** AE, DC, MC, V **Disabled** no special facilities **Pets** not accepted **Closed** never
**Proprietors** Marolleau family

# Ile-de-France

# Hôtel du Jeu de Paume

We feature no less than four hotels in the delightful rue Saint-Louis-en-l'Ile; but whereas the others are homely, this one is highly original with considerable panache.

As its name implies, the building was the site of a 17thC *jeu de paume* court, built in the days when the 'palm game', forerunner to tennis, was all the rage; when the proprietors acquired it ten years ago, however, it was a run-down warehouse. Monsieur Prache is an architect and he wrought something of a miracle on the building, opening out the heart of it right up to the roof, exposing all the old timber construction and slinging mezzanine floors around a central well. The impression of light and transparency is reinforced by a glass-walled lift and glass balustrades around the upper floors. Stone walls and all those beams add a reassuringly rustic feel. The sitting area close to the entrance has the appearance of a sophisticated private apartment with leather sofas, subtle lighting and handsome stone fireplace. Nearby, at the reception desk, the chic, laid-back staff adjust their designer shawls and coolly deal with the guests while a stylish sheepdog pads around. Madame Prache is charming. Bedrooms are small-ish, perfectly pleasant, but nothing like as exciting as the rest of the hotel.

**Nearby** Marais; Nôtre-Dame; Latin Quarter.

54 rue Saint-Louis-en-l'Ile
75004 Paris
**Tel** 01.43.26.14.18
**Fax** 01.40.46.02.76
**Location** halfway along the island's main street, near the junction with rue des Deux Ponts; car parking at Pont-Marie; metro Pont Marie, Cité
**Meals** breakfast
**Prices** FFF; suite FFFF; breakfast F

**Rooms** 30, 1 suite, all with bath and shower; all rooms have phone, TV, minibar, hairdrier **Facilities** breakfast room, sitting-room, bar, lift, courtyard; fitness room, 2 conference rooms, **Credit cards** AE, DC, MC, V **Children** accepted **Disabled** access difficult **Pets** accepted – 50F per day **Closed** never **Proprietors** M. and Mme Prache

# Ile-de-France

## Hôtel Mansart

A stone's throw from the Ritz, spacious bedrooms which recall an earlier, more gracious era, attentive service, fair prices – these are the principle attributes of the excellent Mansart. Recently restored, the aged hotel's former proportions were left mercifully intact. The large modern lobby, with its expanse of marble floor and walls boldly painted in geometric patterns based on Mansart's drawings for the gardens of Versaille (he was also architect of place Vendôme) is impressive, but it doesn't prepare you for the bedrooms, which you might expect to be similarly contemporary. In fact, though recently decorated, they have a dignified, old-fashioned flavour quite different from downstairs. We loved no. 205, which feels like a private flat with its own entrance hall opening onto a large room with antique mirrored *armoir* and regal prints on the white walls, the panelling picked out in gold. The separate bathroom has a pretty tiled floor, as do all the bathrooms. A cheaper option, but equally stately, is no. 212, a huge room with space for table and chairs, with large gilt-framed mirrors, attractive curtains, panelled walls and a green and white bathroom – at 930F excellent value, we felt. Be warned, though – one or two singles are pokey. The breakfast room, with stained-glass windows and marble fireplace, is very elegant.

**Nearby** place Vendôme; Opéra Garnier; place de la Concorde.

Rue des Capucines 75001 Paris
**Tel** 01.42.61.50.28
**Fax** 01.49.27.97.44
**Location** on the corner of place Vendôme; parking at place Vendôme; metro Opéra, Madeleine
**Meals** breakfast
**Prices** FF-FFFF
**Rooms** 57, 50 double with bath, 3 with shower; 4 single all with bath; all rooms have phone, minibar, satellite TV, hairdrier, safe
**Facilities** sitting-room, bar, lift
**Credit cards** AE, DC, MC, V
**Children** accepted
**Disabled** no special facilities
**Pets** not accepted
**Closed** never
**Proprietor** M. Dupaen

# Ile-de-France

## Town hotel, Paris

# Hôtel de Nice

Here is a wonderfully wacky two star hotel, every bit as comfortable and twice as enjoyable as many a more expensive three star. We thought it a terrific find, instantly intrigued and not disappointed by what lay behind the vivid turquoise front door and up the tightly winding stairs.

The Nice is the enchanting creation of a previously high-flying professional couple who love both collecting and entertaining. The fruits of their hobby are everywhere – masses of period engravings and prints – particularly of Paris – mirrors, old doors, postcards, even a splendid portrait of Lady Diana Cooper. The effect is charming and highly individual – the panelled *salon*, for example, where you can also take breakfast, is a harmony of uncoordinated colours, fabrics (the ceiling is tented in Indian cotton) and furniture: antique, painted, modern, garden. The use of wallpaper copied from French 18thC designs makes the smallish bedrooms feel fresh and pretty, with the off-beat addition of Indian cotton bedspreads, and doors and skirtings boldly painted in turquoise, orange or pillar-box red. Two attic rooms on the top floor are particularly charming, with their own little balconies. Others look out on to a pretty square. You'll find only basic amenities here, but plenty of character.

**Nearby** Marais; Les Halles; Ile Saint-Louis; Nôtre Dame.

42 bis rue de Rivoli 75004 Paris
**Tel** 01.42.78.55.29
**Fax** 01.42.78.36.07
**Location** on corner of rue de Rivoli and little square of rue du Bourg Tibourg; parking at Hôtel de Ville (rue de Lobau); metro Hôtel de Ville
**Meals** breakfast
**Prices** F; breakfast F
**Rooms** 23; one family room;

all with bath or shower; all rooms have phone, satellite TV, hairdrier
**Facilities** sitting-room/breakfast room, lift
**Credit cards** MC, V
**Children** accepted
**Disabled** no special facilities
**Pets** accepted
**Closed** never
**Proprietors** M. and Mme Vaudoux

# Ile-de-France

## Hôtel d'Orsay

We felt a pang of nostalgia as we passed into the new Hôtel d'Orsay beneath the blue fascia with large gilt letters which announces that this was once the Solférino. The two hotels have been knocked into one, which now belongs to the same select group as the Mansart (page 57). Although the dividing wall has been demolished, the d'Orsay still feels like two separate hotels with two very different styles.

The part that was originally the Hôtel d'Orsay has been given a total makeover; bedrooms have been redecorated in pastel shades with pretty floral fabrics and attractive bathrooms in white and boldly coloured Italian tiles. These rooms are undoubtedly tasteful, comfortable and offer good value for the area, but our inspectors found themselves yearning for the big old Solférino rooms, with their scruffy blue doors and faded looks. These still exist, but look very shabby and in need of attention now. Their redecoration is planned, and in a year or so we expect all the bedrooms to conform to the new type. We were relieved to find unchanged the spring-like breakfast room with its cane chairs, glass ceiling and pale yellow walls decorated with pretty plates – a favourite of ours.

**Nearby** Musée d'Orsay; Tuileries; Louvre; blvd Saint-Germain and other Left Bank sights.

91 rue de Lille, 75007 Paris
**Tel** (01) 47 05 85 54
**E-mail** hotel.orsay@wanadoo.fr
**Fax** (01) 45 55 51 16
**Location** in stretch of street between blvd Saint-Germain and rue de Solférino; parking rue du Bac; metro Assemblée Nationale
**Meals** breakfast
**Prices** F-FF; breakfast F
**Rooms** 50 double and twin, single, suites, all with bath or shower; all rooms have phone, TV; new rooms have minibar, hairdrier
**Facilities** sitting-room, breakfast-room, lift
**Credit cards** MC, V
**Children** accepted
**Disabled** no special facilities
**Pets** not accepted
**Closed** never
**Manager** David Chevalier

# Ile-de-France

# Hôtel Parc Saint-Séverin

Of the many bedrooms described in this book, no. 70 at the Parc Saint-Séverin remains this writer's favourite. And although it's an expensive choice, its assets are far greater than, say, a standard double room at the Pavillon de la Reine (page 61) or the Relais Christine (page 62) which cost some 200F per night more. Overall, of course, those are far superior hotels, but this room is special: a light, sophisticated and beautifully decorated penthouse suite which is entirely encircled by a broad private terrace affording breathtaking views across the rooftops of all the landmark buildings as far as the Eiffel Tower in one direction, Sacré-Coeur in another. Taking breakfast on a warm summer morning is sheer bliss. Less expensive, but nonetheless very impressive, are two more rooms, each with a broad terrace on three sides. On lower floors, room nos 50 and 12 both have style and space. The rest are pleasant, if unexceptional, pastel coloured, with predominantly grey modern furniture; bathrooms are generally quite spacious with generous basins. The large ground floor lobby, which divides into three areas for reception, breakfast and sitting, is a disappointment, another example of contemporary colours – grey, pink, mauve – abstract paintings and minimalist furniture failing to inspire.

**Nearby** Notre-Dame; Sainte-Chapelle; Musée de Cluny.

22 rue de la Parcheminerie
75005 Paris
**Tel** 01.43.54.32.17
**Fax** 01.43.54.70.71
**E-mail** hotel.parc.severin@wanadoo.fr
**Location** in a pedestrian area close to Saint-Séverin and the junction with rue des Prêtres Saint-Séverin; parking at rue Lagrange; metro Saint-Michel
**Meals** breakfast
**Prices** FF-FFF; suite FFFF

**Rooms** 22 double and twin, 1 family room, 4 single, all with bath; all rooms have phone, satellite TV, minibar, hairdrier, safe; half are air-conditioned **Facilities** breakfast room, sitting area, lift
**Credit cards** AE, DC, MC, V
**Children** accepted
**Disabled** no special facilities
**Pets** not accepted **Closed** never **Manager** Benoît Mulliez

# Ile-de-France

## Pavillon de la Reine

Set back from the gloriously harmonious Place des Vosges, approached through a calming courtyard garden, the Pavillon de la Reine has our vote for the most perfect location in Paris. Like its sister hotel, the Relais Christine (see page 62) it is run with calm professionalism by a dedicated and friendly team, although, it lacks the intimacy of a truly Charming Small Hotel (at 55 bedrooms it is one of our largest, but feels delightfully contained).

The fine 17thC mansion was once the residence of Ann of Austria, wife of Louis XIII. Rescued from near ruin a dozen years ago, it now feels more like a baronial country house, with an impressive entrance hall, a handsome panelled sitting-room with comfy leather sofas and a huge stone fireplace complete with roaring log fire, stone-vaulted breakfast room and two flowery courtyards. For us, the only jarring note was the use of reproduction old masters in some rooms. We were told about the guest of another hotel who had replaced an expensive original canvas with a copy, but still, we felt it was a misconceived idea. Upstairs, via a lift cleverly disguised by *trompe l'oeil*, bedrooms and suites contrive to be both smart and pretty, immaculately maintained and suitably luxurious, with ornaments here and there adding a personal touch.

**Nearby** Musée Carnavalet; Musée Picasso; Notre-Dame.

28 place des Vosges 75003 Paris
**Tel** 01.40.29.19.19
**Fax** 01.40.29 19 20
**Location** northern side of place des Vosges; free private garage; metro Saint-Paul
**Meals** breakfast; light meals served in room at any time
**Prices** FFFF; breakfast FF
**Rooms** 55, all with bath and shower; all rooms have phone, satellite TV, air conditioning, minibar, hairdrier
**Facilities** sitting-room, breakfast room, 2 courtyard gardens, lift, garage
**Credit cards** AE, DC, MC, V
**Children** accepted
**Disabled** ground floor bedrooms
**Pets** accepted
**Closed** never
**Manager** Véronique Ellinger

# Ile-de-France

# Hôtel Relais Christine

The Relais Christine used to be the *sixième*'s most prestigious hotel, but now finds itself competing with less expensive establishments for the same clients. If you can afford it, though, you are unlikely to be disappointed: it has the calm, luxurious feel of a grand hotel but on a far more intimate scale; in this it is matched only by its sister hotel, the Pavillon de la Reine (see page 60). It is also the only hotel in the Rive Gauche area to offer its guests free car parking in a private garage.

Approached through a handsome courtyard, the Relais Christine is an oasis of dignified calm. The reception hall is coolly tiled and strewn with Persian rugs, and the ceiling retains its original painted beams. In the handsome panelled sitting-room, a help-yourself drinks table enhances the feel of a private room. Traces of the building's medieval roots are visible in the elegant stone-vaulted breakfast room which has a huge hearth and a massive central pillar. Bedrooms are decorated with the same sense of restrained luxury as at the Pavillon de la Reine, with plenty of cupboard space, pretty paintings, and bathrooms (all with separate W.C.s) in which it is a pleasure to idle away time. All the bedrooms are a fair size, especially the duplex rooms.

**Nearby** blvd Saint-Germain; Ile de la Cité; Latin Quarter.

3 Rue Christine 75006 Paris
**Tel** 01.40.51.60.80
**Fax** 01.40.51.60.81
**E-mail** relais@club-internet.fr
**Location** in a quiet street between rue Dauphine and rue des Grands Augustins; free private garage; metro Odéon
**Meals** breakfast
**Prices** FFFF; breakfast FF
**Rooms** 38 double and twin, 13 suites, all with bath (separate W.C.); all rooms have phone, satellite TV, air-conditioning, minibar, safe, hairdrier **Facilities** sitting-room, breakfast room, bar, meeting room, lift, garage
**Credit cards** AE, DC, MC,V
**Children** accepted
**Disabled** access difficult
**Pets** accepted **Closed** never
**Manager** M. Monnin

# Ile-de-France

**Town hotel, Paris**

## Le Relais du Louvre

In a quiet side street hard by the Louvre and the river, this sophisticated little hotel proves that, in the right hands, even the most featureless of bedrooms can be made to feel charming and welcoming. Most are standard box-shape, no more than adequate in size, although some have the benefit of beamed ceilings and floor length windows. Ours had a terrific view on to the gables and gargoyles of Saint-Germain-l'Auxerrois opposite and, though small, felt extremely welcoming and comforting, with its pink hydrangea curtains and matching bedspread, elegant desk and bedside tables, each with a decent-sized lamp. On the walls were pretty 19thC fashion plates, and the television could be popped away in the upholstered box on which it sat. The marble-clad bathroom was equipped with generous towels. Breakfast is served in your bedroom. Downstairs, an elegant beamed reception room, with a polished antique table serving as the reception desk, sets the hotel's tone.

Rooms are cleverly arranged so that a pair can be taken together, closed off behind a communal front door; two ground floor rooms have access onto a little patio. The manageress, Sophie Aulnette, and her close-knit staff pride themselves on trying to accommodate clients in the best, most budget-conscious way.

**Nearby** Louvre; Ile de la Cité; Samaritaine store (rooftop view).

19 rue des Prêtres-Saint-Germain-l'Auxerrois 75001 Paris
**Tel** 01.40.41.96.42
**Fax** 01.40.41.96.44
**E-mail** au-relais-du-louvre@dial.oleane.com
**Location** in a quiet side street parallel to Quai du Louvre; public car park opposite; metro Pont Neuf, Louvre Rivoli; Châtelet-les-Halles
**Meals** breakfast

**Prices** FF; suites FFF; breakfast F **Rooms** 21; 16 double, all with bath and shower; 5 single all with shower; 2 suites; 1 penthouse; all rooms have phone, cable TV, mini bar, hairdryer, safe **Facilities** sitting area, lift **Credit cards** AE, DC, MC, V **Children** accepted **Disabled** 2 rooms **Pets** accepted **Closed** never **Manager** Sophie Aulnette

# Ile-de-France

**Town hotel, Paris**

# Le Relais Saint-Germain

Irresistible, if you can afford it: a sumptuous 17thC house whose mini-lift and cramped public rooms – albeit artfully mirrored and glossily decorated – give no hint of the wonderfully spacious bedrooms upstairs. Expensive though the Relais Saint Germain undoubtedly is, bear in mind that what is termed a 'standard double' here would be called a 'junior suite' elsewhere – that is, a bedroom large enough for a sitting area as well. Most 'standard' rooms in Paris give you just enough room to swing a cat. The deluxe rooms are enormous, with two sets of French windows overlooking the street; they are embellished with stunning antiques – mostly French country – plump sofas, lovely fabrics and well-chosen prints and pictures. One is notable for its pair of stone angels culled from a medieval chapel, another for two beautiful matching bookcases. The top floor suite is a dashing yellow, with black and white prints on the walls, ancient sprouting beams and a tiny sun-trap terrace.

In the morning, it's hard to choose whether to take breakfast in bed or in the adjoining café, now part of the hotel and closed to the public until noon. Here you can enjoy the ambience of an authentic 1930s café once frequented by Hemingway, Picasso *et al*, married to slick hotel service.

**Nearby** blvd Saint-Germain; Saint-Sulpice; Latin Quarter.

9 carrefour de l'Odéon 75006 Paris
**Tel** 01.44.27.07.97
**Fax** 01.46.33.45.30
**Location** off blvd Saint-Germain, at the corner of rue Monsieur Le Prince; parking at rue l'Ecole de Médecine; metro Odéon
**Meals** breakfast
**Prices** FFF-FFFF; suite FFFF; breakfast included

**Rooms** 21, 1 suite, all with bath; all rooms have phone, cable TV, video, fax/modem plug, air-conditioning, mini-bar, hairdrier, safe
**Facilities** 2 small sitting-rooms, breakfast room/ bar, lift **Credit cards** AE, DC, MC, V **Children** accepted
**Disabled** not suitable
**Pets** accepted **Closed** never
**Proprietor** Alexis Laipsker

## Ile-de-France

**Town hotel, Paris**

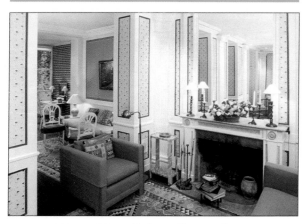

# Hotel Le Saint-Gregoire

A chic, if pricey, little hotel in a tall 18thC town house, run with affable charm by manager Francois de Bené. Le Saint-Gregoire was designed by Christian Badin of David Hicks – dusty pink walls, maroon carpets, floral peachy curtains, and crisp white linen bedspreads and chair covers – and a warm intimate atmosphere prevails. An open fire blazes in the salon on wintry afternoons, a room dotted with antiques and knickknacks, picked up by Madame Bouvier, the owner's wife, in flea markets and antique shops. These range from a basket of fir cones on the mantlepiece to a pretty tin table decorated with an Italian scene, but are liable to change weekly as new acquisitions are made. Trellis on the walls and large French windows leading on to a tiny enclosed garden, full of flowers and ferns, make the back part of the sitting room feel more like a conservatory.

The colour scheme leads from the ground floor upstairs to equally attractive bedrooms, with beautiful antique chests of drawers, tables and mirrors; two bedrooms have private terraces. Bathrooms are typically white tiled and small but well designed. The ubiquitous cellar breakfast room is a particularly pretty one, with woven floor, rush chairs and baskets decorating one wall.

**Nearby** Musée Bourdelle; Jardin du Luxembourg; blvd St-Germain.

43 rue de l'Abbé-Gregoire
75006 Paris
**Tel** 01.45.48.23.23
**Fax** 01.45.48.33.95
**E-mail** hotel@saintgregoire.com
**Location** between blvd Raspail and blvd du Montparnasse; parking rue de l'Abbé-Gregoire in garage by arrangement; metro St Placide/Rennes
**Meals** breakfast

**Prices** rooms FF-FFF; breakfast F
**Rooms** 20, all with bath; all rooms have phone, satellite TV, air-conditioning, hairdrier **Facilities** sitting room, break-fast room, lift
**Credit cards** AE, DC, MC, V
**Children** welcome **Disabled** no special facilities **Pets** small pets accepted **Closed** never
**Proprietor** M. Bouvier

# Ile-de-France

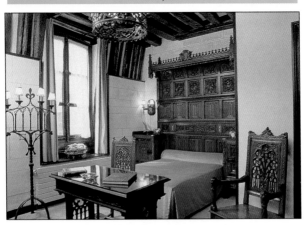

# Hôtel Saint-Merry ★

One of the most distinctive small hotels in Paris, the Saint-Merry has a church-like, medieval atmosphere all its own, with heavily beamed ceilings, pale stone walls, wrought iron fittings and splendid carved wood neo-Gothic furnishings. Everything is kept simple: bedrooms and bathrooms are spotless though mostly small; there are no public rooms to speak of, and breakfast, which is brought to your room, is prepared in a tiny galley behind the reception; a spiralling staircase is the sole means by which you can reach your room; only three bathrooms have baths; and TVs and minibars are only to be found in the suites.

This former presbytery of the adjacent church of Saint-Merri became a private residence after the 1789 revolution, and served for a time as a brothel before it was rescued from decay by its committed proprietor, Christian Crabbe, in the 1960s. He decided on its memorable – if sombre – style after acquiring some neo-Gothic furnishings which were languishing in the basement of the church. The hotel is famous for room 9, where flying buttresses form a low canopy over the bed, whilst rooms 12 and 17 have remarkable bedheads. Even after 36 years, work on the hotel, says M. Crabbe "never ends". Recently he created a charming suite, complete with huge stone chimney breast, tucked under the eves.
**Nearby** Pompidou Centre; Les Halles; Marais; Notre-Dame.

78 rue de la Verrerie 75004 Paris
**Tel** 01.42.78.14.15
**Fax** 01.40.29.06.82
**Location** in a pedestrianized zone, on the corner of rue de la Verrerie and rue Saint-Martin; parking at St Martin; metro Hôtel de Ville
**Meals** breakfast
**Prices** F-FFF, suite FFFF; breakfast F

**Rooms** 11 with bath, 8 with shower, 2 without WC; 2 family rooms, both with shower; 1 suite; all rooms have phone, hairdrier
**Facilities** small sitting area
**Credit cards** AE, V
**Children** accepted
**Disabled** not suitable (no lift)
**Pets** accepted
**Closed** never
**Proprietor** Christian Crabbe

# Ile-de-France

**Town hotel, Paris**

## Hôtel Saint-Paul ★

We like this hotel very much, as have friends to whom we have recommended it. The owner's family have been talented hoteliers in France for generations; she married an Englishman, and now their friendly and capable daughter, Marianne Hawkins, is in charge, accompanied by Spoutnik, the cat.

The Saint-Paul is a 17thC building, renovated to create public rooms which are stylish in an unfussy way with beamed ceilings, a mixture of stone and colour-washed walls, Indian rugs, *haute epoque* and good country antiques, dark pink drapes and attractive pink and green checked armchairs. Facing the entrance, a courtyard garden is set behind a glass wall, carefully tended and full of colour year round. The cellar breakfast room is a particularly elegant variation on the theme, with high-backed tapestry chairs and round wooden tables. If the reception rooms have a rural feel, so do the bedrooms, all of which are differently decorated, with walls covered in grass cloth or enlivened with a dash of bright colour, and smart, carefully lit bathrooms clad in ginger or reddish marble. Our room under the eaves felt cosy, with views over the rooftops; others have four-posters or antique brass bedsteads. All in all easy going and well run: a pleasure to stay in.

**Nearby** Latin Quarter; Musée de Cluny; Jardin de Luxembourg.

43 Rue Monsieur Le Prince
75006 Paris
**Tel** 01.43.26.98.64
**Fax** 01.46.34.58.60
**E-mail** hotel.saint.paul@wanadoo.fr
**Location** halfway along street, in section between rue Racine and rue de Vaugirard; parking at rue l'Ecole de Médicine, rue Soufflot; metro Odéon.
**Meals** breakfast

**Prices** FF-FFF; breakfast F, **Rooms** 31, all with bath or shower; all rooms have phone, TV, air-conditioning (on request), minibar, hairdryer, safe **Facilities** sitting-room, breakfast room, lift/elevator **Credit cards** AE, DC, MC, V **Children** accepted **Disabled** 1 ground floor room **Pets** accepted **Closed** never **Proprietors** Hawkins family

# Ile-de-France

# Hôtel Le Sainte-Beuve

All is discretion and understatement at this essentially simple little hotel with luxurious touches: plain cream walls, restrained patterns in the rich fabrics; beds draped in white, simple furniture mixing modern designs with country antiques, attractive pictures, fresh flowers strategically placed. A log fire burns in the classically-styled *salon*, and there is also a bar, complete with barman in the evening.

Thanks to its owner, Bobette Compagnon, the Sainte-Beuve, though no more than a bed-and-breakfast hotel, has an innate sense of style which rescues it from the rut and sets it apart, along with some pampering extra services. The excellent breakfast — which arrives on a tray beautifully laid with porcelain – can be ordered at any time of day or night, as well as a selection of cold dishes.

During our stay we met someone who had benefited from the hotel's policy of upgrading guests, whenever possible, to a more expensive room than was booked, and another who was accompanied by her three cats – every bit as stylish as their owner – one of which had inadvertently escaped and which we found wandering down the winding staircase – a dizzying sight from the top floor – as we passed.

**Nearby** Montparnasse; blvd Saint-Germain.

9 rue Sainte-Beuve 75006 Paris
**Tel** 01.45.48.20.07
**Fax** 01.45.48.67.52
**E-mail** saintebeuve@wanadoo.fr
**Location** off blvd Raspail, between place Lafou and place Picasso; street parking or car park in blvd Montparnasse; metro Notre Dame des Champs, Vavin
**Meals** breakfast; cold dishes
**Prices** FF-FFFF; suite FFFF; breakfast F
**Rooms** 23; all rooms have phone, satellite TV, minibar, hairdryer and safe
**Facilities** sitting room/breakfast room, bar, lift **Credit cards** AE, MC, V **Children** accepted **Disabled** access difficult **Pets** accepted **Closed** never **Proprietor** Bobette Compagnon

# Ile-de-France

## Le Vert Galant

Even if you don't stay at Le Vert Galant, try to come out here for a meal at the Auberge Etchegorry next door, owned by the same couple. In an annexe overlooking a lush lawn, the pastel Art Deco-inspired bedrooms radiate calm. Ground-floor studios boast French windows and kitchenettes. An attractive conservatory, full of plants, has tables and chairs and makes a great place for breakfast or coffee.

The *raison d'être* of the hotel is the restaurant. A rural inn in the early 19thC, it grew famous as the haunt of such celebrities as Victor Hugo, Béranger and Chateaubriand. Here, beside the now extinct River Bièvre, they were charmed by the voluptuous cabaret artiste, Madame Grégoire. Little appears to have changed in the *auberge*, decorated with bright copper pans and hams, sausages and garlic hanging from beams. Walls are half-panelled; the simple chairs have rush seats, the tables, crisp linen cloths. The cuisine is from the Basque region and includes such deliciously hearty specialities as duck *fois gras* and *confits*. But it is the atmosphere that makes this such an appealing place. Henri Laborde (Maité runs the hotel) is a genial host, who, even though he speaks no English, manages to make his customers feel wonderfully welcome.

**Nearby** square René Le Gall; Manufacture des Gobelins.

41-43 rue Croulebarbe, 75013 Paris **Tel/Hotel** (01) 44 08 83 50 **Restaurant** (01) 44 08 83 51 **Fax** (01) 44 08 83 69 **Location** at junction with rue des Reculettes; parking free private; metro Corvisart, place d'Italie, Les Gobelins **Meals** breakfast; lunch and dinner in restaurant **Prices** rooms F; breakfast F; menus FF **Rooms** 16; 15 double and twin, all with bath or shower; one single with shower; all have phone, TV, hairdrier **Facilities** breakfast/ sitting-room, garden, restaurant; 5 rooms have kitchenettes **Credit cards** AE, DC, MC, V **Children** accepted **Disabled** one specially adapted room **Pets** accepted **Closed** never **Proprietors** M. and Mme Laborde

# Ile-de-France

---

Inn, Barbizon

## Hôtellerie du Bas-Breau

Half of Europe's political grandees have been guests at this hand-some and luxurious (Relais & Châteaux) inn. The best rooms are in the inn itself; but the majority are in a modern chalet set amid the beautifully tended flower gardens. Excellent food. Swimming-pool.

■ 22 Rue Grande, 77630 Barbizon (Seine-et-Marne) **Tel** 01.60.66.40.05 **Fax** 01.60.69.22.89 **Meals** breakfast, lunch, dinner **Prices** rooms FF-FFFF; breakfast FF, dinner FFF **Rooms** 20, all with bath, central heating, phone, TV, hairdrier **Credit cards** AE, MC, V **Closed** never

---

Restaurant with rooms, Barbizon

## Hostellerie de la Clé d'Or

The key attraction is the shady courtyard where meals (well cooked, ample portions) are served in summer. Bedrooms (begin-ning to look a little shabby, according to a recent report) are in a handsome single-storey extension. Smart dining-room with an open fireplace and walls covered in daubs by local artists. Delightful garden.

■ 73 Grande Rue, 77630 Barbizon (Seine-et-Marne) **Tel** 01.60.66.40.96 **Fax** 01.60.66.42.71 **Meals** breakfast, lunch, dinner **Prices** rooms F-FF; menus FF, children's 75F **Rooms** 17, all with bath or shower, central heating, phone, TV, minibar **Credit cards** AE, DC, MC, V **Closed** never

---

Town hotel, Paris

## Hôtel Beaubourg

Although this six-storey town house dates back to the 1600s, the hotel is not lacking in modern comforts; bedrooms and public rooms are pleasantly furnished and effectively lit. Opt for one of the bedrooms overlooking the courtyard garden, full of trailing plants, or the room on the ground floor with its own terrace.

■ 11 Rue Simon Lefranc, 75004 Paris **Tel** 01.42.74.34.24 **Fax** 01.42.78.68.11 **Meals** breakfast **Prices** rooms FF (extra bed 150F); breakfast F **Rooms** 28, all with bath or shower, central heating, phone, TV, radio, minibar **Credit cards** AE, DC, MC, V **Closed** never

---

Town hotel, Paris

## Hôtel Bersoly's Saint-Germain

On a quiet street in the administrative heart of Paris, this 17thC former convent makes an excellent sightseeing base. Each of the bedrooms – generally on the small side – has been thoughtfully done out in a favourite colour of the impressionist painter it is named after. Car parking. Reports welcome.

■ 28 Rue de Lille, 75007 Paris **Tel** 01.42.60.73.79 **Fax** 01.49.27.05.55 **Meals** breakfast, snacks **Prices** rooms FF; breakfast F **Rooms** 16, all with bath or shower, central heating, air-conditioning phone, TV, radio, hair-drier, safe **Credit cards** MC, V **Closed** 2 weeks in Aug

# Ile-de-France

---

Town hotel, Paris

# Hôtel Caron de Beaumarchais

If the *décor* is a mite chi-chi for our taste, most other guests find it enchanting, and everyone agrees that it is an extremely congenial place in which to stay. Monsieurs Bigeard *père et fils* genuinely want their guests to be contented. Beneath the surface gloss is a real heart. New to the guide this year.

■ 12 rue Vieille-du-Temple, 75004 Paris **Tel** 01.42.72.34.12 **Fax** 01.42.72.34.63. **Meals** breakfast; brunch **Prices** FF; breakfast F **Rooms** 19, 17 with bath, 2 with shower; all rooms have phone, fax/modem plug; satellite TV, air-conditioning, minibar, hairdrier **Credit cards** AE, DC, MC, V **Closed** never

---

Town hotel, Paris

# Hôtel Chopin ★

With a charming façade, the Chopin stands at the end of passage Jouffroy, a 19thC glass-and-steel roofed arcade.This is no tourist trap: the welcome is warm and friendly, and a caring hand (that of owner Philippe Bidal) was immediately in evidence in the decoration. All the rooms are quiet. New to the guide this year.

■ 10 blvd Montmartre (46 passage Jouffroy) 75009 Paris **Tel** 01.47.70. 58.10 **Fax** 01.42.47.00.70 **Meals** breakfast **Prices** rooms F-FF; breakfast F **Rooms** 36, all with bath or shower; all rooms have phone, TV **Credit cards** AE, MC, V **Closed** never

---

Town hotel, Paris

# Hôtel Le Clos Médicis

The charming Pascal Beherec owns the Clos Médicis, the equally charming Olivier Méallet manages it, but it is architect, Jean-Philippe Nuel, whose presence is most strongly felt. The entire interior, down to the light fittings and the wave-shaped headboards in the bedrooms, is his creation, circa 1994 – and a great success.

■ 56 rue Monsieur le Prince, 75006 Paris **Tel** 01.43 29 10 80 **Fax** 01.43.54.26.90 **E-mail** clos_medicis@compuserve.com **Meals** breakfast **Prices** rooms FF-FFF; breakfast F **Rooms** 38, all with bath, two with private terrace; all rooms have phone with private line, fax facility and baby listening, cable TV, air-conditioning, minibar, hairdrier **Credit cards** AE, DC, MC, V **Closed** never

---

Town hote, Paris

# Hôtel Le Colbert

Set back from the tiny rue Colbert and approached through a wrought-iron gate and imaginatively planted courtyard, this handsome building, with its origins in the 17thC, was converted in 1966 and retains its period atmosphere. It is quiet, has a genuinely friendly staff and is ideally placed for visiting the Ile de la Cité and Left Bank.

■ 7 rue de l'Hôtel-Colbert, 75005 Paris **Tel** 01.43.25.85.65 **Fax** 01.43. 25.80.19 **Meals** breakfast **Prices** FF-FFFF; breakfast FF **Rooms** 36, all with bath; all rooms have central heating, air-conditioning, phone, TV, minibar, hairdrier, safe **Credit cards** AE, DC, MC, V **Closed** never

# Ile-de-France

---

Town hotel, Paris

## Hôtel des Deux Iles

Roland Buffat's well-known converted townhouse has moved into its third decade as an archetypical charming small hotel, and although we have had some mixed reports, a recent letter confirms that M. Buffat and his staff are striving to be as attentive as ever to the needs of their guests, We would welcome more comments.

■ 59 rue Saint-Louis-en-l'Ile, 75004 Paris **Tel** 01.43.26.13.35 **Fax** 01.43.29.60.25 **Meals** breakfast **Prices** FF; breakfast F **Rooms** 17, all with bath or shower; all rooms have phone, cable TV, air-conditioning, hairdrier **Credit cards** AE, V **Closed** never

---

Town hotel, Paris

## Hôtel du Globe

A gem of a hotel – tiny and quaint. In the entrance – the building is 17thC, once part of the Abbey of Saint-Germain-des-Prés – a door set in a wrought iron grill leads to perhaps the smallest *salon* in Paris. No breakfast room – it is brought to you. Bedooms have an old fashioned charm. For its appeal, location and price, the Globe is hard to beat.

■ 15 rue des Quatre-Vents, 75006 Paris **Tel** 01.43.26.35.50 **Fax** 01.46.33.62.69 **Meals** breakfast; light meals served in room **Prices** F; breakfast F **Rooms** 15, 5 with bath, 9 with shower; all rooms have phone, TV **Credit cards** MC, V **Closed** Aug

---

Bed and breakfast guest-house, Paris

## Hôtel des Grandes Écoles

The name refers to the Sorbonne, next door; the far-from-grand hotel retains the ambience of a country house, aided by its court-yard garden. Bedrooms are modestly furnished and some have thin walls; but a recent visitor was very pleased, especially by Mme LeFoch's 'cheerful disposition'. Parking available (100F).

■ 75 Rue de Cardinal Lemoine, 75005 Paris **Tel** 01.43.26.79.23 **Fax** 01.43.25 28 15 **E-mail** Hotel.Grandes.Ecoles@wanadoo.fr **Website** www.hotel-grandes-ecoles.com **Meals** breakfast **Prices** rooms FF; breakfast F **Rooms** 50, all with central heating , phone **Credit cards** MC, V **Closed** never

---

Town hotel, Paris

## Hôtel des Grands Hommes

Conflicting views on this handsome and well placed hotel, named after the artists and writers who used it in the past, the critics taking the view that prices are rather high for what you get. More reports would be welcome. If you opt for a view of the Panthéon, be prepared for a little street noise.

■ 17 Place du Panthéon, 75005 Paris **Tel** 01.46.34.19.60 **Fax** 01.43.26.67.32 **Meals** breakfast **Prices** rooms FF **Rooms** 32, all with bath or shower, central heating, air-conditioning, cable TV, radio, mini-bar, hairdrier **Credit cards** AE, DC, MC, V **Closed** never

# Ile-de-France

Town hotel, Paris

## Le Jardin des Plantes

Situated directly opposite the botanical gardens, this bright little hotel is now part of the Timhotel group and we welcome hearing about the change in management. Rooms on the top floor have the best views and some open on to the roof terrace. Breakfast can be served here, or in a café-style room. Sauna.

■ 5 Rue Linné, 75005 Paris **Tel** 01.47.07.06.20 **Fax** 01.47.07.62.74 **Meals** breakfast, lunch **Prices** rooms FF; breakfast F **Rooms** 33, all with bath or shower, central heating, phone, TV, minibar, hairdrier **Credit cards** AE, DC, MC, V **Closed** never

Town hotel, Paris

## The Lancaster

Just off the Champs-Elysées, the Lancaster may be large, but its intimacy envelops you once you pass through the old carriage entrance into the reception area. A red, leather-lined lift takes you up to discreetly luxurious bedrooms, furnished with antiques. One suite, in lilac tones, is named after Marlene Dietrich, one of the many famous habitués of the hotel. A large collection of paintings by Boris Pastoukhoff, adorns the walls – he exchanged his works of art to pay the bill. Courtyard garden, fitness centre and sauna.

■ 7 rue de Berri 75008 Paris **Tel** 01.40.76.40.76 **Fax** 01.40.76. 40.00 **E-mail** pippaona@hotel-lancaster.fr **Website** http://www.hotel-lancaster.fr **Meals** breakfast, lunch, dinner **Prices** rooms FFFF; suites FFFF, breakfast FF **Rooms** 50, 10 suites, all with bath and shower, central heating, air-conditioning, phone, TV, hairdrier **Credit cards** AE, DC, MC, V **Closed** never

Town hotel, Paris

## Hôtel Lenox Saint-Germain

The more central of a pair of polished sister hotels, both marked out by smoothly traditional furnishings. The Lenox started life at the turn of the century as a pension, but is now quite a suave hotel, with a clubby bar. Notably tasteful decoration in the bedrooms.

■ 9 Rue de l'Université, 75007 Paris **Tel** 01.42.96.10.95 **Fax** 01.42.61.52.83 **Meals** breakfast **Prices** rooms FF-FFFF; breakfast F **Rooms** 34, all with bath or shower, cent ral heating, phone, TV, hairdrier **Credit cards** AE, DC, MC, V **Closed** never

Town hotel, Paris

## Résidence Lord Byron

In an area of grand hotels, the Lord Byron stands out for its personal service and (by local standards) reasonable prices. Bedrooms tend to be smallish, but are modern and comfortable, with a mix of old and new furnishings. Little courtyard garden.

■ 5 Rue de Chateaubriand, 75008 Paris **Tel** 01.43.59.89.98 **Fax** 01.42.89.46.04 **Meals** breakfast **Prices** rooms FF-FFF; breakfast F **Rooms** 31, all with bath or shower, central heating, phone, TV, minibar, hairdrier, safe **Credit cards** AE, DC, MC, V **Closed** never

# Ile-de-France

---

Town hotel, Paris

## Hôtel du Lys

Ideally situated in a quiet street parallel to blvd Saint Germain, the Hôtel du Lys has been a family-run hotel run along *pension* lines for more than 50 years. Nowadays it is in the hands of Marie-Helène Decharne, daughter of the original owners, and her husband who see it as more a house than a hotel. Some clients have been returning regularly for over 40 years.New to the guide a few years ago.

■ 23 rue Serpente, 75006 Paris **Tel** 01.43.26.97.57 **Fax** 01.44.07. 34.90 **Meals** breakfast **Prices** F-FF with breakfast **Rooms** 22, all with shower or bath, phone, TV, hairdrier **Credit cards** MC, V **Closed** never

---

Town hotel, Paris

## Hôtel Mayflower

In the same ownership as the Lord Byron and right next door to it, the Mayflower shares the same refined but relaxed atmosphere and is similarly well run. Bedrooms are pretty and calm, and mainly spacious. Elegant and comfortable sitting-room.

■ 3 Rue de Chateaubriand, 75008 Paris **Tel** 01.45.62.57.46 **Fax** 01.42.56.32.38 **Meals** breakfast **Prices** rooms FF; breakfast F **Rooms** 24, all with bath, central heating, phone, satellite TV, minibar **Credit cards** MC, V **Closed** never

---

Town hotel, Paris

## Hôtel de la Place des Vosges

Set in a quiet street only 25 metres from one of the loveliest squares in Paris, this 17thC house is entirely in harmony with the surrounding area. The salon is suitably traditional and rustic in style; some of the bedrooms and bathrooms are tiny, and have less character, but are well kept – and reasonably priced. 'Delightful staff, unfailingly cheerful and polite', according to one happy visitor.

■ 12 Rue de Birague, 75004 Paris **Tel** 01.42.72.60.46 **Fax** 01.42.72. 02.64 **Meals** breakfast **Prices** rooms FF; breakfast F; children under 2 free **Rooms** 16, all with bath or shower, central heating, phone **Credit cards** DC, MC, V **Closed** never

---

Town hotel, Paris

## Hôtel Prima-Lepic

Set in bustling Montmartre, this is a cheerful bed and breakfast place. The ground floor is done out as an indoor courtyard giving an airy and peaceful effect; bedrooms are individually and well decorated, though not over-spacious. Breakfast is buffet-style.

■ 29 Rue Lepic, 75018 Paris **Tel** 01.46.06.44.64 **Fax** 01.46.06.66.11 **Meals** breakfast **Prices** rooms F-FF; breakfast F **Rooms** 38, all with bath or shower, central heating, phone, TV, hairdrier **Credit cards** MC, V **Closed** never

# Ile-de-France

---

Town hotel, Paris

## Hôtel Prince Albert

Reasonably priced hotels of any comfort are hard to come by in the 1er arondissement; the Prince Albert – well placed for culture, entertainment and shopping alike – is an exception. The breakfast-room, the reception and main sitting area, and the once rather dim corridors have all been transformed. Bedrooms are well cared for and comfortable.

■ 5 Rue St-Hyacinthe, 75001 Paris **Tel** 01.42.61.58.36 **Fax** 01.42.60.04.06 **Website** www.hotelprincealbert.com **Meals** breakfast **Prices** rooms F-FF, extra bed F; breakfast F **Rooms** 30, all with bath or shower, central heating, phone, satellite TV, minibar, safe, hairdrier **Credit cards** AE, MC, V **Closed** never

---

Town hotel, Paris

## Hôtel Riboutté Lafayette

Not one of the most conspicuous of the city's charming small hotels, but a reasonably priced and cheerful base. Bedrooms are small, friendly and individual; all rooms are quiet, whether over-looking the courtyard or the street.

■ 5 Rue Riboutté, 75009 Paris **Tel** 01.47.70.62.36 **Fax** 01.48.00.91.50 **Meals** breakfast **Prices** rooms F; breakfast F **Rooms** 24, all with bath or shower, phone, satellite TV **Credit cards** AE, MC, V **Closed** never

---

Town hotel, Paris

## Hôtel Les Rives de Notre Dame

Its outlook is the Ile de la Cité across the traffic-heavy quai Saint-Michel and the Seine, but the Degravi's hearts are firmly in Provence and Tuscany, and the decoration is designed to transport you to the south. The well proportioned bedrooms are stylish – less precious than downstairs – Provençal fabrics, wood framed windows and charming fabric bedheads. A new entry this year.

■ 15 quai Saint-Michel, 75005 Paris **Tel** 01.43.54.81.16 **Fax** 01.43.26.27.09 **Meals** breakfast; 24hour rooms service for hot and cold dishes and drinks **Prices** FF-FFFF; breakfast F **Rooms** 10, all with bath; all rooms have phone fax/modem plug; satellite TV, air-conditioning, minibar, hairdrier, safe **Credit cards** AE, DC, MC, V **Closed** never

---

Town hotel, Paris

## Hôtel St-Dominique

Recent refurbishments in a confident, colourful style, have helped to restore the St-Dominique's reputation. The reception-cum-sitting-room is very much part of the appeal – a pleasant, comfortable spot. Bedrooms are small but well-equipped, breakfast delicious and beautifully presented. Drinks can be had outside in the small, flowery courtyard.

■ 62 Rue St-Dominique, 75007 Paris **Tel** 01.47.05.51.44 **Fax** 01.47.05.81.28 **Meals** breakfast **Prices** F-FF; breakfast F **Rooms** 34 all with bath or shower; all rooms have central heating, phone, TV, minibar **Credit cards** AE, DC, MC, V **Closed** never

# Ile-de-France

---

Town hotel, Paris

# Hôtel Saint-Germain-des-Prés

This small Left Bank hotel stands out for charm and individuality, if not for notably good taste or coherence of interior design – its bedrooms are all furnished in different styles and colours. Large salon-cum-breakfast-room.

■ 36 Rue Bonaparte, 75006 Paris **Tel** 01.43.26.00.19 **Fax** 01.40.46.83.63 **Meals** breakfast **Prices** rooms FF-FFFF **Rooms** 30, all with bath or shower, central heating, air-conditioning, phone, TV, radio, minibar; some have air-conditioning **Credit cards** AE, MC, V **Closed** never

---

Bed and breakfast guest-house, Paris

# Hôtel Saint-Louis

Sister hotel to the Saint-Louis Marais, the welcoming atmosphere and its ideal location on the Ile-St-Louis for sightseeing make up for any lack of facilities (only one public room) and the small size of the bedrooms.

■ 75 Rue St-Louis-en-l'Ile, 75004 Paris **Tel** 01.46.34.04.80 **Fax** 01.46.34.02.13 **Meals** breakfast **Prices** rooms FF; breakfast F **Rooms** 21, all with bath or shower, phone, safe **Credit cards** MC,V **Closed** never

---

Town guest-house, Paris

# Hôtel Saint-Louis Marais

A sound, friendly choice if you are looking for a peaceful, reasonably priced base close to the Place des Vosges. The beamed bedrooms are far from spacious, but are prettily decorated with antiques, wall hangings and fresh flowers.

■ 1 Rue Charles V, 75004 Paris **Tel** 01.48.87.87.04 **Fax** 01.48.87.33.26 **Meals** breakfast **Prices** rooms F-FF; breakfast F **Rooms** 15, all with bath or shower, central heating, phone **Credit cards** MC, V **Closed** never

---

Town hotel, Paris

# Hôtel des Saints-Pères

Nearly all the bedrooms in this calmly sophisticated hotel look on to a leafy, glass-sided internal courtyard where you can breakfast or take a drink in the summer sunshine. Bedrooms are restful and fairly spacious, and there are good paintings on the walls. New to the guide this year.

■ 65 rue des Saints-Pères, 75006 Paris **Tel** 01.45.44.50.00 **Fax** 01.45.44.90.83 **Prices** F-FFFF; breakfast F; bar **Rooms** 36, 3 suites, all with bath or shower; all rooms have phone, satellite TV, minibar, hairdrier **Credit cards** AE, MC, V **Closed** never

# Ile-de-France

---

Restaurant with rooms, Paris

## Thoumieux

Set in the shadow of the Eiffel Tower, this efficient, friendly place revolves around its popular brasserie-style restaurant, which offers good country-style cooking and drinkable house-wine. Bedrooms are modern and comfortable, with tasteful fabrics and stylish furniture.

■ 79 Rue St-Dominique, 75007 Paris **Tel** 01 47.05.49.75 **Fax** 01 47.05.36.96 **Meals** breakfast, lunch, dinner **Prices** rooms FF; breakfast F, meals about FF **Rooms** 10, all with bath, central heating, phone, TV, radio **Credit cards** AE, MC **Closed** never

---

Town hote, Paris

## Hôtel des Tuileries

The Poulle-Vidal family offer a pleasant combination of a quiet but convenient setting, comfortable accommodation and a warm welcome. The two small *salons* have velvet seats and paintings and tapestries on plains wells. Bedrooms are pretty and individually decorated, bathrooms small but very smart. Breakfast is a better-than-average buffet.

■ 10 Rue St-Hyacinthe, 75001 Paris **Tel** 01.42.61.04.17 **Fax** 01.49. 27.91.56 **E-mail** htuileri@aol.com **Website** members.aol.com.htuileri/ **Meals** breakfast **Prices** FF-FFF; breakfast F **Rooms** 26, all with bath; all rooms have central heating, air-conditioning, phone, satellite TV, minibar, hairdrier, safe **Credit cards** AE, DC, V **Closed** never

---

Town hotel, Paris

## Hôtel de l'Université

This dignified town house in an area of quiet, elegant streets is not cheap, but does offer reasonable value – antiques in the beamed public areas and in the comfortable bedrooms, efficient and friendly service and breakfasts well above the Parisian norm in quality but not price.

■ 22 Rue de l'Université, 75007 Paris **Tel** 01.42.61.09.39 **Fax** 01.42.60.40.84 **Meals** breakfast, light snacks **Prices** rooms F-FFF; breakfast F **Rooms** 27, all with bath or shower, phone, TV, air-conditioning **Credit cards** AE. MC, V **Closed** never

---

Town hotel, Paris

## Hotel Verneuil

When she took over, Sylvie de Lattre, not only gave this hotel a subtle name change (it was formerly Hotel Verneuil-St-Germain), but also a change in decoration. The former kitsch style has given way to elegant restraint, more in keeping with the 17thC origins of the building. Attractive basement breakfast-room. More reports please.

■ 8 rue de Verneuil, 75007 Paris **Tel** 01.42.60.82.14 **Fax** 01.42.61.40.38 **Meals** breakfast **Prices** FF, buffet breakfast F **Rooms** 26, all with bath; all rooms have central heating, phone, cable TV, hairdrier, minibar safe **Credit cards** AE, DC, MC, V **Closed** never

# The North-East

## Area introduction

Our North-east region contains some large areas with not much to offer the holidaymaker, and which contain few Charming Small Hotels; there are several *départements* with no entries at all. But this region embraces four areas worth singling out for their tourist interest and their hotels.

The hinterland of the main Channel ferry ports includes some pleasant rolling countryside, and of course proximity to those ports makes this area – particularly the *département* of Pas-de-Calais, containing Calais and Boulogne – prime territory for a quick weekend away.

The *départements* of Oise and Seine-et-Marne, respectively to the north and east of the Ile de France, contain some tourist highlights (Compiègne, Chantilly, Vaux-le-Vicomte), and some desirable hotels – though they may owe their existence more to proximity to Paris than to the demands of the local tourist trade.

More or less due east of Paris, where the motorway from Paris to Strasbourg meets that coming down from Calais, is Champagne country. Wherever there is wine there is a satisfyingly cultivated landscape, and here there is also the architectural spectacle of Reims, at the heart of the Champagne business as well as the region, of which the cathedral is only one part.

And then there is Alsace, at the far eastern end of this region, against the German border. This is another wine region – a hilly one, with some wonderful scenery. The wines and the food alike are German-influenced, as you might expect.

---

**Contenders in the North-east**
**Audinghen-par-Wissant, La Maison de la Houve** 03.21.32.97.06 Well modernised old farmhouse B&B, comfortably furnished and well run, in flowery garden.
**Illhaeusern, Hôtel des Berges** 03.89.71.87.87 Luxurious barn-style lodgings at foot of garden of one of the most celebrated restaurants in Alsace.
**Langres, Le Cheval Blanc** 03.25.87.07.00 Neat Logis in ancient town-centre building; small terrace.
**Sars-Poteries, Hôtel Fleuri** 03.27.61.62.72 Old farm building, now a prettily furnished B&B hotel, with independently run Michelin-starred restaurant (Auberge Fleurie) next door.

**Reporting to the guide**
We're very keen to hear from readers about their hotel-going experiences. We can't visit every hotel in the guide every year; even if we could, we wouldn't be staying in them all. And it's only when you stay in a place that you find out how the plumbing deals with the demand for hot water, what that much-vaunted 70F breakfast is really like, and what happens when you request something extraordinary like an extra pillow. So please do let us know how you get on next time you're travelling in France.

In particular, please do write when you like a small hotel, whether or not you've chosen it with our help. People are pretty good at letting us know when we've got a place wrong (usually, we hope, because the place has gone downhill). Places that come up to expectations don't always trigger a reaction.

# The North-East

# Hostellerie des 3 Mousquetaires

Most visitors are thoroughly well pleased by this jolly 19thC château, equidistant from the ferry ports of Boulogne, Calais and Dunkerque, although some reports indicate that the service in the restaurant at the weekend is sometimes overstretched.

The hotel is a family-run *logis*, a world away from the classical château pattern. The charming and vigilant Mme Venet is in charge front of house, aided by her daughter-in-law, while husband Marcel and son Philippe prepare regionally based meals offering 'enormous portions' and 'astonishing value' in the spotless open-to-view kitchen. (The cheeseboard is 'magnificent'; and there is even an impressive menu for vegetarians.)

The building is an eccentric mixture of stone-and-brick stripes and pseudo-timbering beneath a steep slate roof, set in a large wooded garden with ponds and streams (ducks and swans). A reader reports delightedly that children can follow the example of the owners' own children and run around without raising eyebrows. The interior is traditionally grand in style, the best of the old bedrooms (eg 'Milady') huge and elegant (though some are much smaller); those in the annexe are sumptuously decora ed in various styles – one has a Japanese theme, for example. But several guests have been worried by street noise in these rooms.

**Nearby** Aire – Renaissance bailiff's court, collegiate church of St-Pierre; St Omer (20 km) – basilica, fine arts museum.

Château du Fort de la Redoute
62120 Aire-sur-la-Lys
**Tel** 03.21.39.01.11
**Fax** 03.21.39.50.10
**Location** in countryside off N43, 2km S of Aire; in parkland, with ample car parking
**Meals** breakfast, lunch, dinner
**Prices** rooms F-FF, suites F; breakfast F, menus FF- (except weekends) FFF
**Rooms** 31 double (9 twin), 24 with bath, 2 with shower; one suite with bath; one family room with bath; all rooms have central heating, phone, TV
**Facilities** 2 sitting- rooms, 2 dining-rooms, bar; golf
**Credit cards** AE, MC, V
**Children** welcome; cots and special menu available
**Disabled** no special facilities
**Pets** accepted
**Closed** mid-Dec to mid-Jan
**Proprietors** M. and Mme Philippe Venet

# The North-East

# Château de Remaisnil

This pretty 18thC mansion, set in 35 acres deep in the Picardy countryside, was previously the home of Bernard and Laura Ashley, founders of the fabrics and wallpaper retail chain. At the back of the house sheep graze placidly in the meadow, and horses in a neighbouring field are available for guests to ride. Near a grove of chestnut trees *javelot picard* can be tried – a medieval game which involves throwing giant darts underarm with as much force as you can muster at a sturdy target.

Susan and Adrian Doull left their small Manhattan apartment more than a decade ago to take up residence here with their family. They are charming hosts, and although the house is extremely grand inside, with lavish rococo embellishments, tapestries and antique furniture, it is very much a family home.

Bedrooms are opulent, with Laura Ashley designs still much in evidence; bathrooms are large, with fluffy, white robes. Dinner is a set four courses, and guests mingle in the library for pre-dinner drinks and for coffee and liqueurs afterwards. A remarkable white-tiled underground passageway, reminiscent of the Paris metro, links the château to the conference centre and coach house, where bedrooms are smaller, more rustic. A small, private disco/bar has been created in the cellar.

**Nearby** Doullens (8 km); Amiens; Picardy battlefields.

80600 Doullens
**Tel** 03 22 77 07 47
**Fax** 03 22 77 41 23
**Website** www.Chateau-de-remaisnil.com
**Location** on D938 direction Auxi-le-Château, on right before Mézerolles
**Meals** breakfast, lunch, dinner, by arrangement
**Prices** FFFF château, FF coach house; DB&B FFF, breakfast F; dinner FFF

**Rooms** 20 (9 in coach house), all with bath and shower; all have central heating, phone, TV, minibar **Facilities** 3 sitting rooms, library, breakfast/dining-room; swimming pool, riding, tennis, snooker **Credit cards** AE, DC, MC, V **Children** accepted **Disabled** not suitable **Pets** by arrangement **Closed** never **Proprietors** Susan and Adrian Doull

# The North-East

# Hôtel Cléry

This elegant 18thC mansion has produced a stream of satisfied reports from readers in the past. However, for the time being we are reserving judgement. The young, hands-on couple who ran the hotel so successfully in recent years have left, and the hotel is now under new ownership. Further reports particularly welcome.

Properly called the Château d'Hesdin-l'Abbé, a dignified façade dominates the fine tree-lined approach to the house. But there is no need to be intimidated: this is not a stuffy place. There is a very fine Louis XV wrought-iron staircase, but essentially the style is bright and light in harmonious pastel tones, understated and modern. Some of the furnishing downstairs is somewhat functional but the overall effect is more than pleasant.

The hotel already has an established British trade; the excellent golf at nearby Hardelot is an attraction in addition to proximity to the Channel. Bedrooms are newly decorated, with plenty of individual touches; don't overlook those in the cottage annexes. There is an attractive bar, and a log fire in the sitting-room when the weather calls for it. Lunch and dinner can be taken here; also many restaurants in nearby Boulogne.

**Nearby** Hardelot, golf and beach (9km); Le Touquet (15km)

62360 Hesdin-L'Abbé
**Tel** 03.21.83.19.83
**Fax** 03.21.87.52.59
**Location** in tiny rural village, 9 km SE of Boulogne; 1 km from Exit 28 (A16); with gardens and ample car parking
**Meals** breakfast, dinner
**Prices** rooms F-FF; menu F-FF
**Rooms** 22 double (17 twin), 16 with bath, 6 with shower ; all have central heating, phone, satellite TV

**Facilities** bar, 2 sitting-rooms; tennis court, mountain bikes for hire
**Credit cards** AE, DC, MC, V
**Children** accepted
**Pets** not accepted
**Disabled** no special facilities
**Closed** mid-Dec to end Jan
**Proprietor** Jean-Jacques Durond

# The North-East

# Le Cerf

All the signs are that the Cerf is as compelling as ever for visitors who like the cooking of Alsace as much as its wines. Michel Husser carries on the gastronomic tradition of father Robert; Michelin awards two stars. Bedrooms are not particularly luxurious, but are well furnished and thoroughly comfortable. There is a cobbled courtyard for drinks and breakfast. We hope, given the prices charged, that Le Cerf continues to keep up standards – one reader's letter indicates that they can sometimes slip.

**Nearby** Strasbourg (20 km); wine villages.

30 Rue du Général-de-Gaulle
67520 Marlenheim
**Tel** 03.88.87.73.73
**Fax** 03.88.87.68.08
**E-mail** info@lecerf.com
**Location** on main road through village, 18 km W of Strasbourg; with courtyard and car parking
**Meals** breakfast, lunch, dinner
**Prices** rooms F-FF; menus FF-FFF
**Rooms** 17 double, 8 with bath, 7 with shower (6 twin); one single with shower; 2 family rooms, both with bath; all rooms have central heating, phone
**Facilities** dining-room, 2 function rooms
**Credit cards** AE,V
**Children** accepted
**Disabled** access to dining-room; 2 ground-floor bedrooms
**Pets** accepted
**Closed** restaurant, Tue, Wed
**Proprietor** Robert Husser

# *The North-East*

**Restaurant with rooms, Montreuil-sur-Mer**

## Auberge de la Grenouillère

This low Picardy-style farmhouse (known to many as the Froggery), is a popular gastronomic halt with the British. Two visitors particularly commend lunch on the terrace ('most agreeable', 'delightful').

The spacious gravel terrace is certainly an excellent spot for leisurely lunches, rather overshadowing the gleaming brass and polished wood of the restaurant – complete with frog-motif mural (done by an Englishman, of course). And the food is excellent, too – Michelin-starred, and not wildly expensive, with a wide choice of good value wines.

Bedrooms are captivating (one is very large, and eminently suitable for families), complete with well equipped and very attractive bathrooms.

If you are normally resolute about going native once on French soil, and feel you might be put off by all those other English voices, relax. You can safely resist the temptation to carry on driving: this is a serious French enterprise and M. Gauthier has not allowed the popularity of his establishment to make him complacent.

**Nearby** Ramparts, citadel; Le Touquet (15 km).

La Madelaine-sous-Montreuil, 62170 Montreuil-sur-Mer
**Tel** 03.21.06.07.22
**Fax** 03.21.86.36.36
**E-mail** Auberge.de.la.Grenouillere@wanadoo.fr
**Website** www.lagrenouillere.fr
**Location** by river at end of lane off D139, NW of Montreuil-sur-Mer; with ample car parking
**Meals** breakfast, lunch, dinner
**Prices** rooms F; breakfast F; menus FF-FFF

**Rooms** 2 double, 1 twin, one flat; all with bath; all rooms have central heating, phone,
**Facilities** dining-room, small bar
**Credit cards** AE, DC, MC, V
**Children** welcome
**Disabled** two ground-floor room
**Pets** welcome
**Closed** mid-Dec to end Jan; Tue and Wed from Sep to Jun
**Proprietor** M. Gauthier

# The North-East

**Country house hotel, Montreuil-sur-Mer**

# Château de Montreuil

'Montreuil, Château de: Charming host, exceptional food, great advice on local shopping for food and wine. Comfortable, well equipped rooms. Not cheap. Wife of patron: English.' Military man, this reporter; as usual, verdict spot-on; other readers concur. No doubt about it: full entry merited.

This substantial, luxurious country house, dating from the 1930s, is a well established favourite with British travellers, who make up most of the resident guests. The house is immaculately done out, with great taste throughout. Bedrooms are splendid – decorated with real flair and furnished with character; those on the top floor are very spacious, but the first floor rooms give better views of the beautiful English-style gardens. There is a snug brick-and-beams bar for an aperitif, an airy glass-fronted sitting-room and a lovely, elegant dining-room. Although you're quite close to the town centre, the setting is quiet, the gardens secluded.

Christian Germain's cooking aims high and hits the target (the restaurant does not rely on British custom but has a loyal French following); even breakfast ('home-made everything') is delicious. **Nearby** Ramparts (still intact), citadel; Le Touquet (15 km); Golf.

4 Chaussée des Capucins
62170 Montreuil-sur-Mer
**Tel** 03.21.81.53.04
**Fax** 03.21.81.36.43
**Location** in quiet part of town, 38 km S of Boulogne, off N1; with large garden and ample car parking
**Meals** breakfast, lunch, dinner
**Prices** rooms FF-FFF, DB&B FF; menus FFF
**Rooms** 12 double, all with bath (6 twin); 3 single; 2 family rooms all with bath or shower; all rooms have central heating, phone, TV
**Facilities** sitting-room, dining-room, bar
**Credit cards** AE, DC, MC, V
**Children** welcome
**Disabled** 1 ground-floor bedroom
**Pets** not accepted
**Closed** mid-Dec to end Jan
**Proprietors** Christian and Lindsay Germain

# The North-East

**Château hotel, Reims**

## Château des Crayères

Gérard Boyer (by common consent one of the finest chefs in the land) and his wife Elyane had a good starting point: a graceful turn-of-the-century mansion (built in Louis XVI style), situated in a spacious park almost at the heart of Reims, and surrounded by the *caves* of the famous Champagne names.

With Elyane's exquisite taste and skill in interior decoration, they could hardly go far wrong. There are a wonderful grand staircase, enormous windows, marble columns and tapestries; the dining-room is wood panelled and candle-lit. Bedrooms are sumptuous, individually decorated to a theme, and have views over the park; two have a large balcony.

Château des Crayères is prohibitively expensive, but a reporter who 'stayed in the best room and drank one of the best wines' wrote to approve of the place – singling out for praise (of all things) baby croissants that 'melt in the mouth'.

The cooking is not merely for the benefit of Champagne grandees; it's good enough to attract businessmen from Paris. Not surprisingly, it is necessary to book well ahead.

**Nearby** Basilica, cathedral; Champagne Route.

64 Blvd Henry Vasnier 51100 Reims
**Tel** 03.26.82.80.80
**Fax** 03.26.82.65.52
**Location** on edge of city centre, near St-Remi basilica; in own grounds with ample car parking
**Meals** breakfast, lunch, dinner
**Prices** rooms FFFF; menus FFF
**Rooms** 19 double, all with bath (15 twin); all rooms have air-conditioning, phone, TV, radio, minibar
**Facilities** dining-room, bar, function room; tennis, helistation
**Credit cards** AE, DC, MC, V
**Children** welcome
**Disabled** access possible, lift/elevator
**Pets** dogs welcome
**Closed** 3 weeks at Christmas/New Year; restaurant only, Mon and Tue lunch
**Proprietor** M. Boyer

# *The North-East*

---

Country hotel, Artzenheim

## Auberge d'Artzenheim ★

'A beflowered oasis in the middle of nowhere,' says a recent report on this cosy auberge. Its focal point is the restaurant, all beams and polished wood, but there is a terrace for outdoor eating. Bedrooms (some small) are prettily decorated with rustic furniture and jolly fabrics.

■ 30 Rue du Sponeck, 68320 Artzenheim (Haut-Rhin) **Tel** 03.89. 71.60.51 **Fax** 03.89.71.68.21 **Meals** breakfast, lunch, dinner **Prices** rooms F; menus FF **Rooms** 10, all with bath or shower, central heating, phone, TV **Credit cards** MC, V **Closed** Feb; restaurant only, Mon dinner and Tue

---

Town hotel, Boulogne-sur-Mer

## Hôtel Métropole

A very pleasant hotel, centrally situated in one of the main shopping streets of Boulogne but with the bonus of a pretty and colourful garden. It came well out of a recent inspection visit. No restaurant but 'excellent' breakfasts. Private garage (50F).

■ 51-53 Rue Thiers, 62200 Boulogne-sur-Mer (Pas-de-Calais) **Tel** 03.21.31.54.30 **Fax** 03.21.30.45.72 **Meals** breakfast **Prices** rooms F; breakfast F **Rooms** 25, all with bath or shower, central heating, air-conditioning, phone, TV, minibar **Credit cards** AE, DC, MC, V **Closed** mid-Dec to early Jan

---

Château hotel, Courcelles-sur-Vesle

## Château de Courcelles

Set in a small formal park, this impressive – and expensive – 17thC château can name Napoléon and Jean-Jacques Rousseau among former visitors. Bedrooms are spacious and individually decorated, food rated 'very impressive' by a visitor. Pool, tennis. A reporter was 'much impressed by the warm welcome, beautiful room and excellent dinner.'

■ 02220 Courcelles-sur-Vesle (Aisne) **Tel** 03.23.74.13.53 **Fax** 03.23.74.06.41 **E-mail** reservation@chateaudecourcelles.fr.**Meals** breakfast, lunch, dinner **Prices** rooms FF-FFF, suites FFF-FFFF; breakfast F, menus FF-FFF **Rooms** 18, all with bath or shower, central heating, phone, TV, minibar **Credit cards** AE, DC, MC, V **Closed** never

---

Country hotel, Dampierre

## Auberge du Château

A traditional inn with a calm, prosperous air which stands in the centre of a stone-built country village. The layout reflects its age: floors rise and fall at will and rickety wooden staircases lead to rooms. Those at the front overlook the château and its park, situated in a lovely rural area which seems far from Paris but is in fact only half an hour away by car.

■ 1 Grande Rue, 78720 Dampierre (Yvelines) **Tel** 01.30.47.56.56 **Fax** 01.30.52.56.95 **Meals** breakfast, lunch, dinner **Prices** rooms F-FF; breakfast F; menus FF **Rooms** 20, all with bath, phone, TV **Credit cards** AE, MC, V **Closed** Sun eve, Mon

# *The North-East*

---

Village hotel, L'Épine

## Aux Armes de Champagne

The main attractions here are the renowned cuisine and cellar, and the hotel's refreshing lack of pretension. The modern bed-rooms are comfortable and impeccable; sixteen of the rooms are in an annexe 200 metres down the road, away from the traffic noise that afflicts the main building. ■ Avenue du Luxembourg, 51460 L'Épine (Marne) **Tel** 03.26.69.30.30 **Fax** 03.26.69.30.26 **Meals** breakfast, lunch, dinner **Prices** rooms F-FF; breakfast F, menus FF (weekday lunch only), FF-FFF **Rooms** 37, all with bath or shower, central heating, phone, TV, minibar **Credit cards** AE, DC, MC, V **Closed** early Jan to mid-Feb; Sun eve and Mon, Nov to Mar

---

Town hotel, Etréaupont

## Le Clos du Montvinage ★

This imposing, spacious red-brick building has the cheerful Auberge du Val de l'Oise restaurant at its heart. Bedrooms are well equipped; those at the back have views of the walled garden and suffer no disturbance from the busy main road.

■ RN 2, 02580 Etréaupont (Aisne) **Tel** 03.23.97.91.10 **Fax** 03.23.97.48.92 **Meals** breakfast, lunch, dinner **Prices** rooms F; dinner F-FF **Rooms** 20, all with bath, central heating, air-conditioning, phone, TV, minibar, hairdrier **Credit cards** AE, DC, MC, V **Closed** Sun night; 1 week Feb, 1 week Aug; restaurant only, Mon lunch, Sun eve

---

Country hotel, Futeau

## A L'Orée du Bois

Surrounded by woods, this modest hotel enjoys perfect peace, although the mood is often jolly in the elegantly rustic restaurant at its heart. Cooking, by the *patron*, is excellent, with seafood very much the high-point. Rooms are adequate: motel-style, in a ground-floor extension; some enormous rooms, with more character, are available in an adjacent house.

■ Futeau, 55120 Clermont-en-Argonne (Meuse) **Tel** 03.29.88.28.41 **Fax** 03.29.88.24.52 **Meals** breakfast, lunch, dinner **Prices** rooms F, suite FF; breakfast F, lunch F-FF, menus FF-FFF **Rooms** 13, 1 suite; all with bath and shower, central heating, phone, TV, hairdrier **Credit cards** MC, V **Closed** one week Nov, Jan; restaurant only, Tue and Sun dinner out of season

---

Village inn, Kaysersberg

## Hôtel Résidence Chambard

Pierre Irrmann's sober, highly traditional-looking inn is almost better thought of as a restaurant with rooms; there is sitting space, but you'll spend most of your time (when you're not out tasting Alsatian wines) in the restaurant 50 metres away and in your elegantly furnished, spacious bedroom.

■ 13 Rue de Général de Gaulle, 68240 Kaysersberg (Haut-Rhin) **Tel** 03.89.47.10.17 **Fax** 03.89.47.35.03 **Meals** breakfast, lunch, dinner **Prices** rooms F-FF, suites FF; breakfast F, menus FF-FFF **Rooms** 20, all with bath or shower, phone, TV, radio **Credit cards** AE, MC, V **Closed** 3 weeks Mar; restaurant only, Mon, and Tue lunch

# The North-East

---

Country hotel, Lapoutroie

## Les Alisiers

This simple, farmhouse-style place enjoys a splendid setting, high in the Vosges, with floor-to-ceiling windows in the dining-room to exploit the view. The rustic interior has an intimate, private-house feel, the bedrooms are small but comfortable. Alsatian specialities dominate the menus. Good value.

■ 5 Faudé, 68650 Lapoutroie (Haut-Rhin) **Tel** 03.89.47.52.82 **Fax** 03.89.47.22.38 **E-mail** Hotel-Restaurant.LesAlisiers@wanadoo.fr **Meals** breakfast, lunch, dinner **Prices** rooms F; menus F-FF; reductions for children sharing parents' room **Rooms** 13, all with phone **Credit cards** MC, V **Closed** Tue; Jan

---

Converted mill, Lumbres

## Moulin de Mombreux

An eighteenth century mill, much improved over the past few years, though lacking in character, according to one reporter. Pleasant, compact bedrooms in a modern block built to match the mill; public rooms that are charmingly traditional or light and airy; 'deserved' Michelin star for food; friendly atmosphere.

■ Rte de Bayenghem, 62380 Lumbres (Pas-de-Calais) **Tel** 03.21.39.62.44 **Fax** 03.21.93.61.34 **E-mail** moulindemombreux@goufarnet.com **Meals** breakfast, lunch, dinner **Prices** rooms F-FF; breakfast F; menus FF-FFF (including wine) **Rooms** 24, all with bath or shower, central heating, TV, phone **Credit cards** AE, DC, V **Closed** around Christmas

---

Town hotel, Montreuil-sur-Mer

## Les Hauts de Montreuil

A reader who resorted to this timbered hotel near the centre of Montreuil when our recommendations in the area were closed recommends it for a combination of well-furnished rooms (some in a modern annexe), a warm welcome from the patron and his wife, 'fantastic' traditional food and 'excellent' value.

■ 21-23, Rue Pierre Ledent, 62170 Montreuil-sur-Mer (Pas-de-Calais) **Tel** 03.21.81.95.92 **Fax** 03.21.86.28.83 **Meals** breakfast, lunch, dinner **Prices** rooms F; breakfast F; menus FF-FFF **Rooms** 27, all with bath or shower, central heating, phone, TV, minibar, safe, hairdrier **Credit cards** AE, DC, MC, V **Closed** never

---

Country hotel, Ribeauvillé

## Le Clos Saint-Vincent

The service at this elegant hotel is almost impossible to fault. The bedrooms are beautifully furnished, the staff friendly and the food delicious, reports a recent visitor. Although the restaurant is closed on Tuesday and Wednesday evenings, there are excellent alternatives in the town. Indoor swimming-pool.

■ Rte de Bergheim, 68150 Ribeauvillé (Haut-Rhin) **Tel** 03.89.73.67.65 **Fax** 03.89.73.32.20 **E-mail** clos.vincent@ad.com **Meals** breakfast, lunch, dinner **Prices** rooms FF-FFF; menus FF **Rooms** 15, all with bath, central heating, phone, minibar; TV on request **Credit cards** MC, V **Closed** mid-Nov to mid-Mar; restaurant only, Tue and Wed

# The North-East

---

Restaurant with rooms, Ribeauvillé

## Les Vosges

An American couple were so impressed that they intend to return to this neat little place in the middle of one of the most attractive wine towns of Alsace. Only breakfast is offered but there is a wide choice of food. Bedrooms are pleasantly comfortable, with excellent bathrooms; public areas handsomely display Madame's quilted han ings.

■ 2 Grande Rue, 68150 Ribeauvillé (Haut-Rhin) **Tel** 03.89.73.61.39 **Fax** 03.89.73.34.21 **Meals** breakfast **Prices** rooms F; breakfast F **Rooms** 18, all with bath or shower, phone, TV **Credit cards** AE, DC, MC, V **Closed** Sun evening; restaurant only, mid-Nov to Apr

---

Country hotel, Sept-Saulx

## Le Cheval Blanc ★

This old inn has been extended over the years but is still blessed with a charming garden. Once hailed for its food and accommodation, things seem to be in decline. A recent visitor reports scruffiness in some bed- and bathrooms; another, on disappointing food.

■ 51400 Sept-Saulx (Marne) **Tel** 03.26.03.90.27 **Fax** 03.26.03.97.09 **Meals** breakfast, lunch, dinner **Prices** rooms F-FF; suites FF; breakfast F, **Rooms** 25, all with bath or shower, phone, TV, minibar **Credit cards** AE, DC, MC, V **Closed** Tue, Thu lunch; 3 weeks Feb

---

Town mansion, Vervins

## La Tour du Roy ★

We receive a letter each year from the Desvignes family: they exude enthusiasm for their hotel and we know that they put real care into running this turreted building perched on the ramparts of Vervins. Many appreciative reports endorse their efforts. The house is full of character, with pretty, individually decorated rooms. No complaints about the food either, which features *cuisine du Terroir* from Annie Desvignes. Enclosed parking at night.

■ 45 Rue du Général Leclerc, 02140 Vervins (Aisne) **Tel** 03.23.98.00.11 **Fax** 03.23.98.00.72 **E-mail** chatotel@chatotel.com **Website** http://www.chatotel.com **Meals** breakfast, lunch, dinner **Prices** rooms F-FF; breakfast F, menus FF-FFF **Rooms** 22, 8 suites (1 suite suitable for the disabled), all with bath, central heating, phone, TV, radio, minibar; 15 with air-conditioning **Credit cards** AE, DC, MC, V **Closed** mid-Jan to mid-Feb

# Western France

## Area introduction

Our Western France region has three major components of interest to tourists. First there is the Loire valley and its immediate surroundings, including the atmospheric Sologne, south of Orleans. There are almost as many charming small hotels here as there are Renaissance châteaux. Secondly, the hilly Limousin, fading into the northern fringes of Périgord, around Angoulême and Limoges. And finally the hinterland of the Atlantic coast, including the canals of Poitou-Charente. We have entries in all these areas, but also dotted around the *départements* in between, and on the western side of the region on the fringes of the Massif Central.

### Contenders in Western France

**Aubigny-sur-Nère, Château de la Verrerie** 02.48.58.06.91 Splendid turreted château in gracious parkland, run by aristocratic owners.

**Blois, Le Vieux Cognet** 02.54.56.05.34 Simple but well furnished B&B in quiet spot on banks of the Loire.

**Challans, Château de la Vérie** 02.51.35.33.44 Richly furnished manor-house in extensive grounds; pool, tennis.

**Cheverny, Château du Breuil** 02.54.44.20.20 18thC château in large grounds, with an elegant salon and comfortable bedrooms with antiques.

**Chouzé-sur-Loire, Château des Réaux** 02.47.95.14.40 Fairytale château, stylishly decorated and handsomely furnished.

**Dompierre-les-Eglises, Le Moulin des Combes** 05.55.68.62.09 Ancient watermill turned luxury B&B, with British owner.

**Grez-Neuville, La Croix d'Etain** 02.41.95.68.49 Handsome little manor-house B&B in pleasant village on the Mayenne.

**Le Gua, Le Moulin de Châlons** 05.46.22.82.72 Pale stone mill beside the Seudre with grassy grounds and charming rooms.

**Loches, Hôtel George Sand** 02.47.59.39.74 Riverside Logis with abundant beams and traditional decor.

**Mondoubleau, Le Grand Monarque** 02.54.80.92.10 Friendly Logis with neat (some cramped) rooms, in mature grassy garden.

**Mont-près-Chambord, Manoir de Clénord** 02.54.70.41.62 Secluded country house, tastefully furnished and family-run.

**Montbazon-en-Touraine, Domaine de la Tortinière** 02.47.26.00.19 Dinky fairytale château, smartly furnished, in wooded grounds with views and pool.

**Onzain-en-Touraine, Domaine des Hauts de Loire** 02.54.20.72.57 Elegantly furnished but characterful converted hunting lodge (Relais & Châteaux).

**La-Roche-sur-Yon, Logis de la Couperie** 02.51.37.21.19 Country house, just outside the town, run as an elegant but home-like guest-house.

**St-Lambert-des-Levées, La Croix de la Voulte** 02.41.38.46.66 Ancient country house B&B in lush gardens.

**Tours, Jean Bardet** 02.47.41.41.11 Smooth, elegant setting for some of the best food in France.

**Velluire, Auberge de la Rivière** 02.51.52.32.15 Unpretentious waterside Logis with some pleasant rooms.

# *Western France*

**Converted mill, Bannegon**

# Auberge du Moulin de Chaméron

The Moulin de Chameron is a curious animal, and difficult to categorise. At the heart of it is the original 18thC water-mill – now a combination of country museum and charmingly traditional restaurant. But the bedrooms are housed across the garden in a pair of unremarkable modern buildings of rather towny appearance – comfortable, but thin on charm. So should it be thought of as a restaurant with rooms? We think to do so would be to underestimate its appeal as a place to stay for more than a one-night stopover (though one reporter found the peace marred by the noise of early morning departures) – at least in summer, when the wooded garden and neat pool come into play, along with the restaurant's tented dining terrace beside the mill stream. Jean Merilleau's cooking is excellent.

**Nearby** Meillant castle (25 km); Noirlac abbey (30 km).

Bannegon 18210 Charenton-du-Cher
**Tel** 02.48.61.83.80
**Fax** 02.48.61.84.92
**Location** in countryside between Bannegon and Neuilly, 40 km SE of Bourges; with garden and ample car parking
**Meals** breakfast, lunch, dinner
**Prices** rooms FF; menus FF, children's F **Rooms** 13 double, 8 with bath, 5 with shower (5 twin); one family room with bath; all rooms have central heating, phone, TV
**Facilities** 2 dining-rooms, bar, 2 sitting-rooms; swimming-pool, table-tennis, fishing
**Credit cards** AE, MC, V
**Children** welcome
**Disabled** no special facilities
**Pets** accepted in bedrooms; charge
**Closed** mid-Nov to early Mar; Tue in low season
**Proprietors** M. Rommel and M. Merilleau

# Western France

## Château de Noirieux

'A gem of a hotel, situated at the western end of the Loire château-belt; whereas most hotels on the Loire tourist trail are over-priced and under-enthusiastic, this one gets most things right and is thoroughly professional in the nicest way.' So says one of our most conscientious reporters. Since he's started so well, we'll let him finish.

'Dating from the seventeenth century, with Art Deco additions in 1927, it opened as a hotel in 1991. It is set in magnificent grounds, with views down to the Loir. It is outstandingly comfortable; a good test was that during three days of almost continuous rain we always felt cosseted. The salons are beautifully furnished and comfortable, the dining-room light and airy, with a terrace for fine weather. Bedrooms are split between the main building and two others – all well furnished, some quite opulently.

'The cuisine is inventive and of a high standard. The wine list is exemplary, with prices that don't take your breath away. We received a warm welcome, and all the staff were unfailingly helpful and courteous. The chateau is not cheap, but is excellent value in every respect.'

**Nearby** golf; Angers (12 km) – cathedral, château

26 Route du Moulin, 49125 Briollay
**Tel** 02.41.42.50.05
**Fax** 02.41.37.91.00
**E-mail** noirieux@relaischateaux.fr
**Location** in countryside off D 52, (junction 14 off A11); with gardens and car parking
**Meals** breakfast, lunch, dinner
**Prices** rooms FF-FFFF; breakfast FF, menus FF (lunch – weekdays only) FF-FFF

**Rooms** 19 double with bath; some rooms with central heating, phone, TV, minibar, hairdrier
**Facilities** dining-room, sitting-room/bar; jacuzzi, swimming-pool, tennis **Credit cards** AE, DC, MC, V **Children** accepted
**Disabled** 2 ground-floor bedrooms **Pets** accepted
**Closed** Feb; Nov; restaurant Sun eve, Mon mid-Oct to mid-Apr **Managers** Gérard and Anja Côme

# Western France

**Town mansion, Chinon**

## Hôtel Diderot

Surprisingly few hotels have been in these pages since the first edition while generating a steady stream of entirely complimentary reports. And we hear that nothing has changed at the Diderot, not even the moderate prices. 'Excellent' and 'superb' are some verdicts, and the latest visitor .will 'definitely return'.

Creeper-covered and white-shuttered, it is a handsome townhouse set in a courtyard, which conveys the benefit of convenient private parking. The French-Cypriot proprietors are charming and unstintingly helpful, and breakfast (served on the shady terrace or in a rustic room with tiled floor and massive beams) is exceptionally tasty – thanks to Madame's home-made preserves. Bedrooms are simply furnished, but are spotlessly clean and some have fine views. Some now have smart new bathrooms.

**Nearby** Grand Carroi, ruined château, church of St-Maurice; châteaux – Azay-le-Rideau (20 km), Langeais (30 km).

4 Rue Buffon 37500 Chinon
**Tel** 02.47.93.18.87
**Fax** 02.47.93.37.10
**Location** in middle of town; with courtyard and private car parking
**Meals** breakfast
**Prices** rooms F; breakfast F
**Rooms** 28 double, 17 with bath, 11 with shower (8 twin); 3 family rooms, all with bath; all rooms have central heating, phone
**Facilities** bar, breakfast room

**Credit cards** AE, DC, MC, V
**Children** welcome
**Disabled** some ground-floor bedrooms
**Pets** not accepted
**Closed** mid-Dec to mid-Jan
**Proprietor** Theo Kazamias

# *Western France*

**Country house hotel, Fleuray**

# Le Fleuray ★

We revisited in 1999 and appreciated once more Le Fleuray's two key attractions: a warm welcome and relaxed atmosphere, courtesy of the Newingtons, a lively and committed English family who rescued the place from ruin in 1992; and the peaceful, indeed isolated, rural setting in open fields. (Keep faith in the signposting from Cangey – it's more than 6 km outside the village). Combined, these qualities are at a premium in the Loire (major sights are within half an hour) and together with fair prices for prettily decorated rooms (the best with small outdoor sitting areas) explain the place's obvious popularity. When we visited in high season there was a good humoured buzz in the dining-room from a cross-section of nationalities. The staff, several English students on long vacation, were at full stretch. Don't expect a 'French eating experience'. Despite positive readers' letters about the cooking, we found that the menu changes little, and that the food, though satisfying, lacks panache.

At certain times, guests are expected to eat dinner in the hotel – check when booking if the obligatory half pension terms are operating.

**Nearby** Châteaux: Amboise, Chaumont, Chenonceaux, Tours.

Cangey 37530 Amboise
**Tel** 02.47.56.09.25
**Fax** 02.47.56.93.97
**E-mail** LEFLEURAYHOTEL@wanadoo.fr
**Website** www.lefleurayhotel.com
**Location** on D74, 12 km NE of Amboise, 7 km from A10 exit 18; in large gardens with ample car parking, garage
**Meals** breakfast, dinner
**Prices** rooms F; breakfast F, menus FF, children's F
**Rooms** 14 double, 8 with bath, 6 with shower; central or electric heating, phone
**Facilities** restaurant, garden terrace
**Credit cards** MC, V
**Children** very welcome (family rooms and special menus; games)
**Disabled** some ground floor rooms **Pets** accepted
**Closed** late Feb; late Oct to early Nov; Christmas and New Year
**Proprietors** Peter and Hazel Newington

# Western France

**Château hotel, Montbron**

# Hostellerie Ste-Catherine

The Tardoire valley is a pretty one, but the area around Montbron, east of Angoulême, is off the beaten tourist track and we presume this is why we hear so little from readers about this fine old house, once the residence of the Empress Joséphine.

The approach, along a winding drive through splendid wooded grounds, is appropriately imposing and the house – built in a pale, irregular stone – looks handsome but austere. But inside it is a different story: despite fine furnishings and immaculate housekeeping, there is none of the expected pretension, and a relaxed, informal atmosphere prevails.

Rooms are decorated and furnished with proper regard for both style and comfort: the dining-rooms (one leads in to the other) have tapestries on the walls, and a carved wooden mantlepiece stands over an old fireplace; the two sitting-rooms are inviting and relaxing. Most of the individually furnished and thoroughly comfortable bedrooms have views of the surrounding parkland; they do vary in size, and the prices reflect this. One menu and an 'interesting' *carte* are offered.

**Nearby** Angoulême (30 km) – cathedral, walk along ramparts; châteaux – de Brie (40 km); Rochechouart (40 km).

Route de Marthon 16220 Montbron
**Tel** 05.45.23.60.03
**Fax** 05.45.70.72.00
**Location** in park off D16, 4 km SW of Montbron, 28 km E of Angoulême; with ample car parking
**Meals** breakfast, lunch, dinner
**Prices** rooms F-FF; breakfast F, menu FF
**Rooms** 14 double and 4 family rooms, most with bath or shower; all rooms have central heating, phone, TV
**Facilities** 2 dining-rooms, 2 sitting-rooms, bar; swimming-pool
**Credit cards** AE, DC, MC, V
**Children** accepted
**Disabled** no special facilities
**Pets** accepted
**Closed** never
**Proprietor** Marie-Michelle Rey

# Western France

**Château hotel, Nieuil**

## Château de Nieuil

'Our room was extremely comfortable, even though it was one of their smaller ones, and one of the best-value rooms of our holiday,' says a reporter on this fairy-tale Renaissance château, making the point that high prices can be worth paying if you get something special in return. Steep-roofed, turreted, and surrounded by parkland stretching away beyond its formal garden and ornamental 'moat', it is the picture of elegance. Inside, it is appropriately furnished throughout, with exquisite antiques, porcelain and tapestries. Some of the bedrooms are exceedingly grand.

It could be embarrassingly pretentious. But the delight of the place is that it is not at all pretentious or intimidating. The château has been in the Bodinaud family for over a hundred years, and the hotel is very much a family concern. Mme Bodinaud (an ex-design-lecturer) does all the interior decoration and oversees the cooking, earning a Michelin star for her imaginative food, while her husband administers a collection of 300 cognacs.

Recently, the Bodinauds have opened a 'winter' restaurant, La Grange aux Oies, in converted stables. Their shared interest in art has also led to a gallery.

**Nearby** Angoulême (40km), Limoges (65 km).

Rte de Fontafie, 16270 Nieuil
**Tel** 05.45.71.36.38
**Fax** 05.05.45.71.46.45
**E-mail** nieuil@relaischateaux.fr.
**Location** in wooded park, 2 km E of Nieuil; with extensive grounds, car parking and garage for 8 cars
**Meals** breakfast, lunch, dinner
**Prices** rooms FF-FFF; suites FFFF; breakfast F; menus FF
**Rooms** 11 double, 3 suites, all with bath; all rooms have central heating, air-conditioning phone, TV, minibar
**Facilities** dining-room, sitting-room, bar; swimming-pool, tennis court
**Credit cards** AE, DC, MC, V
**Children** accepted
**Disabled** access possible to one bedroom and apartment
**Pets** welcome **Closed** Nov to Apr; restaurant 'La Grange aux Oies' mid-Apr to mid Dec
**Proprietor** Jean-Michel and Luce Bodinaud

# *Western France*

**Seaside guest-house, La Rochelle**

# 33 Rue Thiers ★

This distinctive little guest-house continues to delight a steady stream of guests, who pronounce it excellent value for money. 'The warm welcome makes 33 Rue Thiers a particular favourite,' says one reporter. 'It proved to be the most memorable hotel I stayed in, and one I will certainly visit again,' says another. Because of these reports, we are recommending the place for another year, despite new owners. Reports especially welcome.

33 Rue Thiers is a renovated 18thC townhouse in the heart of La Rochelle. Its former owner and renovator was a half American/half-French cook-book author, Maybelle Iribe. She opened for business in 1987, the word spread like wildfire and she built up a faithful band of enthusiastic guests who returned year after year. Public rooms have a slightly faded elegance, and are filled with antiques and (mainly) stylish modern furniture. Huge bedrooms are decorated in soothing pastel shades; to say they have been furnished individually is an understatement.

As we went to press it was uncertain whether the new owners would still serve dinner.

**Nearby** old quarter, port, and lantern tower of La Rochelle; Ile de Rey.

33 Rue Thiers, 17000 La Rochelle
**Tel** 05.46.41.62.23
**Fax** 05.46.41 10.76
**Location** in street next to central market; with small walled garden and car parking
**Meals** breakfast
**Prices** rooms FF; breakfast F, dinner FF
**Rooms** 5 double, one family room, all with bath; all rooms have central heating

**Facilities** dining-room, sitting-room, TV room
**Credit cards** not accepted
**Children** welcome; special meals, baby-sitting available
**Disabled** no special facilities
**Pets** well-behaved dogs accepted
**Closed** never
**Proprietor** M. Fonteneau

# *Western France*

**Restaurant with rooms, Les Rosiers-sur-Loire**

# Auberge Jeanne de Laval

This is a quintessential restaurant with rooms – you go for Michel Augereau's Michelin-starred cooking, with the option of staying the night. You're unlikely to want to spend a holiday here, but the auberge makes an excellent stopover, whether you are touring the Loire château country or on your way south. The restaurant is a warmly welcoming room with light modern furniture beneath mellow exposed beams, and with an uncompromisingly modern glazed extension. In the same main building are four of the bedrooms – two overlooking the road, two the pretty garden. Most of the rooms are a fair walk away in the château-style Ducs d'Anjou annexe shown in our photo (in need of upgrading, according to recent reporters). Service in the annexe is limited to breakfast, which is served in the rooms or in the pretty garden.

**Nearby** Saumur (15 km); Angers (30 km) – cathedral, château.

54 Rue Nationale, Les Rosiers-sur-Loire 49350 Gennes
**Tel** 02.41.51.80.17
**Fax** 02.41.38.04.18
**Location** in middle of village, 15 km NW of Saumur; with flower gardens and car parking
**Meals** breakfast, lunch, dinner
**Prices** rooms F; breakfast F, menus FF-FFF
**Rooms** 10 double, all but one with bath; all rooms have central heating, phone, TV, minibar
**Facilities** TV room, dining-room
**Credit cards** MC, V
**Children** welcome
**Disabled** easy access to restaurant
**Pets** dogs accepted in bedrooms
**Closed** Mon (except public holidays and high season); Mon lunchtime Jun-Sep
**Proprietors** Augereau family

# Western France

## Château de la Vallée Bleue

The young Gasquets took over this handsome château in 1985, just in time to make an appearance in the first edition of this guide, and have been assiduously improving it ever since – a barn and stables have been renovated to provide extra space. A report from a British resident in France with three young children sums up the Vallée Bleue precisely: 'Here is complete commitment. Service was friendly and discreet – the children treated like young adults. The restaurant was one of the best we've eaten in.'

Inside, the atmosphere of the house is, as always, warm and easy. Fresh flowers and a cosy log fire in the spacious entrance hall set the tone, and personal touches are in evidence in every room. The château overlooks gardens front and back, giving all the bedrooms – big, and comfortably furnished with antiques – a pleasant outlook; just visible, beyond cows grazing in the fields, are the terracotta roof-tops of the village. Public rooms are gracious and charming, furnished with solid antiques and looking on to the garden. Cooking is regionally based but *nouvelle*-oriented and way above average in execution.

**Nearby** Tour de la Prison (Museum of George Sand and Vallée Noire); Sarzay (10 km) – château; Nohant (5 km) – château.

Rte de Verneuil, St-Chartier
36400 La Châtre
**Tel** 02.54.31.01.91
**Fax** 02.54.31.04.48
**E-mail** valleebleue@yahoo.com
**Website** valleebleue@aol.com
**Location** just outside hamlet, on D69 9 km N of La Châtre; in 4 acres, with ample parking
**Meals** breakfast, lunch, dinner
**Prices** rooms F-FF; breakfast F, menus F-FF (weekday lunch) -FF, children F
**Rooms** 15 double, all with bath or shower; one single with shower; 2 family rooms with bath; all rooms have central heating, phone, TV, minibar, hairdrier **Facilities** 2 dining-rooms, sitting-room, meeting room, fitness room; swimming-pool, bowling area **Credit cards** MC, V **Children** welcome; special menus available **Disabled** 3 ground-floor rooms **Pets** not accepted **Closed** mid Nov to early Mar **Proprietor** Gérard Gasquet

# Western France

# La Tonnellerie ★

The flow of readers' reports on this fine 19th-century wine merchant's house has dried to a trickle (perhaps because the cheapest rooms are no longer cheap) but its attractions seem to us to remain undiminished.

The hotel, in the small village of Tavers, close to the Loire and not far from Beaugency, is set around a central courtyard-garden which is at the heart of its appeal. There is a pretty little swimming-pool, shady chestnut trees; tables for summer meals stand on the lawn and further away from the house on terrace areas. The country atmosphere extends indoors to the dining-rooms, both looking on to the garden, one in 'winter garden' style, the other handsomely rustic, with tiled floor and mellow woodwork. Cooking is *nouvelle* in style but recognizes the traditions of the region, and is above average in execution.

In recent years Mme Pouey has steadily improved the hotel, adding four 'apartments/suites' (pastel walls, flowery drapes, polished antiques, smart tiled bathrooms) and refurbishing other bedrooms.

**Nearby** Beaugency – Hôtel de Ville, Tour St-Firmin, church of Notre-Dame; châteaux – Chambord (25 km), Blois (30 km).

12 Rue des Eaux-Bleues,
Tavers 45190 Beaugency
**Tel** 02.38.44.68.15
**Fax** 02.38.44.10.01
**Location** in middle of village, 3 km W of Beaugency; with garden, and private and public car parking
**Meals** breakfast, lunch, dinner
**Prices** rooms F-FF, apartments FF-FFF; breakfast F, menus FF
**Rooms** 12 double (7 twin), 3 suites, 5 apartments, all with bath; all rooms have central

heating, phone, TV, hairdrier
**Facilities** 2 dining-rooms, sitting-room; swimming-pool, tennis, bicycle hire
**Credit cards** AE, MC, V
**Children** welcome; cots and special meals
**Disabled** ground-floor rooms; lift/elevator
**Pets** accepted
**Closed** 2 Jan to end Feb
**Proprietor** Marie-Christine Pouey

# *Western France*

# Le Prieuré

A few years ago we came close to dropping this hotel from the guide through lack of support from readers, but our perseverance has been rewarded by a renewed burst of enthusiastic reports. 'I certainly endorse the inclusion of Le Prieuré,' says one. 'At just over 800F for two it must rank as our most expensive stopover, but well worth it.' Another reporter (who describes the prices as 'reasonable') sums up Le Prieuré as 'excellent in every respect,' with 'first-rate food'.

Tonnay-Boutonne is a small, quiet village lying between the old military town of Rochefort and St-Jean-d'Angély, a former wine port. Set slightly back from the (not very busy) main road in a large grassy garden, Le Prieuré is a typical Charentaise building: plain but handsomely symmetrical, with white-shuttered windows. It was the family home of the proprietors before they opened it as a hotel, and retains a friendly atmosphere. The bedrooms and bathrooms have been revamped, leading a reporter to call them 'lovely' and justifying a move from two-star to three-star status a couple of years ago.

**Nearby** Rochefort – 17thC Corderie Royale, Navy Museum; La Roche Courbon (25 km) – château; Saintes (30 km).

17380 Tonnay-Boutonne
**Tel** 05.46.33.20.18
**Fax** 05.46.33.25.55
**Location** in village 21 km E of Rochefort; with large garden and ample car parking
**Meals** breakfast, lunch, dinner
**Prices** rooms 250F-450F; breakfast 45F, menu 140F
**Rooms** 16 double (6 twin), 2 family rooms; 15 with bath, 3 with shower; all rooms have phone, TV

**Facilities** reception/sitting-area, TV/sitting-room, 2 dining-rooms
**Credit cards** MC, V
**Children** welcome
**Disabled** no special facilities
**Pets** accepted
**Closed** Christmas/New Year
**Proprietors** M. and Mme Paul Vernoux

# *Western France*

---

Château hotel, Amboise

## Château de Pray

A 13thC château steeped in history and in a magnificent position high up above the Loire, with superb views from the windows and terraces. All the rooms have been smartly redecorated and four swish suites have been added across the garden. A recent visitor thought Château de Pray both impressive and good value.

■ 37400 Amboise (Indre-et-Loire) **Tel** 02.47.57.23.67 **Fax** 02.47.57.32.50 **E-mail** chateau.depray@wanadoo.fr.**Meals** breakfast, lunch, dinner **Prices** rooms FF; breakfast F, menus FF **Rooms** 19, all with bath, phone, TV **Credit cards** AE, DC, MC, V **Closed** Jan

---

Village inn, Angles sur l'Anglin

## Le Relais du Lyon D'or ★

A couple who visit France frequently, praised the warm welcome and high quality service they received here, and we continue to receive enthusiastic reports. The Lyon D'or is situated at the heart of a tranquil village that has been designated one of the most beautiful in France. The building, which was once a royal tythe depot and dates back to the 14thC, now provides comfortable accommodation with open log fires, rustic beams and terracotta tiled floors. 'Excellent' food is based on seasonal local produce. During March, Heather Thoreau runs two- and three-day paint finish courses.

■ 4 Rue d'Enfer, 86260 Angles sur l'Anglin (Vienne) **Tel** 05.49.48.32.53 **Fax** 05.49.84.02.28 **Meals** breakfast, lunch, dinner **Prices** rooms F; breakfast F; menus FF **Rooms** 10, all with bath or shower, central heating, phone **Credit cards** MC, V **Closed** 2 Jan to 1 Mar

---

Country house, Ardenais

## Domaine de Vilotte ★

The home of the welcoming Champenier family, this elegant rose-covered mansion offers five individually decorated bedrooms, a farmhouse-style kitchen with copper pans lining the walls and a lovely terrace. An interesting collection of antique radios, telephones and sewing machines fills the entrance. We welcome further reports.

■ Ardenais, 18170 Le Châtelet-en-Berry (Cher) **Tel & Fax** 02.48.96.04.96 **Meals** breakfast, dinner by arrangement **Prices** rooms F, with breakfast **Rooms** 5, all with bath, central heating **Credit cards** none **Closed** never

---

Village hotel, Bassac

## L'Essille

It's years since we first heard of this modest hotel in a peaceful small village on the banks of the Charente. 'Comfortable hotel in delightful garden; very quiet; good parking.' 'Warm welcome, friendly but efficient service,' say two earlier reports. The hotel is now up for sale and we welcome reports on developments.

■ 16120 Bassac (Charente) **Tel** 05.45.81.94.13 **Fax** 05.45.81.97.26 **Meals** breakfast **Prices** rooms F; breakfast F **Rooms** 10, all with bath, central heating, phone, TV **Credit cards** AE, DC, MC, V **Closed** never

# *Western France*

---

Village hotel, Bléré

## Le Cheval Blanc

This smart-looking three-fireplace Logis on the main square of Bléré comes highly recommended, particularly for the 'outstanding' warmth of welcome and friendly service from the young staff. Food is 'imaginative and delicious', (especially the desserts), value for money,'difficult to beat in the area'. Garden and heated swimming-pool.

■ Place de l'Église, 37150 Bléré (Indre-et-Loire) **Tel** 02.47.30.30.14 **Fax** 02.47.23.52.80 **Meals** breakfast, lunch, dinner **Prices** rooms F; breakfast F, menus FF **Rooms** 12, all with bath or shower, central heating, phone, TV, minibar, hairdrier **Credit cards** AE, DC, MC, V **Closed** Jan and Feb; restaurant only, Sun and Mon dinner except Jul and Aug

---

Village hotel, Brinon-sur-Sauldre

## Auberge de la Solognote

The attractions of this rather dull-looking house are within – elegantly rustic furnishing and restrained, tasteful decoration, and excellent (Michelin-starred) food. The light, attractive bedrooms earn top marks for comfort – especially those in the converted outhouse.

■ 18410 Brinon-sur-Sauldre (Cher) **Tel** 02.48.58.50.29 **Fax** 02.48.58.56.00 **Meals** breakfast, lunch, dinner **Prices** rooms F; breakfast F, menus FF **Rooms** 13, all with bath or shower, central heating, phone, TV **Credit cards** MC, V **Closed** mid-Feb to mid-Mar

---

Country hotel, Buzançais

## L'Hermitage

Monsieur and Madame Sureau have added a second dining-room and a veranda to this excellent Logis de France, occupying a mini manor house in leafy grounds beside the Indre. Breakfast can be had in the garden, which also provides flowers and vegetables. An open fire on winter evenings. Reporters continue to be enthusiastic – warm welcome, good housekeeping, excellent good-value food in an otherwise pricey area.

■ 36500 Buzançais (Indre) **Tel** 02.54.84.03.90 **Fax** 02.54.02.13.19 **Meals** breakfast, lunch, dinner **Prices** rooms F; breakfast F, menus F-FF **Rooms** 14, all with central he ating, phone, TV **Credit cards** MC, V **Closed** 1-15 Jan; 12-21 Sep; restaurant only, Sun eve; Mon

---

Riverside hotel, Châteauneuf-sur-Sarthe

## Hôtel de la Sarthe

Our most recent reporter was happy with this modest Logis on a beautiful stretch of the Sarthe, but light sleepers can be disturbed by noise from the nearby through-road. Bedrooms have recently been redecorated; food is well prepared and excellent value, and served on the terrace in summer. Very welcoming proprietors.

■ 1 Rue du Port, 49330 Châteauneuf-sur-Sarthe (Maine-et-Loire) **Tel & Fax** 02.41.69.85.29 **Meals** breakfast, lunch, dinner **Prices** rooms F; breakfast F, menus F-FF **Rooms** 7, all with bath or shower, central heating **Credit cards** MC, V **Closed** 3 weeks Oct; restaurant only, Sun dinner, Mon lunch and dinner out of season

# *Western France*

---

## La Croix Blanche de Sologne

The 200-year-old tradition of women chefs continues at this cosy hotel, furnished with gleaming country antiques and floral-patterned fabrics. The 'superb' food is the attraction; the style of cooking is largely Périgordian (foie gras and so on). A recent visitor thought the hotel itself 'in need of a facelift'.

■ 41600 Chaumont-sur-Tharonne (Loir-et-Cher) **Tel** 02.54.88.55.12 **Fax** 02.54.88.60.40 **Meals** breakfast, lunch, dinner **Prices** rooms F; DB&B F; breakfast F, menus FF **Rooms** 18, all with bath, central heating, phone, TV, radio, minibar **Credit cards** AE, DC, MC, V **Closed** never

---

## La Roseraie

A reader alerted us to this hotel, formerly the Ottoni. The bedrooms are tastefully decorated. Regional food is served either in the charming beamed dining-room or on the sunny terrace. There is now a heated swimming-pool, too. The splendid château is only a couple of minutes away.

■ 7 Rue du Dr Bretonneau, 37150 Chenonceaux (Indre-et-Loire) **Tel** 02.47.23.90.09 **Fax** 02.47.23.91.59 **Meals** breakfast, lunch, dinner **Prices** rooms F; breakfast F, menus FF Rooms 19, all with central heating, phone, satellite TV **Credit cards** AE, DC, MC, V **Closed** mid-Nov to mid-Feb

---

## Au Marais

The Marais in question is a huge area of marshes west of Niort. This friendly little inn on the banks of the Sèvre-Niortaise river makes a pleasant and peaceful stop-over. The rooms are decorated in bright pastel tones and immaculately kept.

■ 46-48 Quai Louis-Tardy, 79510 Coulon (Deux-Sèvres) **Tel** 05.49. 35.90.43 **Fax** 05.49.35.81. 98 **Meals** breakfast **Prices** rooms F; breakfast F **Rooms** 18, all with bath, central heating, phone, TV **Credit cards** AE, MC, V **Closed** Jan

---

## Manoir du Grand Martigny

Henri and Monique Desmarais are fluent in English, and actively seek to attract English-speaking guests to their 16thC manor house, in wooded grounds not far from the Loire. They renovated the house in the mid-1980s, and it makes a captivating place to stay, with splendid bedrooms and elegant public rooms. Excellent breakfasts.

■ Vallières, 37230 Fondettes (Indre-et-Loire) **Tel** 02.47.42.29.87 **Fax** 02.47.42.24.44 **Meals** breakfast **Prices** rooms F-FF with breakfast **Rooms** 7, all with bath, central heating **Credit cards** not accepted **Closed** mid-Nov to Mar

# Western France

---

Village inn, Fontgombault

## Auberge de l'Abbaye

'An interesting overnight stop' sums up this unpretentious, tiny 16thC auberge – described as 'barely more than a cottage' by a recent reporter. Bedrooms are small and basic but the food is excellent and the service 'delightful' – as is the village setting, close to Fontgombault Abbey, which is famous for Gregorian chant. Reservation in advance is recommended.

■ 36220 Fontgombault (Indre) **Tel** 02.54.37.10.82 **Meals** breakfast, lunch, dinner **Prices** rooms F; breakfast F, menu FF **Rooms** 5 **Credit cards** V **Closed** never

---

Riverside hotel, Gien

## Hôtel du Rivage

Christian Gaillard's modern-classic (Michelin-starred) cooking is the main attraction of this unpretentious but quite chic modern hotel. Rooms are generally comfortable, with new mattresses promised for the beds, and good value. Lovely views of the Loire are shared by some bedrooms and the pretty dining-room.

■ 1 Quai de Nice, 45500 Gien (Loiret) **Tel** 02.38.37.79.00 **Fax** 02.38.38.10.21 **E-mail** hoteldurivage@wanadoo.fr **Meals** breakfast, lunch, dinner **Prices** rooms F, suites FF; breakfast F; menus FF **Rooms** 19, all with bath or shower, central heating, phone, TV **Credit cards** AE, DC, MC, V **Closed** early Feb to Mar

---

Converted mill, Loches

## Le Moulin ★

Andrew and Sue wrote to suggest that their 19thC watermill might make an entry here, and they were right. The house is on a small island in the Indre, with lawns down to the water. Bedrooms are furnished with stripped pine or antiques. French-trained Andrew Page cooks, and you can eat separately or communally, with meals on the mill race terrace in summer.

■ St-Jean, St-Germain, 37600 Loches (Indre-et-Loire) **Tel** 02.47. 94.70.12 **Fax** 02.47.94.77. 98 **Meals** breakfast, dinner **Prices** rooms F with breakfast; menu FF **Rooms** 5, all with bath, central heating **Credit cards** not accepted **Closed** Jan, Nov, Dec

---

Restaurant with rooms, Marans

## La Porte Verte

This neat, shuttered house sits quietly on the quayside with its own invitingly shady courtyard. A good, predominantly fishy menu (and wonderful puds) from Didier Montéran's kitchen. Bedrooms are tasteful, although there are idiosyncratic touches. Two are in the Montérans' own house along the quay. Reports on the new quayside *terrasse* please.

■ 20 Quai Foch, 17230 Marans (Charente-Maritime) **Tel** 05.46.01.09.45 **Meals** breakfast, lunch, dinner **Prices** rooms F with breakfast; menus F-FF **Rooms** 5, all with shower, central heating **Credit cards** MC,V **Closed** 2 weeks in Feb, 2 weeks in Nov

# Western France

---

## Château de Chissay

A small-scale fairytale château in the heart of château country, renovated in the late 1980s, with rooms ranging from the affordable to the rather less so. Cooking is above average, including fish from the Loire. Swimming-pool.

■ Chissay-en-Touraine, 41400 Montrichard (Loir-et-Cher)
**Tel** 02.54.32.32.01 **Fax** 02.54.32.43.80 **E-mail** chissay@chateaucountry.com
**Meals** breakfast, lunch, dinner **Prices** rooms F-FFF; breakfast F; menus
FF **Rooms** 31, all with bath, central heating, phone
**Credit cards** AE, DC, MC, V **Closed** mid-Nov to mid-Mar

---

## Château de la Menaudière

Despite its elegant furnishings, the atmosphere of this lovely little château is not intimidating. There are two intimate and rather hushed dining-rooms, and the food is good; breakfast can be had in the courtyard in summer, and there is a pubby bar in the stables. Bedrooms are well furnished, with smart bathrooms.

■ 41401 Montrichard (Loir-et-Cher) **Tel** 02.54.71.23.45 **Fax** 02.54.
71.34.58 **Meals** breakfast, lunch, dinner **Prices** rooms FF; breakfast F;
menus FF **Rooms** 25, all with bath, central heating, phone, TV, minibar
**Credit cards** AE, DC, MC, V **Closed** Nov to Mar; restaurant only, Sun
dinner, Mon lunch and dinner out of season

---

## Moulin de Marcouze

The food (two Michelin stars) is the main draw of this smartly converted mill – Dominique Bouchet is a graduate of the Tour d'Argent in Paris. The modern bedrooms, like the dining-room, employ a light, simple style, with antique and reproduction furniture on plain quarry-tiled floors; some overlook the mill stream. Swimming-pool. 'A curate's egg of a hotel,' reports a visitor who found the cuisine and rooms excellent, but the service 'cold'.

■ Mosnac, 17240 Saint-Genis-de-Saintonge (Charente-Maritime)
**Tel** 05.46.70.46.16 **Fax** 05.46.70.48.14 **Meals** breakfast, lunch, dinner
**Prices** rooms F-FF; breakfast 70F, menus FF-FFF **Rooms** 9, all with bath,
central heating, air-conditioning, phone, TV, minibar **Credit cards** AE,
MC, V **Closed** Feb

---

## Le Rivage

Position and food are the keys to this ordinary-looking hotel. It's in a peaceful spot on the banks of the Loiret, with a riverside terrace; the food is regionally-based and rated 'excellent' and 'beautifully presented' in a stylish setting. Chatty, friendly owner. Tennis court.

■ 635 Rue de la Reine Blanche, 45160 Olivet (Loiret)
**Tel** 02.38.66.02.93 **Fax** 02.38.56.31.11 **Meals** breakfast, lunch, dinner
**Prices** rooms F; breakfast F, menus FF **Rooms** 17, all with bath or
shower, central heating, phone, TV, minibar **Credit cards** AE, DC, MC, V
**Closed** 3 weeks in Jan; restaurant only, Sun dinner Nov to Easter

# *Western France*

Manor house hotel, Ouchamps

## Relais des Landes

This 17thC mansion has a splendidly peaceful setting, in neat gardens leading off to the ponds and woods of the Sologne. Restful, spacious, well equipped bedrooms (most in low outbuildings); traditional food is served in a tiled, beamed dining-room. Reports welcome.

■ 41120 Ouchamps (Loir-et-Cher) **Tel** 02.54.44.40.40 **Fax** 02.54. 44.03.89 **Meals** breakfast, dinner **Prices** rooms F-FF; DB&B FF **Rooms** 28, all with bath, central heating, pho ne, TV, minibar **Credit cards** AE, DC, MC, V **Closed** 30 Nov to 30 Mar

Town hotel, Pons

## Auberge Pontoise

The Massiots took over this simple, unpretentious hotel in the late 1990s. The rooms (some facing the garden) are of a fair size, and there is a pleasant courtyard where meals are served in summer. 'A convenient overnight stop in an attractive village, with seriously good food,' comments a recent visitor.

■ 23 Ave Gambetta, 17800 Pons (Charente-Maritime) **Tel** 05.46.94.00.99 **Fax** 05.46.91.33.40 **E-mail** auberge.pontoise@wanadoo.fr **Website** www.auberge-pontoise.fr **Meals** breakfast, lunch, dinner **Prices** rooms F; menus FF **Rooms** 22, all with bath or shower, central heating, phone, TV **Credit cards** MC, V **Closed** Sun dinner and Mon out of season

Converted mill, La Roche-l'Abeille

## Moulin de la Gorce

A tranquil setting and renowned cooking (two stars from Michelin) are the main attractions of this neat, low-lying 16thC mill building, beside a lake amid wooded grounds. Bedrooms – some richly furnished, some more bland – are split between the main building and an ancient nearby mill. Relais & Châteaux. Thoroughly recommended by a visitor for its 'setting, the food and the welcome'.

■87800 La Roche-l'Abeille (Haute-Vienne) **Tel** 05.55.00.70.66 **Fax** 05.55.00.76.57 **Meals** breakfast, lunch, dinner **Prices** rooms F-FF, apartment FFF; breakfast F; menus FF (Mon to Sat, lunchtime) -FFF **Rooms** 10, all with bath, phone, TV **Credit cards** AE, DC, MC, V **Closed** Jan; Sun eve and Mon, Oct to Apr

Château hotel, St-Hilaire-de-Court

## Château de la Beuvrière

A beautifully restored medieval château with 11thC origins – complete with conical slate roofs atop its round towers. Inside, the scale is more domestic than in many châteaux, the atmosphere welcoming. Outside, extensive grounds. A recent visitor described it as 'a wonderful place for a short break'.

■ St-Hilaire-de-Court, 18100 Vierzon (Cher) **Tel** 02.48.75.14.63 **Fax** 02.48.75.47.62 **Meals** breakfast, lunch, dinner **Prices** rooms F, suite FF; breakfast F; menus FF **Rooms** 15, all with bath or shower, central heating, phone **Credit card** AE, DC, V **Closed** Sun night and Mon

# Western France

---

Country hotel, St-Maixent-l'Ecole

## Le Logis Saint-Martin

This neat old house, completely secluded in wooded grounds but
conveniently close to the RN11 and the A10, has a new new fountain to
soothe those opting for outdoor dining on the terrace. Bedrooms
have been redecorated and are individually and tastefully furnished, bathrooms remodelled, and a new split-level suite has been
created in the 17thC tower. Food is taken increasingly seriously.

■ Chemin de Pissot, 79400 St-Maixent-l'Ecole (Deux-Sèvres)
**Tel** 05.49. 05.58.68 **Fax** 05.49.76.19.93 **Meals** breakfast, lunch, dinner
**Prices** rooms F-FF; suite FF; breakfast F; menus FF-FFF **Rooms** 11, all
with bath or shower, central heating, phone, hairdrier, satellite TV **Credit
cards** AE, DC, MC, V **Closed** Jan

---

Country house hotel, St-Martin-du-Fault

## La Chapelle-Saint-Martin

A neat, shuttered country house in lovely manicured grounds. The
suave interior is designer-decorated and luxuriously furnished,
mixing antiques, modern conveniences and rich fabrics in the best
of taste; bedrooms are equally impressive. Relais & Châteaux.

■ St-Martin-du-Fault, 87510 Nieul (Haute-Vienne) **Tel** 05.55.75.80.17
**Fax** 05.55.75.89.50 **Meals** breakfast, lunch, dinner **Prices** rooms FF,
suites FFF-FFFF; DB&B FF **Rooms** 14, all with bath, central heating,
phone, TV **Credit cards** AE, MC, V **Closed** Jan

---

Château hotel, St-Patrice

## Château de Rochecotte

'Travellers who stay here for only one night do themselves an injus-
tice,' writes a well-satisfied reporter. An opportunity to sample life
in a château of the grandest style, looked after by the charming
Mme Pasquier and her equally charming daughters and staff.
Bright fabrics and elegant modern furniture complement the classical proportions of the rooms. Gastronomique cuisine.

■ St-Patrice, 37130 Langeais (Indre-et-Loire) **Tel** 02.47.96.16.16
**Fax** 02.47.96.90.59 **E-mail** chateau.rochecotte@wanadoo.fr **Website** www. chateau-
de-rochecotte.fr **Meals** breakfast, lunch, dinner **Prices** rooms FF-FFF, suites
FFF; menus FF-FFF **Rooms** 30, all with bath, central heating, phone, TV
**Credit cards** AE, DC, MC, V **Closed** Feb

---

Village inn, Souvigny-en-Sologne

## Auberge de la Croix Blanche ★

A warm welcome from the Marois family at this brick-and-timber
auberge, occupying a prime spot in the middle of a deliciously
pretty village in the Sologne (the annexe is some 150 metres from
the hotel itself). Bedrooms are small and simple with smartly tiled
bathrooms. The *cuisine traditionelle et copieuse* is highly regarded.

■ Rue Eugenie Labiche, Souvigny-en-Sologne, 41600 Lamotte-Beuvron
(Loir-et-Cher) **Tel** 02.54.88.40.08 **Fax** 02 54 88 91 06 **Meals** breakfast,
lunch, dinner **Prices** rooms F; breakfast F, menus F-FF **Rooms** 9, all with
central heating, phone **Credit cards** V **Closed** mid-Jan to Mar; Tue and
Wed

# *Eastern France*

## Area introduction

Our Eastern France region takes in Burgundy, the Jura and most of the Alps – an exceptionally rewarding area for lovers of food, wine and the great outdoors. We have a great many potential entries for this area, listed below.

**Contenders in Eastern France**

**Beaune, Le Cep** 03.80.22.35.48 Fairly pricey B&B in centre, now much enlarged.

**Bourg-St-Maurice, Hôtel l'Autantic** 04.79.07.01.70 Modern stone-faced chalet on edge of town, with comfy rooms.

**Le-Bourget-du-Lac, Ombremont** 04.79.25.00.23 Tastefully decorated R&C villa overlooking lake; pool.

**Bresson, Chavant** 04.76.25.25.38 Upmarket, elegantly furnished auberge; flower-filled dining terrace; excellent food.

**Buxy, Château de Sassangy** 03.85.96.12.40 Tall 18thC château in lovely grounds, with freshly decorated rooms.

**Chamonix-Mont-Blanc, Hôtel Albert 1er** 04.50.53.05.09 Solid old town hotel with the best food in town.

**Chorey-les-Beaune, Château de Chorey-les-Beaune** 03.80.22.06.05 Tastefully decorated, family-run B&B in solid 17thC château.

**Cordon, Le Cordonant** 04.50.58.34.56 Good-value modern chalet hotel in a country setting with excellent views.

**Courchevel 1850, La Sivolière** 04.79.08.08.33 Warmly welcoming hotel, run with dedication; quiet, but close to centre.

**Lods, La Truite d'Or** 03.81.60.95.48 Old riverside mill in a narrow Jura valley, now a modest, rustic Logis.

**Loué, Laurent** 02.43.88.40.03 Smart Relais & Châteaux place with extravagant decor, attractive gardens with pool.

**Lyon, La Tour Rose** 04.78.37.25.90 Ambitious restaurant with spectacularly individual rooms decorated by Lyon silk makers.

**Megève, Le Fer à Cheval** 04.50.21.30.39 Tastefully rustic furnishings in a wood-built chalet on edge of town.

**Mionnay, Alain Chapel** 04.78.91.82.02 Luxury restaurant (one of best in France) with very expensive rooms.

**Monêtier-les-Bains, l'Auberge du Choucas** 04.92.24.42.73 Former farmhouse, still charming, with simple quiet rooms.

**Le-Moulin-du-Milieu, Le Moulin** 03.81.44.35.18 Eccentric house with large garden in a remote setting, recently opened.

**Onlay, Château de Lesvault** 03.86.84.32.91 Home-like 19thC manor in grounds, with special appeal for writers and artists.

**Replonges, La Huchette** 03.85.31.03.55 Boldly decorated, shuttered house in grassy grounds with large pool; good food.

**St-Martin-en-Bresse, Au Puits Enchanté** 03.85.47.71.96 Neat little Logis; exceptionally stylish decor and good-value food.

**St-Sauveur-en-Rue, L'Auberge du Château de Bobigneux** 04.77.39.24.33 Dinky rustic 16thC château offering simple rooms and country cooking at very low prices.

**Saulieu, Bernard Loiseau** 03.80.64.07.66 A temple of gastronomy, in an old inn, beautifully renovated, plus rustic-style extensions.

**Veyrier-du-Lac, Auberge de l'Eridan** 04.50.60.24.00 Swanky villa on lake shore; super-chef Marc Veyrat cooks.

**Vienne, La Pyramide** 04.74.53.01.96 Famous restaurant, revived under a new chef; tasteful, comfortable rooms.

# *Eastern France*

**Manor house hotel, Aloxe-Corton**

# Villa Louise

'Highly recommended,' enthuses a German visitor, 'especially for its modern style in a traditional building, the superb garden views and the excellent breakfasts.' And the only change here is the name – it was formerly Hôtel Clarion, but the owners sought to avoid confusion with the US hotel chain of that name.

The tiny village of Aloxe-Corton is a place of pilgrimage for lovers of great white wine. Its symbol is the château of Corton-André, a picturesque building of gleaming coloured tiles and tidy tunnels full of *premiers crus*. Next to it lies the Villa Louise, a 17th-century mansion which has been cleverly converted into a small and unconventional hotel. The style mixes modern and old – art deco furnishings set against old timberwork and beamed ceilings. Bedrooms are well co-ordinated, mainly in matching fabrics of pastel shades. Although varied in size and price, all are thoroughly comfortable and well-equipped. Bathrooms, in marble, are large. Other merits of the hotel are the comfortable salon (beams, open fireplace) opening out on to the park and vineyards, and large garden. 'Superb' breakfasts include eggs, cheese and fresh fruit in addition to the usual coffee and croissants.

**Nearby** Beaune – infirmary, museum; Le Rochepot (25 km).

21420 Aloxe-Corton
**Tel** 03.80.26.46.70
**Fax** 03.80.26.47.16
**E-mail** villalou@iafrica.com
**Website** www.villalouise.com
**Location** on edge of village, 3.5 km N of Beaune on N74; in large garden with ample car parking
**Meals** breakfast
**Prices** rooms F-FF
**Rooms** 10 double (7 twin), all with bath; one family room with bath ; all rooms have

central heating, phone, TV, minibar
**Facilities** sitting-room; bicycles
**Credit cards** MC, V
**Children** welcome; cots, special meals, baby-sitting available
**Disabled** one ground-floor bedroom specially equipped
**Pets** accepted
**Closed** never
**Proprietor** Christian Voarick

# *Eastern France*

**Converted abbey, Annecy-le-Vieux**

## L'Abbaye

Annecy-le-Vieux is not the lovely medieval heart of Annecy, but a sprawling residential area north of the lake, and to be honest both the inspectors we've recently sent here have fretted about this weak spot in an otherwise captivating (although idiosyncratic) hotel. A reader summarises it as 'a very attractive hotel with delightful bedrooms,' with no niggles about the location. A room overlooking the garden is recommended.

L'Abbaye was indeed an ancient abbey. A stone archway leads into a quaint cobbled courtyard surrounded by a wooden balcony. The dining-room is a splendid, vaulted room sporting a motley array of decoration: gold mythological masks, chandeliers, Renaissance fresco, Indian print napkins. In summer, tables are set up in the shade of huge trees. The bedrooms have been beautifully furnished – again in a variety of styles – and with every modern convenience. (We're not surprised to hear that the hotel has recently stepped up to four-star status.) It's rather surprising to find a disco in a hotel like this, but it is separate and does not disturb the peace. The food is good, and well priced; service is casual in terms of dress, but effective.

**Nearby** lake; Annecy (old town, churches, château)

15, Chemin de l'Abbaye, 74940 Annecy-le-Vieux
**Tel** 04.50.23.61.08
**Fax** 04.50.27.77.65
**Location** in rural setting, 2 km NE of Annecy; with garden and car parking
**Meals** breakfast, dinner
**Prices** rooms F-FF; breakfast F, menu FF
**Rooms** 15 double, 2 suites, one apartment, all with bath; all have central heating, phone, TV, minibar

**Facilities** dining-room, bar, terrace
**Credit cards** AE, DC, MC, V
**Children** welcome
**Disabled** no special facilities
**Pets** accepted
**Closed** restaurant only, Mon
**Proprietors** M. Menges and M. Burnet

# *Eastern France*

**Town mansion, Auxerre**

## Parc des Maréchaux

This substantial 1850s house, restored from near-dereliction by Espérance Hervé and her doctor husband, enjoys clear support from readers, not least because it offers excellent value.

The Hervés have cut no corners: the welcoming ambience, confident style and solid comfort of the house would do credit to any professional hotelier. For a bed-and-breakfast establishment, the public rooms are exceptionally comfortable; as well as the sitting-room, the smart little bar looking over the garden is appreciated.

The large bedrooms are beautifully done out in restrained colours, and handsomely furnished using warm wooden beds and chests in traditional styles. One reader warned against those on the noisy road side and advises booking one that overlooks the garden – the secluded, leafy 'park' from which the hotel takes its name. But Madame advises that the road-side rooms have now been soundproofed. Breakfast, which can be had outside in summer, as an alternative to the pretty breakfast room, is 'outstanding,' says one reporter, 'adequate, with more copious options,' says another.

**Nearby** cathedral, abbey church of St-Germain; Chablis (20 km)

6 Ave Foch 89000 Auxerre
**Tel** 03.86.51.43.77
**Fax** 03.86.51.31.72
**Website** www.ch-demeures.com/
**Location** close to middle of town; with gardens and car parking
**Meals** breakfast
**Prices** rooms F (under 7s free); breakfast F
**Rooms** 19 double (7 twin), 2 single, 3 family rooms; all with bath; all rooms have central heating, phone, TV

**Facilities** sitting-room, bar, breakfast room
**Credit cards** AE, DC, V
**Children** welcome
**Disabled** 3 ground-floor bedrooms; lift/elevator
**Pets** accepted
**Closed** never
**Proprietor** Espérance Hervé

# *Eastern France*

**Château hotel, Avallon**

## Château de Vault de Lugny

Press a button and the iron gates open automatically; once through, the front door comes into view across the sweep of lawn. Standing there on the steps is the aimiable butler and a maid; they take your cases and show you to your room. Have no fears: this is understated, friendly service such as guests once experienced at large country houses. You will be at ease.

Inside, this ambience is faithfully preserved: it's a very handsome house, but Elizabeth Audin's good taste has kept the decoration not too smart, not too informal: it has the feel of a private home. However, there are two rather grand bedrooms, filled with impressive antiques; the rest are all spacious and comfortable.

Dinner is taken house-party style at a table large enough to allow a couple to talk amongst themselves, but if you prefer to sit at a separate table for complete privacy, you can. The food is rich and delicious, and presentation in restrained good taste: not dolled up, but in the style of authentic home cooking. If in doubt, try the classic Burgundy menu.

The extensive, well-wooded grounds include a stretch of trout fishing, a tennis court and a Medieval defensive tower.

**Nearby** Avallon - ramparts; Vezelay (10 km).

89200 Avallon
**Tel** 03.86.34.07.86
**Fax** 03.86.34.16.36
**Website** www.lugny.com
**Location** 4 km W of Avallon, 1 km N of Pontaubert, on D427 outside village of Vault-de-Lugny, in large grounds with ample car parking
**Meals** breakfast, lunch, dinner, snacks
**Prices** rooms FF-FFFF with continental breakfast; dinner FF; reductions for 5 nights +

**Rooms** 12 double (4 twin), all with bath; all rooms have central heating, phone, satellite TV, minibar, hairdrier, safe **Facilities** sitting-room/bar, sitting-room, restaurant; tennis, fishing
**Credit cards** AE, MC, V
**Children** welcome; babysitting available **Disabled** easy access, room on ground floor **Pets** welcome (50F charge)**Closed** mid-Nov to early Apr
**Proprietor** Elisabeth Audan

# Eastern France

**Converted mill, Chaublanc**

## Moulin d'Hauterive

We recommend this place for another year despite one negative reader's report.

The wheels of the mill were still turning less than 30 years ago; only for the last decade or so has it been enjoying a new lease of life as a country hotel – offering an unusual blend of rural seclusion, good living and sporting activities. It is a handsome creeper-clad building, three storeys high, surrounded by a collection of lower outbuildings. Beyond them are the little pool (with a lift-up cover/roof which is doubtless a great aid to child safety and energy conservation when the pool is not in use, but diminishes the pleasure of swimming) and tennis court.

The interior is the epitome of rustic chic. The building contributes a network of beams, smooth stone-flagged floors, whitewashed or rough pale stone walls. Against this are placed bright fabrics, delicate mellow antiques, gleaming ornaments, and vivid bowls of flowers. Bedrooms are romantically done out in pastel shades – beds are often draped or canopied with lacy fabrics. The Moilles were new to hotel keeping when they set up the Moulin. Madame has gained a formidable reputation for her inventive dishes (two red *toques* from Gault-Millau).

**Nearby** Archéodrome (10 km) – archeological centre; Beaune (15 km) – medieval infirmary, wine museum.

Chaublanc 71350 St-Gervais-en-Vallière
**Tel** 03.85.91.55.56
**Fax** 03.85.91.89.65
**E-mail** hauterive@hol.fr
**Location** 16 km SE of Beaune, off D970; in grounds with ample car parking
**Meals** breakfast, lunch, dinner
**Prices** rooms FF, suites FFF; DB&B FF; menus FF-FFF
**Rooms** 5 double, 14 suites, all with bath or shower; all rooms have central heating, phone, TV, minibar
**Facilities** 2 dining-rooms, bar, 3 seminar rooms; swimming-pool, tennis, spa, billiards, heliport, sauna, solarium, fitness room **Credit cards** AE, DC, V **Children** accepted
**Disabled** one room
**Pets** dogs accepted in bedrooms at extra charge
**Closed** 16 Nov to Feb; restaurant only, Mon to Fri Sep to Jun **Proprietors** Christiane and Michel Moille

# *Eastern France*

**Country hotel, Gevrey-Chambertin**

## Les Grands Crus

The walls are vertical and plastered, the exposed beams are straight and smooth, the windows are easily opened casements: this is a modern hotel, built as recently as 1977, and so not as immediately charming as many older places in these pages. But the Grands Crus has been done out in traditional Burgundian style, with quarry-tiled floors, lime-washed walls, tapestry fabrics and a carved-stone fireplace, and it drips with geraniums in summer – so to a degree it combines the charm of the old with the comfort of the new.

The bedrooms are not the last word in stylish decoration, but they are peaceful, spacious and thoughtfully furnished, and look out over the famous Gevrey-Chambertin vineyards. A better-than-average breakfast is served in the small flowery garden in fine weather; if you're confined indoors, there may be delays because of a shortage of space in the breakfast room, off reception.

There are plenty of restaurants nearby for other meals, including some notably good ones. The Farniers will advise on the best *ventes-directs* for buying local wines.

**Nearby** Dijon – Grand Duke's palace, Place de la Libération; Gevrey-Chambertin vineyards.

Rte des Grands Crus 21220 Gevrey-Chambertin
**Tel** 03.80.34.34.15
**Fax** 03.80.51.89.07
**E-mail** hotel.lesgrandscrus@ipac.fr
**Location** in middle of village, 10 km SW of Dijon; with garden and ample car parking
**Meals** breakfast
**Prices** rooms F; breakfast F; children under 4 free
**Rooms** 24 double (8 twin) all with bath; all rooms have phone
**Facilities** sitting-room
**Credit cards** MC, V
**Children** welcome
**Disabled** no special facilities
**Pets** accepted but not to be left in rooms
**Closed** Dec to Feb
**Proprietor** Mme Marie-Paule Farnier

# *Eastern France*

**Chalet hotel, Chamonix**

## Auberge du Bois Prin

Despite increasing competition (notably from the newish Jeu de Paume, see page 125) the Bois Prin remains our favourite spot in (or at least near) Chamonix. This is partly because of its stunning views across the valley to the spires and glaciers of Mont Blanc, Europe's highest peak. But an inspection visit also confirms its merits as a cossetting place to stay.

The Bois Prin is a traditional-style dark-wood chalet, in a pretty, flowery garden close to the foot of the Brévent cable-car, on the north side of the deep, steep-sided Chamonix valley. The Carriers have run the hotel since it was built (by Monsieur's parents) in 1976. The first impression may be of a surprising degree of formality, with crisply dressed staff. But in fact the informal and friendly approach of the young Carriers sets the tone. Bedrooms face Mont Blanc, and are lavishly furnished, with rich fabrics and carved woodwork (much of it Denis's own work) and a sprinkling of antiques; the best have a private terrace. Food is excellent, with a good choice of menus and a 'wonderful' cheese-board. 'Luxurious...yet homely and cosy' praises a visitor.

**Nearby** Mt Blanc and Le Brévent – cable-car rides, walking, rock climbing, skiing; Mont Blanc tunnel for easy access to Italy.

69 Chemin de l'Hermine, Les Moussoux 74400 Chamonix
**Tel** 04.50.53.33.51
**Fax** 04.50.53.48.75
**E-mail** *boisprin@relaischateaux.fr*
**Website** *www.boisprin.com*
**Location** on hillside, NW of town; with garden and ample car parking and garages
**Meals** breakfast, lunch, dinner
**Prices** rooms FF-FFFF with breakfast; menus FF-FFF
**Rooms** 9 double (5 twin), all with bath; 2 family rooms, with bath; all rooms have phone, TV, minibar
**Facilities** dining-room, seminar room
**Credit cards** AE, DC, MC, V
**Children** welcome; special meals, high-chair available
**Disabled** no special facilities
**Pets** accepted
**Closed** 17 Apr to 3 May, 29 Oct to 29 Nov
**Proprietors** Monique and Denis Carrier

# *Eastern France*

## Le Castel ★

We have had mixed reports, over the years, on this pleasant old *maison bourgeoise*. We're coming to the view that it's a matter of expectations. It is a modest hotel – a two-fireplace Logis, with rooms and meals at very attractive prices. But because the house and its name are rather grand, some visitors perhaps expect too much. Our latest reporter, who stayed two nights, takes a balanced view: 'Pleasant welcome (in English), good rooms, good food; reasonable prices.'

Built at the end of the last century, Le Castel is a large shuttered house lying in the shadow of the village church,. with a well-kept garden and a flowery terrace shaded by lime trees, where you can have breakfast.

There are two dining-rooms, separated by a small salon with Empire-style furnishings and a handsome fireplace. Bedrooms vary widely – from spacious ones with touches of grandeur, such as chandeliers and drapes over bedheads, to much smaller and simpler rooms. Some much-needed refurbishment has been undertaken recently, and continues. Madame is 'the perfect hostess'.

**Nearby** Vézelay (24 km) – Romanesque buildings; Avallon (30 km) – ramparts; Chablis (45 km) – vineyards.

Place de l'Église 89660 Mailly-le-Château
**Tel** 03.86.81.43.06
**Fax** 03.86.81.49.26
**Location** in church square of village, 30 km S of Auxerre; with garden, terrace and car parking
**Meals** breakfast, lunch, dinner
**Prices** rooms F, suite F; menus F-FF
**Rooms** 10 double (5 twin), 7 with bath, 2 with shower; 2 family rooms with bath ; all rooms have central heating, phone
**Facilities** 2 dining-rooms, sitting-room
**Credit cards** MC, V
**Children** accepted
**Disabled** one ground-floor bedroom
**Pets** accepted
**Closed** Wed
**Proprietors** M. and Mme Breerette

# *Eastern France*

**Chalet hotel, Manigod**

# Chalet Hôtel de la Croix-Fry

The inspector who was lucky enough to find herself spending a night in this cosy wooden chalet could scarcely contain her enthusiasm, summing it up in the end as her favourite in a week-long tour which included several delectable places.

Mountain chalets come in many styles, but the pretty-as-a-cuckoo-clock variety, two a penny in Switzerland, is all too rare in France. But this is one – built in dark wood, its terrace overflowing with bright flowers. Inside, the immediate impression is of rustic simplicity, with wood the warm, dominant material; an open fire burns on cool evenings, with benches and sofas covered by animal skins in front of it. The bedrooms, too, are charmingly rustic in style – even in the modern annexe-chalets, which offer flexible and comfortable accommodation (with kitchenettes) for all sizes of family.

Style apart, the peaceful setting is the attraction, with superb views across the valley from the terrace and the picture windows of the dining-area. The welcoming owners and staff strike the perfect balance of attentive service without intrusion. Good, nourishing mountain food completes a happy picture.

**Nearby** skiing; Vallée de Manigod, Thônes (10 km); Annecy.

Rte du Col de la Croix-Fry,
Manigod 74230 Thônes
**Tel** 04.50.44.90.16
**Fax** 04.50.44.94.87
**Website** www.oda.fr/aa/croix-fry
**Location** at the col, 5 km NE
of Manigod, on D16 6 km S of
La Clusaz; in countryside,
with garden; ample parking,
garage (50F per day)
**Meals** breakfast, lunch,
dinner
**Prices** rooms FF-FFFF;
breakfast FF; menus FF-FFF

**Rooms** 12 double with bath
(4 whirlpool); all rooms have
central heating, phone,
satellite TV, balcony
**Facilities** dining-room, sitting-room, bar; heated swimming-pool, fitness room, tennis, ski
bus **Credit cards** AE, MC, V
**Children** accepted **Disabled**
no special facilities **Pets** not in
dining-room **Closed** mid-Sep
to mid-Dec, mid-Apr to mid-Jun **Proprietor** Mme Marie-Ange Guelpa-Veyrat

# *Eastern France*

**Converted convent, Marcigny**

# Les Récollets

The Brionnais is a rural region, with gently rolling hills and lush meadows where Charollais cattle graze. It is a part of Burgundy that few foreigners bother with, which explains why we get so few reports on this interesting place. The small market town of Marcigny provides an excellent base for touring the region – it is close to the Loire, and not far from the famous cattle market of St-Christophe-en-Brionnais. It is also the location of this, one of the most delightful hotels in the region. We use the word 'hotel' loosely: this is really a private home open to guests.

Josette Badin, who runs the place with Burgundian *bonhomie*, has furnished the rooms superbly, from the dining-room with its hand-painted cupboards to the antique-laden bedrooms. There are log fires, home-made *brioches* for breakfast, hand-made chocolates by the bedside (along with sleeping tablets, indigestion pills and painkillers). Indeed, every need is catered for, and the only house-rule is 'do as you please'.

Officially, only breakfast is served, but ask in advance and Josette will be happy to prepare a simple meal: soup or omelette – even *foie gras,* followed by Charollais beef.

We hear that Les Récollets is up for sale, so be prepared for changes.

**Nearby** Mill Tower Museum; La Clayette (25 km); Charlieu Abbey (30 km); Château Drée (30 km).

Place du Champ de Foire
71110 Marcigny
**Tel** 03.85.25.05.16
**Fax** 03.85.25.06.91
**Location** on edge of small town 22 km S of Paray; in grounds with ample car parking
**Meals** breakfast; lunch and dinner on request
**Prices** rooms F with breakfast; menus FF
**Rooms** 6 double (2 twin), all with bath; 3 family rooms, all with bath; all rooms have central heating, phone
**Facilities** TV room, library, breakfast/dining-room
**Credit cards** AE, V
**Children** accepted
**Disabled** one ground-floor bedroom
**Pets** accepted
**Closed** never
**Proprietor** Mme Josette Badin

# Eastern France

## Village inn, Mercurey

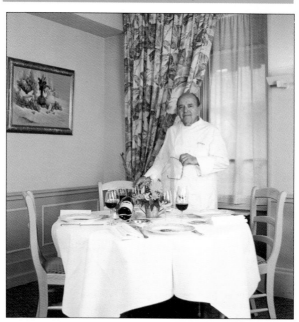

# Hôtellerie du Val d'Or

Jean-Claude Cogny and his family keep standards as high as ever in this early 19th-century coaching inn, on the main street of the prestigious but rather dull wine village of Mercurey. It is easy to see what brings the customers back: in a region of culinary excellence and exorbitant prices, many are daunted by the formal (or even pretentious) style of most hotels, and long to find some village-inn simplicity. The friendly Val d'Or obliges, and combines this with excellent cooking (Michelin-starred) and comfortable, neatly decorated bedrooms – though some are rather small. There is an attractive gravelled garden.

**Nearby** Château de Germolles (10 km); Buxy (20 km).

Grande-Rue 71640 Mercurey
**Tel** 03.85.45.13.70
**Fax** 03.85.45.18.45
**Location** in middle of village, 9 km S of Chagny; with garden
**Meals** breakfast, lunch, dinner
**Prices** rooms F; meals FF (lunch) -FFF, children's meals F
**Rooms** 10 double (3 twin), one single, 2 family rooms; all with bath or shower; all rooms have central heating, phone, TV; 5 have air-conditioning
**Facilities** 2 dining-rooms, lounge/bar
**Credit cards** MC, V
**Children** accepted
**Disabled** no special facilities
**Pets** not accepted
**Closed** Mon and Tue lunch
**Proprietor** Jean-Claude Cogny

# *Eastern France*

**Village hotel, Poisson**

# La Reconce

The strangely-named village of Poisson lies on the borders of Charolais (famous for its white cattle) and Brionnais (noted for its Romanesque churches), both beautiful, little visited stretches of rolling countryside. When farmers walked their cattle to market in St Christophe-en-Brionnais (still held every Thursday), they stopped to rest at the village inn, La Poste, which for the past 27 years has been the restaurant, specializing in Charolais beef and fish, of Denise and Jean-Noel Dauvergne. Seven years ago they bought the handsome house next door and converted it into a small hotel. The parquet flooring in each room is original; apart from that, however, the rooms are standardized and modern, but with more comfort and attention to detail than one expects at this price. Loos are separate from bathrooms, and there are desks and plenty of mirrored cupboard space.

A door in the lobby of La Reconce connects with the bar of La Poste, where locals gather. The restaurant is altogether more soignée, with apricot walls, pale wicker chairs and white tablecloths, and a tank of tropical fish. In summer it is delightful to eat in the little garden under the shade of Pawlonia trees.

**Nearby** circuit of Romanesque churches in Brionnais; Charolais.

Le Bourg, 71600 Poisson (Saône-et-Loire)
**Tel** 03 85 81 10 72
**Fax** 03 85 81 64 34
**e-mail** LaReconce@wanadoo.fr
**Location** in village centre, opposite church, 8 km S of Paray-le-Monial; with ample parking
**Meals** breakfast, lunch, dinner
**Prices** F560
**Rooms** 7; 6 double and twin, 1 suite, 3 with shower, 4 with bath; all rooms have phone, TV, minibar, hairdrier
**Facilities** breakfast room, bar, verandah, garden
**Credit cards** AE, MC, V
**Children** accepted
**Disabled** one specially adapted suite **Pets** accepted
**Closed** Mon, Tues, except Aug **Proprietor** Denise and Jean-Noel Dauvergne

# Eastern France

**Town mansion, Vézelay**

# Le Pontot

Most visitors to this rambling fortified house – the only hotel inside the walls of the old town of Vézelay, just a short walk from the famous basilica – are captivated by its combination of character and luxury. Rebuilt after the Hundred Years War, and added to in the 18thC it has only recently become a hotel. Since 1984 the American owner, architect Charles Thum, and manager Christian Abadie have skilfully converted the building into a rather special bed-and-breakfast. (Who needs a restaurant when the famous Espérance lies just down the road?) The bedrooms include a large Louis XVI apartment, with canopied beds, fireplace and private dressing room; and another with stone paving, 16thC beamed ceiling and antique, country-style, furnishings.

Breakfast is served on gold-encrusted, royal blue Limoges porcelain. On cool days, it is eaten in front of a blazing fire in the handsome, panelled, Louis XVI salon; but in summer you sit outside in the delightful walled garden. A report, however, suggests that grandeur does not compensate for some skimping on the quality of food at breakfast and the comforts in the house.

**Nearby** St-Père-sous-Vézelay (2 km); Avallon (15 km); Auxerre (50 km); Chablis and Sancerre (50 km) – vineyards.

Place du Pontot 89450 Vézelay
**Tel** 03.86.33.24.40
**Fax** 03.86.33.30.05
**Location** in middle of town; with walled flower garden and car parking
**Meals** breakfast
**Prices** rooms F-FFF (extra bed in room 100F); breakfast F
**Rooms** 9 double, one single, all with bath and shower (4 twin); all rooms have phone, radio

**Facilities** sitting-room, bar, breakfast room
Credit cards DC, MC, V
**Children** over 10 accepted
**Disabled** not suitable for wheelchairs
**Pets** accepted; 50F charge
**Closed** Nov to Easter
**Manager** Christian Abadie

# *Eastern France*

---

Town hotel, Arnay-le-Duc

## Chez Camille

Armand Poinsot's excellent cooking (traditional but light) is only one attraction of this captivating little hotel. The mostly compact bedrooms are tastefully decorated and cluttered with antiques – and effectively double-glazed against noise from the RN 6. Much cheaper rooms in the modern Clair de Lune annexe.

■ 1 Place Edouard-Herriot, 21230 Arnay-le-Duc (Côte-d'Or) **Tel** 03.80.90.01.38 **Fax** 03.80.9 0.04.64 **Meals** breakfast, lunch, dinner **Prices** rooms F-FF; menus FF-FFF **Rooms** 14, all with bath, central heating, phone, TV **Credit cards** AE, DC, V **Closed** never

---

Converted mill, Avallon

## Moulin des Templiers

Anne et Jean Liberatore are now running this modest, captivating stop-over on the way through Burgundy. Breakfast is served on the riverside terrace on fine days, otherwise in a tiny room – there may be a queue. The pretty bedrooms. Reports welcome.

■ Vallée du Cousin, Pontaubert, 89200 Avallon (Yonne) **Tel** 03.86. 34.10.80 **Fax** 03.86.31.03.05 **Meals** breakfast **Prices** rooms F; breakfast F **Rooms** 14, all with bath, phone **Credit cards** AE, MC, V **Closed** Dec to 1 Mar

---

Château hotel, Bagnols

## Château de Bagnols

Some expensive château hotels are simply smart, or luxurious, or full of character, or in exceptionally privileged settings. Bagnols is entirely extraordinary – a medieval fortress restored and furnished to be perfect in every detail. Send for the brochure before you dismiss the idea of paying the prices. 'Loved it; would certainly go back,' says our ecstatic nominating reader. Outdoor 'Roman' pool.

■ 69620 Bagnols (Rhône) **Tel** 04.74.71.40.00 **Fax** 04.74.71.40.49 **Meals** breakfast, lunch, dinner **Prices** rooms FFFF; suites FFFF; breakfast FF **Rooms** 20, all with bath, central heating, phone, TV, hairdrier **Credit cards** AE, DC, MC, V **Closed** Jan to Apr

---

Converted mill, Bonnevaux-le-Prieuré

## Le Moulin du Prieuré

Eight neat bedrooms are located in little modern chalets in the garden of this converted watermill which offers complete peace, wonderful scenery and competent cooking. You prepare your own breakfast (an arrangement that suits trout-fishing guests).

■ 25560 Bonnevaux-le-Prieuré (Doubs) **Tel** 03.81.59.28.79 **Fax** 03.81.59.21.47 **Meals** breakfast, lunch, dinner **Prices** rooms F; breakfast F; menus FF-FFF (at least one meal obligatory) **Rooms** 8, all with bath or shower, phone, TV, minibar **Credit cards** AE, DC, MC, V **Closed** mid-Nov to early Mar, Sun evening, Mon

# *Eastern France*

---

## La Fontaine aux Muses

'We absolutely loved it,' says a weary traveller refreshed by the 'delightful' pool of this creeper-covered rural auberge, which also offers golf, tennis and a music room where the family often play. Simple rooms opening on to the garden. Good simple cooking with an emphasis on fish; slow service; breakfast disappointing.

■ Route de la Fontaine, 89116 La Celle-Saint-Cyr (Yonne) **Tel** 03.86.73.40.22 **Fax** 03.86.73.48.66 **Meals** breakfast, lunch, dinner **Prices** rooms F-FF; breakfast F, menu FF **Rooms** 17, all with bath or shower, central heating, phone **Credit cards** MC, V **Closed** Mon; restaurant only, Tue lunch

---

## Hostellerie des Clos

You go here for the food; the modern, tasteful but unremarkable rooms are a bonus. The designer-decorated dining-room is light and stylish; the light, innovative cooking (one Michelin star, two toques from Gault-Millau) makes full use of the local white wines.

■ Rue Jules Rathier, 89800 Chablis (Yonne) **Tel** 03.86.42.10.63 **Fax** 03.86.42.17.11 **Meals** breakfast, lunch, dinner **Prices** rooms F; breakfast F, menus FF-FFF **Rooms** 26, all with bath, central heating, phone, TV, radio, minibar **Credit cards** MC, V **Closed** 2 weeks Christmas and New Year

---

## Hostellerie du Château de Bellecroix

An approving report from a discriminating reader restores this creeper-covered château to the guide. It combines 12thC and 18thC architecture to magical effect. Comfortable bedrooms, some in the turrets, with plenty of antiques and views over the parkland. Large pool. 'Excellent' food.

■ Route Nationale 6, 71150 Chagny (Saône-et-Loire) **Tel** 03.85.87.13.86 **Fax** 03.85.91.28.62 **Meals** breakfast, lunch, dinner **Prices** rooms FF-FFF; breakfast F, menus FF-FFF **Rooms** 20, all with bath or shower, central heating, phone, TV, minibar **Credit cards** AE, DC, MC, V **Closed** 20 Dec to 13 Feb; restaurant only, Wed and Thur lunch

---

## Lameloise

Jacques Lameloise maintains the reputation of this calm shuttered house, established by his father Jean, as one of the best restaurants in France. It is a comfortable hotel, too, with tastefully furnished bedrooms and solidly traditional public areas. Relais & Châteaux, but not at all snooty.

■ 36 Place d'Armes, 71150 Chagny (Saône-et-Loire) **Tel** 03.85.87.65.65 **Fax** 03.85.87.03.57 **E-mail** reception@lameloise.fr **Website** www.lameloise.fr **Meals** breakfast, lunch, dinner **Prices** rooms FF-FFFF; menus FF-FFF **Rooms** 17, all with bath, phone, TV; most have air-conditioning **Credit cards** AE, DC, MC, V **Closed** Tue lunch, Wed, Thu until 3 pm; 22 Dec to 27 Jan

# *Eastern France*

---

Chalet hotel, Chamonix

## Hôtel du Jeu de Paume

Parisian chic comes to the mountains: this offshoot of the Jeu de Paume in Paris, newly built in traditional chalet style, has immediately become one of the most desirable places to stay in the Chamonix valley. Pine-panelled bedrooms. Small indoor pool, Jacuzzi, steam room and sauna.

■ 705, Route du Chapeau, Le Lavancher, 74400 Chamonix (Haute-Savoie) **Tel** 04.50.54.03.76 **Fax** 04.50.54.10.75 **Meals** breakfast, lunch, dinner **Prices** rooms FFF-FFFF; breakfast 65F, menus 165F-280F **Rooms** 22, all with bath, central heating, phone, TV, radio, minibar, hairdrier **Credit cards** AE, DC, MC, V **Closed** mid-May to mid-Jun, mid-Sep to mid-Dec

---

Town hotel, Charolles

## Hôtel de la Poste

A prime example of an unassuming provincial hotel doing a sound job. The white-painted building is immaculately maintained, as is the smart bar-salon; and the dining-room has been made positively ritzy by small-town standards. It is also possible to dine in the lovely internal garden.

■ 2 Ave de la Libération, 71120 Charolles (Saône-et-Loire) **Tel** 03.85.24.11.32 **Fax** 03.85.24.05.74 **Meals** breakfast, lunch, dinner **Prices** rooms F, 2 suites F-FF; breakfast F, menus FF-FFF **Rooms** 13, all with bath or shower, central heating, phone, TV **Credit cards** AE, MC, V **Closed** Sun evening, Mon; Nov

---

Village hotel, Chassignelles

## Hôtel de l'Ecluse No. 79

The *écluse* is the nearby lock on the canal in front of this infant enterprise – a peaceful row of houses boldly but sympathetically converted to provide (at present) seven tastefully furnished bedrooms with smart bathrooms, as well as pleasantly rustic dining-rooms and a bar. Charming *patronne*, modest prices at this Logis de France.

■ 89160 Chassignelles (Yonne) **Tel** 03.86.75.18.51 **Fax** 03.86.75.02.04 **Meals** breakfast, lunch, dinner **Prices** rooms F; breakfast F, menus F-FF, children's F **Rooms** 7, all with bath or shower, central heating, phone, TV, hairdrier **Credit cards** DC, MC, V **Closed** never

---

Village hotel, Châteauneuf

## Hostellerie du Château

The picturesque hostellerie, cleverly converted from a 15thC presbytery close to the château, is in keeping with the medieval village around it: old stone walls, quiet rustic rooms and terraced gardens. In the beamed restaurant wholesome Burgundian dishes are the order of the day. Several recent reporters could not fault it.

■ Châteauneuf, 21320 Pouilly-en-Auxois (Côte-d'Or) **Tel** 03.80.49.22.00 **Fax** 03.80.49.21.27 **E-mail** hostellerie-du-chateau@hostellerie-chateauneuf.com **Website** www. hostellerie-chateauneuf.com **Meals** breakfast, lunch, dinner **Prices** rooms F; menu FF **Rooms** 17, all with bath or shower, central heating, phone **Credit cards** AE, DC, MC, V **Closed** Dec to mid-Feb

# Eastern France

---

Town inn, Châtillon-sur-Seine

## Hôtel de la Côte d'Or

This creeper-covered family-run auberge in a leafy garden offers prettily decorated rooms at modest prices, friendly but proper service and food that is interesting and competently cooked (and served on the terrace when the weather permits).

■ Rue Charles-Ronot, 21400 Châtillon-sur-Seine (Côte-d'Or) **Tel** 03.80.91.13.29 **Fax** 03.80.91.29.15 **Meals** breakfast, lunch, dinner **Prices** rooms F-FF; breakfast F; menus F-FF **Rooms** 10, all with central heating, phone, TV **Credit cards** AE, DC, MC, V **Closed** Jan

---

Country house hotel, Chonas-l'Amballan

## Domaine de Clairefontaine

Of the Girardons' two operations (see also the Marais St Jean) this has the higher reputation for food, with prestigious awards and one Michelin star for Philippe Giradon's cooking. The handsome old house in splendid, peaceful park-like grounds, is family-run without pretension, and offers entirely comfortable rooms at modest prices.

■ Chonas-l'Amballan, 38121 Reventin-Vaugris (Isère) **Tel** 04.74.58.81.52 **Fax** 04.74.58.80.93 **Meals** breakfast, lunch, dinner **Prices** rooms F; breakfast F, menus FF-FFF **Rooms** 28, all with bath or shower, central heating, phone **Credit cards** AE, DC, MC, V **Closed** Dec, Jan; restaurant only, Sun evening and Mon

---

Farmhouse hotel, Chonas-l'Amballan

## Le Marais Saint-Jean

For some years now in the same ownership as the Clairefontaine, this neat farmhouse conversion has a private-home atmosphere, much of which has recently undergone redecoration. Modern comforts blend with the original timbered ceilings, beams and quarry tiles. Good food served in a beamed dining-room or on a sunny terrace.

■ Chonas-l'Amballan, 38121 Reventin-Vaugris (Isère) **Tel** 04.74.58.83.28 **Fax** 04.74.58.81.9 6 **Meals** breakfast, lunch, dinner **Prices** rooms FF; breakfast F, menus FF-FFF **Rooms** 10, all with bath, phone, satellite TV, minibar **Credit cards** AE, DC, MC, V **Closed** Feb to mid Mar, Nov; restaurant only, Wed and Thurs lunch

---

Town hotel, Cluny

## Hôtel de Bourgogne

The most comfortable and central hotel in Cluny, this attractive stone mansion, dating from 1817, is built around a garden and courtyard. The elegant setting and Burgundian specialities of the restaurant draw many non-residents. The Colin family have taken over recently, so reports please.

■ Place de l'Abbaye, 71250 Cluny (Saône-et-Loire) **Tel** 03.85.59.00.58 **Fax** 03.85.59.03.73 **Meals** breakfast, lunch, dinner **Prices** rooms F-FFF; breakfast F, menus FF-FFF **Rooms** 15, all with bath, central heating, phone, TV **Credit cards** AE, MC, V **Closed** mid-Nov to Mar, Tue; restaurant Tue, and Wed lunch

## *Eastern France*

---

Riverside hotel, Condrieu

# Hôtellerie Beau Rivage

The 'beau rivage' is that of the Rhône – not an entirely appropriate description, given the nearby chemical works. But the immediate surroundings of this elegantly furnished place are 'most agreeable', the staff welcoming and the Michelin-starred food 'excellent'.

■ 69420 Condrieu (Rhône) **Tel** 04.74.56.82.82 **Fax** 04.74.59.59.36 **E-mail** Hotel-Beaurivage@wanadoo.fr **Website** .Hotel-Beaurivage.com **Meals** breakfast, lunch, dinner **Prices** rooms FF; breakfast F, menus FF-FFF **Rooms** 24, all with bath or shower, central heating, phone **Credit cards** AE, DC, MC, V **Closed** never

---

Village hotel, Curtil-Vergy

# Hôtel Le Manassès

What better way to spend an overnight stop in Burgundy than in the heart of a working vineyard in the Hautes Côtes de Nuits? 'Beautifully furnished' and well equipped rooms in a converted outbuilding offer remarkable value, and the Chaleys have added five further luxury bedrooms. In the next-door wine museum Yves Chaley will treat you to a taste of his wines. Restaurants nearby.

■ 21220 Curtil-Vergy (Côte-d'Or) **Tel** 03.80.61.43.81 **Fax** 03.80.61.42.79 **Meals** breakfast **Prices** rooms F-FF with breakfast **Rooms** 12, all with bath, central heating, air conditioning, phone, TV, minibar **Credit cards** AE, DC, MC, V **Closed** Dec to Feb

---

Country hotel, Doussard

# Marceau Hôtel

Recommended 'without reservation,' says a visitor of this plain-looking but welcoming family-run hotel, near lake Annecy. The beautiful mountain views are not the only attraction: bedrooms are spacious and dotted with antiques, there is a cosy sitting-room, a rambling garden. A limited menu allows you the choice of eating in the dining-room, on the panoramic terrace, or in your room.

■ Bout du Lac, 74210 Doussard (Haute-Savoie) **Tel** 04.50.44.30.11 **Fax** 04.50.44.39.44 **E-mail** hotelmarceau@aol.com **Website** LacAnnecy.com. **Meals** breakfast, dinner **Prices** rooms FF; breakfast F, **Rooms** 16, all with bath or shower, central heating, phone, TV, radio, hairdrier, minibar **Credit cards** AE, DC, MC, V **Closed** never

---

Château hotel, Fleurville

# Château de Fleurville

Unlike so many château hotels, this is not a formal, luxury establishment – the atmosphere is pleasantly relaxed and it is reasonably priced. Many original 16thC features have been retained and, despite modernization, there is still a medieval atmosphere. Bedrooms are simply furnished. Tennis and swimming-pool.

■ 71260 Fleurville (Saône-et-Loire) **Tel** 03.85.33.12.17 **Fax** 03.85. 33.95.34 **Meals** breakfast, lunch, dinner **Prices** rooms F, apartment FF; breakfast F, menus FF **Rooms** 15, all with bath, central heating, phone **Credit cards** DC, MC, V **Closed** Nov to end Feb; restaurant only, Mon lunch

# *Eastern France*

---

Village inn, Givry

# Hôtel de la Halle

The façade and interior of this town-centre Logis underwent major renovations a few years ago. What captivates British visitors and local regulars alike is the scrupulous housekeeping, excellent traditional Burgundian cuisine and exceptionally low prices. Reports please.

■ Place de la Halle, 71640 Givry (Saône-et-Loire) **Tel** 03.85.44.32.45 **Fax** 03.85.44.49.45 **Meals** breakfast, lunch, dinner **Prices** rooms F; breakfast F, menus F-FF **Rooms** 9, all with bath or shower, central heating, phone **Credit cards** AE, DC, MC, V **Closed** mid-Nov to early Dec

---

Chalet hotel, Goumois

# Hôtel Taillard

A steady flow of readers approve of this pretty chalet in a wooded valley on the Swiss border. They like the wonderful views from the breakfast terrace, the delightful garden, the comfortable rooms, the friendly atmosphere and (not least) the food – 'delicious, if slightly repetitive'. Fitness room.

■ 25470 Goumois (Doubs) **Tel** 03.81.44.20.75 **Fax** 03.81.44.26.15 **Meals** breakfast, lunch, dinner **Prices** rooms F; breakfast F; menus FF-FFF **Rooms** 24, all with bath or shower, central heating, phone, TV **Credit cards** AE, DC, MC, V **Closed** mid-Nov to mid-Mar; restaurant only, Wed in Mar, Oct and Nov; Wed lunch Sep to Jul

---

Château hotel, Igé

# Château d'Igé

This turreted, creeper-covered castle retains its medieval atmosphere despite its conversion into a luxurious Relais & Châteaux hotel. Above-average food is served in front of a huge open hearth in the massively beamed dining-room – a marked contrast to the pleasant new conservatory.

■ 71960 Igé (Saône-et-Loire) **Tel** 03.85.33.33.99 **Fax** 03.85.33.41.41 **Meals** breakfast, lunch, dinner **E-mail** ige@relaischateaux.fr **Prices** rooms F-FF, suites FF-FFF; breakfast F, menus FF-FFF **Rooms** 13, all with bath, central heating, phone, TV, hairdrier **Credit cards** AE, DC, V **Closed** Dec to Mar

---

Bed and breakfast farmhouse, Levernois

# Le Parc

Beaune has a dearth of reasonably priced accommodation but the Parc, 5 km away, offers excellent value and a pleasant rural setting. It is a simple hotel, converted from an old farmhouse, and run rather like a private home. Breakfast is served in a pretty courtyard.

■ Levernois, 21200 Beaune (Côte-d'Or) **Tel** 03.80.24.63.00 **Fax** 03.80. 24.21.19 **Meals** breakfast **Prices** rooms F **Rooms** 25, all with bath or shower, central heating, phone, TV **Credit cards** MC, V **Closed** Dec to 20 Jan

## Eastern France

---

Village hotel, Meursault

## Hôtel les Charmes

This 18thC *maison bourgeoise* sits peacefully in a park-like garden with mature trees. A refined private-house atmosphere prevails: in the bedrooms, the furniture is antique and elegant, the decorative schemes individual and harmonious. There is a swimming pool in the summer months. Secure parking. Fairly new to the guide – reports welcome.

■ 10 Place du Murger, 21190 Meursault (Côte-d'Or) **Tel** 03.80.21.63.53 **Fax** 03.80.21.62.89 **Meals** breakfast **Prices** rooms F; breakfast F **Rooms** 14, all with bath, central heating, phone, TV, minibar **Credit cards** MC, V **Closed** Dec to Mar

---

Village bed-and-breakfast, Meursault

## Les Magnolias

In a pleasantly quiet location, Les Magnolias is a polished and unusually stylish place – a group of old houses around a small courtyard, with spacious bedrooms that have been individually decorated with some panache. Expect to walk to a restaurant.

■ 8 Rue Pierre Joigneaux, 21190 Meursault (Côte-d'Or) **Tel** 03.80. 21.23.23 **Fax** 03.80.21.29.10 **Website** www.les-magnolias.fr **Meals** breakfast **Prices** rooms F-FF; breakfast F **Rooms** 12, all with bath or shower, central heating, phone; TV on request **Credit cards** AE, MC, V **Closed** Dec to 15 Mar

---

Medieval inn, Pérouges

## Ostellerie du Vieux Pérouges

The Ostellerie is at the heart of the perfectly preserved little medieval town of Pérouges. Excellent meals are served in the charming old dining rooms, while slices of *galette Pérougienne* (a sort of sugary pizza) are dispensed from the kitchen window. Bedrooms are in four other houses, the best splendidly old (and pricey).

■ Place du Tilleul, Pérouges, 01800 Meximieux (Ain) **Tel** 04.74.61.00.88 **Fax** 04.74.34.77.9 0 **Website** www.ostellerie.com **Meals** breakfast, lunch, dinner **Prices** rooms F-FFF; menus FF-FFF **Rooms** 28, all with bath, phone, TV **Credit cards** V **Closed** never

---

Town hotel, St-Florentin

## La Grande Chaumière

This attractive pink, turn-of-the-century building with a leafy garden makes a pleasant gastronomic stop-over on the route south. It's not strong on character: bedrooms are in an essentially modern style, the Michelin-starred restaurant light and smartly furnished.

■ 3 Rue des Capucins, 89600 St-Florentin (Yonne) **Tel** 03.86.35.15.12 **Fax** 03.86.35.33.14 **Meals** breakfast, lunch, dinner **Prices** rooms F-FF; breakfast F; menus FF **Rooms** 10, all with bath or shower, central heating, phone, TV **Credit cards** AE, DC, MC, V **Closed** first week Sep, mid-Dec to mid-Jan; Wed out of season

# *Eastern France*

---

Country inn, St-Lattier

# Le Lièvre Amoureux

One reporter reckons the food at this old hunting lodge is of star quality. Michelin disagrees, but there are other attractions – not least the leafy garden and the pool, which is directly accessible from the pine-panelled rooms in the modern 'outbuildings'; in the main building there are more traditional alternatives.

■ La Gare, 38840 St-Lattier (Isère) **Tel** 04.76.64.50.67 **Fax** 04.76. 64.31.21 **Meals** breakfast, lunch, dinner **Prices** rooms F; breakfast F, DB&B F; menus FF **Rooms** 14, all with bath, central heating, phone, TV, hairdrier **Credit cards** DC, MC, V **Closed** Oct to Easter

---

Converted abbey, Tonnerre

# L'Abbaye Saint-Michel

Not everyone likes the way this ancient benedictine abbey has been modernized, using plate glass or stainless steel as readily as stone and wood. The 'Mont-Saint-Michel' room retains 13thC frescos, one dining-room is a stone vault and the other gives views of the park and the vineyards of Epineuil. Heliport; tennis, mini-golf.

■ Montée de Saint-Michel, 89700 Tonnerre (Yonne) **Tel** 03.86.55.05.99 **Fax** 03.86.55.00.10 **E-mail** abbaye-st-michel@wanadoo.fr **Meals** breakfast, lunch, dinner **Prices** rooms F-FFF, suites FF-FFFF, continental breakfast F; menus FF-FFF **Rooms** 11, all with bath, phone, TV, minibar **Credit cards** AE, DC, MC, V **Closed** during winter

---

Ski resort hotel, Val-Thorens

# Fitz Roy

The ski resort of Val-Thorens is the highest Relais & Château in Europe. It is an exceptionally civilized and welcoming chalet-style hotel with light, pine-furnished bedrooms. Serious food – about the best in the resort. Swimming-pool, sauna and steam room.

■ 73440 Val-Thorens (Savoie) **Tel** 04.79.00.04.78 **Fax** 04.79.00.06.11 **Meals** breakfast, lunch, dinner **Prices** DB&B FF-FFFF **Rooms** 36, all with spa bath, central heating, phone, TV, radio, minibar, hairdrier **Credit cards** AE, DC, MC, V **Closed** early May to 2 Dec

---

Lakeside hotel, Veyrier-du-Lac

# La Demeure de Chavoire

A splendid combination of traditional elegance and modern comfort, set in a pretty garden on the shores of lovely lake Annecy. Every room has been thoughtfully and richly furnished; the bed-rooms are all individually decorated in romantic style, and named after local beauty spots and Annecy's famous writers.

■ Route d'Annecy-Chavoire, 74290 Veyrier-du-Lac (Haute-Savoie) **Tel** 04.50.60.04.38 **Fax** 04.50.60.05.36 **Meals** breakfast, snacks **Prices** rooms FF-FFF, suites FFF-FFFF; breakfast F **Rooms** 13, all with bath, central heating, phone, TV, radio, minibar, hairdrier **Credit cards** AE, DC, MC, V **Closed** never

# *The South-West*

## Area introduction

The Limousin hills represent the watershed between the basins of the Charente and the Loire, to the north, and that of the Garonne and its tributaries, to the south; and the start of our South-west region. For many British visitors, the valleys of the Dordogne and the Lot represent an ideal, not only of France but of life itself – life in a kind climate and a fertile landscape. And the concentration of our kind of hotel here is second only to that in Provence. To the west lie the peerless vineyards of Bordeaux, and the forests and limitless beaches of the Landes. To the south, Gascony and the Basque country of the Pyrenees.

**Contenders in the South-west**
**Barcus, Chez Chilo** 05.59.28.90.79 Idiosyncratic village hotel, smartly furnished; good food.
**Cadéac-les-Bains, Hostellerie du Val d'Aure** Tel 05.62.98. 60.63, fax 05.62.98.68.99. Secluded riverbank Logis in wooded grounds with pool and tennis, near the ski resort of St-Lary. Ideal for walkers in summer. Enthusiastically endorsed by several recent visitors; deserves a full entry.
**Les Courrières, Les Murailles** 05.53.05.58.09 English-run farmhouse B&B (option to dine with owners) tastefully restored; in large garden with pool.
**Gramat, Château de Roumegouse** 05.65.33.63.81 Prettily furnished mini-château surrounded by woods; pool.
**Grenade-sur-l'Adour, Pain Adour et Fantaisie** 05.58.45.18.80 Handsome riverside house with stylishly modern furnishings and knockout food – 2 stars, 4 *toques*.
**Lascabanes, La Petite Auberge** 05.65.31.82.51 A captivating group of stone farm buildings in a quiet country setting; charmingly simple stone-walled rooms.
**Loubressac, Château de Gamot** 05.65.38.58.50 Little 17thC château furnished in period, run as a B&B in summer by its Parisian owners; pool, but not available July and August.
**Mussidan, Le Bastit** 05.53.81.32.33 Carefully furnished country house in flowery garden (with pool) run by friendly Anglo-French couple.
**Paulhiac, L'Ormeraie** 05.53.36.45.96 Carefully converted farmhouse in lovely country setting, run in house-party style by retired publisher.
**Port-de-Lanne, La Vieille Auberge** 05.58.89.16.29 Warmly furnished village Logis with pleasant garden and pool.
**St-Jean-de-Luz, Parc Victoria** 05.59.26.78.78 Immaculate, elegantly furnished villa in leafy gardens with excellent pool.
**St-Pierre-de-Côle, Domaine de Doumarias** 05.53.62.34.37 Simply but tastefully furnished country B&B with pool in lush garden. **St-Robert, La Maison Anglaise** 05.55.25.19.58 Freshly decorated 19thC villa in peaceful setting with long views; carefully run by English proprietors.
**Segos, Domaine de Bassibé** 05.62.09.46.71 Small, intimate, comfortable hotel with lovely views and good chef.
**Toulouse, Hôtel des Beaux Arts** 05.61.23.40.50 Designer style in central Toulouse.
**Valence-sur-Baïse, La Ferme de Flaran** 05.62.28.58.22 Freshly decorated farmhouse with dining terrace and pleasant pool, in countryside; decent food.

# *The South-West*

# Hôtel Ohantzea ★

This is by some margin the cheapest of our main recommendations in the Pyrénées-Atlantiques, and accordingly simple – but no less charming for that.

The timbered and shuttered building is set on the road through the attractive mountain village of Cambo-les-Bains, which is renowned for its mild climate – Edmond Rostand, author of *Cyrano de Bergerac*, came her to take the spa waters and liked it so much that he built a house (Villa Arnaga) nearby.

The house, has been in the Ithurria family for no less than three centuries, and dates from the 17thC. It was originally a farm, but it is now very much a family home with old furniture dotted about: uneven wooden floors, beamed ceilings and an unmatchable patina of age on well looked-after family possessions. The bedrooms are notably spacious, some with balconies.

The menus offer fair value and the dining-room is pleasant enough. "This is not a modern house," says Mme Ithurria in a pleasantly self-effacing way – "and we have no 'formula' – except to provide the atmosphere of a family home and fair prices."

**Nearby** Villa Arnaga, on the D932 a short distance north of town; St-Pée-sur-Nivelle (10 km); Sare (10 km) – cog railway.k

Aïnhoa 64250 Cambo-les-Bains
**Tel** 05.59.29.90.50
**Location** in middle of village, 10 km SW of Cambo-les-Bains; with garden and car parking behind
**Meals** breakfast, lunch, dinner
**Prices** rooms F; menus FF
**Rooms** 10 double, 9 with bath and shower (3 twin); all rooms have central heating, phone
**Facilities** sitting-room, dining-room
**Credit cards** AE, DC, MC, V
**Children** welcome
**Disabled** no special facilities
**Pets** accepted
**Closed** Dec and Jan
**Proprietor** M. Ithurria

# The South-West

**Manor house hotel, Brantôme**

# Le Chatenet

This lovely 17thC manor house has prompted a steady flow of approving reports from readers over the years of its inclusion in the guide, and the latest gives the clearest possible view: 'We left wanting to stay longer, and we will certainly go back.'

The appeal of the place stems not only from its rural surroundings – down a country track off the busy riverside road, blissfully far removed from the tourist bustle of Brantôme – but also from its informal atmosphere: despite evidently heavy investment in rich furnishings, the Laxtons attach importance to maintaining the family-home feel, and it shows. There are vases of fresh flowers on low tables, deep armchairs, and country antiques in both the sitting-room and breakfast room, which form part of the Laxtons' home. Bedrooms are spacious, with elegant decoration. In the cosy clubhouse there's an 'honesty' bar and room for wet-weather activities. Outside, deckchairs are scattered invitingly around the garden beneath shady trees, and there is plenty of space for children.

Breakfasts (Magdeleine has a repertoire of 10 sorts of home-made *confiture*) are served on a covered terrace in fine weather, and guests may have the use of an outdoor barbecue. If do-it-yourself doesn't appeal, there are several excellent restaurants nearby. The 'very cordial' welcome is 'enhanced by the dog'.

**Nearby** Brantôme – monks' garden, belfry, troglodyte caves; Bourdeilles (10 km) – château; Chancelade (30 km) – abbey.

24310 Brantôme
**Tel** 05.53.05.81.08
**Fax** 05.53.05.85.52
**Location** 1.5 km SW of town, off D78; in large grounds with ample car parking
**Meals** breakfast
**Prices** rooms F-FF, suites FF
**Rooms** 8 double, all with bath (6 twin); 2 suites; one cottage with 2 double rooms; all rooms have central heating, phone; TV on request
**Facilities** sitting-room, breakfast room, clubhouse with billiards; heated swimming-pool, tennis
**Credit cards** MC, V
**Children** welcome if well behaved
**Disabled** access easy; 2 ground-floor bedrooms, one specially equipped
**Pets** welcome if well behaved
**Closed** at times Nov to Apr – phone to check
**Proprietors** Philippe and Magdeleine Laxton

# The South-West

## Moulin de l'Abbaye ★

Our visits to this exquisite little mill have always left us wishing to stay longer; a recent report praises the welcome, the comfort and the views.

The setting is the thing. The shady riverside terrace, illuminated in the evening, is an idyllic place for a drink or a meal while admiring Brantôme's unusual angled bridge, the tower of the abbey or the swans gliding by. Wonderful views over the river and the old houses of one of the prettiest villages in France are also to be had from many of the bedrooms – all beautifully decorated and comfortably furnished (some have four-poster beds and antiques, others are more modern).

Traditional Périgord dishes with a *nouvelle* touch earn the restaurant 3 *toques* from Gault-Millau and a star from Michelin. The dining-room is as pleasant a place to enjoy this excellent cuisine as the terrace it leads to, though we can raise no enthusiasm for the 'Monet-style' colour scheme. There are fresh flowers, sparkling glass and silverware, and soft lighting in the evening. Staff are correct and courteous; service is efficient.

**Nearby** Monk's garden, belfry; Antonne-et-Trigonant (3 km) – 15thC Périgord manor; Bourdeilles (10 km) – château.

1 Rte de Bourdeilles 24310 Brantôme
**Tel** 05.53.05.80.22
**Fax** 05.53.05.75.27
**E-mail** moulin@relaischateaux.fr
**Location** on edge of town, 20 km N of Périgueux; with garden, and ample car parking across road
**Meals** breakfast, lunch, dinner
**Prices** rooms FF, apartments FFF; breakfast F, menus FF-FFF

**Rooms** 16 double, 3 apartments, all with bath; all rooms have central heating, TV, minibar
**Facilities** dining-room, sitting-room
**Credit cards** AE, DC, MC, V
**Children** welcome
**Disabled** no special facilities
**Pets** dogs accepted
**Closed** Nov to May; restaurant only, Mon and Fri lunch
**Manager** M. Dessum

# *The South-West*

Manor house hotel, Le Buisson-de-Cadouin

## Manoir de Bellerive

There is a new owner at this fine Napoléon III manor house, but a recent report suggests that everything continues well here: 'Everything a fine hotel should be. Delightful friendly staff. Really good food – beautifully served. Good value.'

The Manoir is set in ten acres of lovely peaceful parkland which stretches down to the banks of the Dordogne. Sun beds and tables are liberally scattered over the lawns, and there is a swimming-pool and tennis court tucked away between the pine trees and flower borders. If you prefer to watch the world go by from a more elevated position, you can sit out on the balustraded first-floor terrace overlooking the slow-moving Dordogne river, and valley. Once you step inside the lofty entrance hall, you are transported back in time. The elegant stone staircase sweeps up to spacious and very comfortable designer-decorated bedrooms. Eight more have been created in the Orangerie. Breakfast can be taken on the terrace or in a room with murals on the pale walls.

For six months of the year (mid-March to mid-June and mid-September to mid-November), the hotel is also used as a conference centre. At other times, peace reigns.

**Nearby** walking, golf; Lascaux – caves; Les Eyzies; Sarlat (35 km).

Route de Siorac 24480 Le Buisson-de-Cadouin
**Tel** 05.53.22.16.16
**Fax** 05.53.22.09.05
**Location** in countryside, 800 m SE of Le Buisson-de-Cadouin on D25; grounds and ample car parking
**Meals** breakfast, lunch, dinner
**Prices** rooms F-FFF; suites FF-FFF-FFFF; breakfast F; menu FF
**Rooms** 25 double, all with bath or shower; all rooms have central heating, phone, satellite TV, minibar; some with air-conditioning
**Facilities** sitting-room, breakfast room; restaurant; sauna, jacuzzi, conference facilities; swimming-pool, tennis court
**Credit cards** MC, V
**Children** accepted
**Disabled** one room
**Pets** accepted
**Closed** Nov to mid-Apr
**Proprietor** M. Clevenot

# The South-West

## Le Moulin du Roc

A steady flow of approving reports from readers confirm the attractions of this delectable old walnut-oil mill, one of that rare breed of hotels that give you the sensation of pampering without charging £100 a night for a room. 'Absolutely stellar,' says the most recent – although the Moulin is less stellar than it used to be (these days it rates 'only' one Michelin star).

The setting on the banks of the Dronne is wonderfully romantic; the waterside gardens are lush, secluded, shady and bursting with colour. Inside the rough-stone 17thC building, old beams, fireplaces, mill machinery, fine old carved furniture, rich fabrics and massive oil paintings – together with plenty of ornaments and flower arrangements – create a style that is highly individual, or even eccentric. Some may find it rather heavy. The same cannot be said of the food: in the land of *foie gras*, Alain Gardillou, who has taken over from his mother, manages to build on culinary traditions to produce remarkably light and inventive dishes. Breakfasts are a treat, with home-made rolls and jams, beautifully served. Bedrooms vary in size, but do not disappoint – pretty, cosy, with their full share of antiques.

**Nearby** Brantôme; Bourdeilles (15 km) – château; golf; riding.

24530 Champagnac-de-Belair
**Tel** 05.53.02.86.00
**Fax** 05.53.54.21.31
**E-mail** moulinroc@aol.com
**Location** in hamlet, on D82 and D83, 6 km NE of Brantôme; with large garden and ample car parking
**Meals** breakfast, lunch, dinner
**Prices** rooms F-FF; breakfast F, DB&B F-FF; menus FF-FFF, children's FF
**Rooms** 10 double (2 twin), 4 suites; all with bath; all rooms have central heating, air-conditioning (8 rooms), phone, TV, minibar
**Facilities** sitting-room, dining-room; heated swimming-pool, tennis court, fishing, terrace
**Credit cards** AE, DC, MC, V
**Children** welcome
**Disabled** two ground-floor rooms **Pets** accepted
**Closed** 2 Jan to 8 Mar; restaurant only, Tue, Wed lunch **Proprietors** M. and Mme Gardillou

# The South-West

## Manoir d'Hautegente

A reader describes this creeper-clad manor house as 'so good that I wouldn't tell you about it if it were not already in the guide'. We'll just have to hope that he doesn't mind our promotion of the Manoir – new to the guide a few years ago – to a full entry.

The house, set in beautiful wooded grounds, has been in the Hamelin family for about 300 years, and is now run by Edith Hamelin and her son Patrick. It was built as a forge in the 13th century, later became a mill (using the stream that runs beside it), was then embellished and turned into a family residence and was finally converted into a hotel – but with the private-home feel entirely intact. Public rooms and the spacious, comfortable bedrooms are imaginatively decorated with family antiques and paintings. Dinner in the pretty vaulted dining-room is a five-course affair – 'first-class cuisine' which inevitably includes home-produced *foie gras*, another of the Hamelins' commercial successes. Wines are reasonably priced.

In the pleasant grassy grounds there is a smart pool that gets plenty of sun. A warm welcome from the family awaits.

**Nearby** châteaux; Lascaux (15 km); Sarlat (25 km).

Coly 24120 Terrasson
**Tel** 05.53.51.68.03
**Fax** 05.53.50.38.52
**Location** in countryside, 6 km SE of Le Lardin on the D62; with grounds and car parking
**Meals** breakfast, dinner
**Prices** rooms F-FFF; breakfast F, menus FF-FFF
**Rooms** 15 double, all with bath (2 twin); all rooms have central heating, phone; hairdrier, TV
**Facilities** dining-room, sitting-room; heated swimming-pool
**Credit cards** AE, MC, V
**Children** welcome
**Disabled** two ground-floor room
**Pets** accepted if well behaved
**Closed** Nov to Easter
**Proprietors** Edith Hamelin and Patrick Hamelin

# The South-West

**Village hotel, Les Eyzies-de-Tayac**

# Les Glycines

When Chef, Pascal Lombard and his wife, Maud, became the new owners of Les Glycines in April 1999, we were pleased to hear that they had quickly made a start on upgrading some of the bedrooms, which were beginning to.look shabby and dated. The house stands close to the station on the edge of Les Eyzies, and is set in lush and beautiful gardens that are one of the hotel's chief attractions; the name means wisteria, and that lovely flower is to be found here in abundance. There is also a swimming-pool and a terrace for drinks, so it's an excellent place in good weather.

Indoors there are also plenty of sitting-areas, well supplied with reading material, meaning this is also an hotel where it's not unpleasant to while away time in poor weather. The dining-room and covered terrace, where you can enjoy Pascal's Périgord dishes, are very attractive too. There are more rooms than we generally allow in a country hotel, but the hotel does not feel large, partly because some of the rooms are in a connected annexe. Reports on the improvements would be especially welcome.

**Nearby** Château de Fages (15 km); Sarlat (21 km); Lascaux caves (25 km); Beynac (30 km) – village and castle.

24620 Les Eyzies-de-Tayac
**Tel** 05.53.06.97.07
**Fax** 05.53.06.92.19
**Location** on edge of town, on main road; with large gardens and ample car parking
**Meals** breakfast, lunch, dinner
**Prices** rooms F; breakfast F; DB&B F; menus FF
**Rooms** 25 double, all with bath or shower (12 twin); all rooms have central heating, phone

**Facilities** 2 sitting-rooms, dining-room, bar; swimming-pool
**Credit cards** AE, MC, V
**Children** accepted
**Disabled** access possible
**Pets** accepted
**Closed** mid Oct to mid Apr; restaurant Sat lunch out of season
**Proprietors** Maud and Pascal Lombard

# *The South-West*

## La Daille

Another Dordogne establishment that combines the best of France and Britain. The mellow stone, red-roofed buildings are surrounded by gardens with glorious herbaceous borders that could only be the work of British green fingers.

*Emigrés* from Britain, Barbara and Derek Brown, have been running this unusual place in wonderful unspoilt and hilly countryside just south of the Dordogne, for over 24 years now. They have recently decided to give up their restaurant, and no longer serve evening meals; but they are continuing with their famous afternoon set teas (served on the terrace between 4.00 p.m. and 6.30 p.m., Friday to Monday and on Fête Days), for which they have built up a regular local clientele. If shelter is necessary, the Old Bake House, facing the farmhouse across the terrace, provides a pleasant alternative.

La Daille is a small-scale establishment, catering for no more than 6 residents. The double bedrooms are in a modern single-storey building – all thoroughly comfortable, with big bath-rooms and terraces – across the garden from the original farm-house. Lovely woodland walks in the surrounding countryside.

**Nearby** golf, canoeing; Domme (15 km) – *bastide*; Sarlat (25 km)

Florimont-Gaumiers 24250
**Tel** 05.53.28.40.71
**Location** in countryside, 2 km S of Gaumiers (signposted from village); in large grounds with ample car parking
**Meals** breakfast; afternoon tea
**Prices** FF (for two – min three-night stay; FFFF per week (two people sharing)
**Rooms** 3 double; all with bath and shower; all rooms have

central heating, terrace
**Facilities** breakfast-room, *Salon de Thé*; terrace
**Credit cards** not accepted
**Children** accepted over 7
**Disabled** access difficult
**Pets** not accepted
**Closed** Oct to 1 May
**Proprietors** Mr and Mrs Derek Vaughan Brown

# *The South-West*

**Château hotel, Lacave**

# Château de la Treyne

We've had our eye on this little château beside the Dordogne since an inspector came back a few years ago with a report littered with emphatically underscored adjectives – 'gorgeous ... impeccable ... exceptionally comfortable'. Of course, it is not cheap; perhaps we should be grateful that elevation to Relais & Châteaux status has not pushed prices up further.

Michèle Gombert-Devals' house has made a splendid small hotel. It starts with the advantage of a beautiful position, in woods on a low cliff cut by the meandering river Dordogne. But the compelling attraction of the château is the near-ideal balance struck between the impressiveness of a fortified manor-house and the intimacy of a genuine home. The building dates from the early 14th century, but was substantially rebuilt in the 1600s; it is now tastefully equipped with a happy mix of furnishings – comfy sofas in front of an open fire, as well as grand antiques.

There are long walks to enjoy in the grounds, and a very beautiful formal garden before which you can take breakfast. Excellent regional food is served – on the delightful terrace perched above the river – in good weather.

**Nearby** Souillac – abbey church; Rocamadour, Sarlat.

Lacave 46200 Souillac
**Tel** 05.65.27.60.60
**Fax** 05.65.27.60.70
**Location** 3 km W of village on D43, 6 km SE of Souillac; in large grounds beside river, with ample private parking
**Meals** breakfast, lunch, dinner
**Prices** rooms FF-FFFF; apartments FFFF DB&B F; breakfast F, menus FF
**Rooms** 16 double, all with bath; all rooms have central heating, air conditioning, phone, TV
**Facilities** 3 sitting-rooms, dining-room, bar, billiard room, meeting-room; swimming-pool, tennis
**Credit cards** AE, DC, MC, V
**Children** welcome
**Disabled** access difficult
**Pets** accepted if well behaved
**Closed** 15 Nov to Easter
**Proprietor** Mme Michèle Gombert-Devals

# *The South-West*

## Hostellerie Le Vert

Le Vert goes from strength to strength. The attractions of this secluded 17th-century farmhouse have been greatly increased by the construction of a swimming-pool. It will doubtless remain the kind of hotel you look forward to returning to at the end of the day; it also looks set to become the kind you're disinclined to leave at all. Recent visitors were ecstatic with praise.

There is just a small side door to lead you inside. Within, all is original stone walls and beams. The dining-room opens out on to a terrace with wide views; through an arch at one end is a small sitting-room – ideal for an aperitif. The bedrooms are all comfortably and tastefully modernized, and have lovely views. The largest are quite grand and furnished with antiques. But the most attractive are in the little annexe a couple of yards from the entrance – the lower one stone-vaulted, the upper one beamed, with a marble floor. The garden has chairs and tables, and is improving in colour despite dry summers. The Philippes are a friendly and hard-working couple  – he cooks (interestingly and competently), she serves (and speaks excellent English).

**Nearby** Bonaguil (15 km)  –  château; Biron castle (35 km); Monpazier (50 km)  –  *bastide*; Cahors (50 km)  –  medieval bridge.

Mauroux 46700 Puy-l'Evêque
**Tel** 05.65.36.51.36
**Location** in countryside, off D5 10 km SW of Puy-l'Evêque; 10 km SE of Fumel; in garden, with ample private car parking
**Meals** breakfast, lunch, dinner
**Prices** rooms F; breakfast F, menus FF
**Rooms** 7 double, all with bath or shower; all have central heating, phone, TV
**Facilities** dining-room, sitting-room, terrace, swimming-pool
**Credit cards** AE, MC, V
**Children** welcom; children's menu 50F
**Disabled** no special facilities
**Pets** welcome at extra charge
**Closed** mid Nov to mid Feb
**Proprietors** Eva and Bernard Philippe

# The South-West

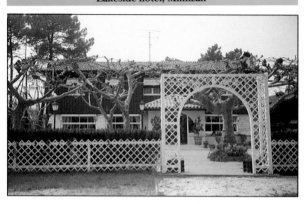

## Au Bon Coin du Lac

We see no sign of slippage in the high standards of Jean-Pierre Caule, the third generation of his family to run Au Bon Coin, or indeed the exacting standards of Mme Caule, who oversees things front of house.

The two-storey, stone and painted-wood house has a superb lakeside setting, with neat little footpaths inviting you to walk around the grounds. But the hotel's *raison d'être* is its Michelin-starred restaurant, and M. Caule's culinary skill as head chef (seafood is his speciality). The generally expensive feel of the place is reflected in the menu – and the prices. The dining-room has an uncluttered view of the lake and is charmingly furnished: round tables, white table-cloths, floral china and floral-covered chairs. The service is formal, as you would expect in a restaurant in this price range, but nevertheless friendly.

The bedrooms are large and luxurious; not impersonal, but rather uniform. Despite the many activities on the lake – sailing, fishing – the swings nearby and the special children's menu, this is not really a place for a family holiday. But it is ideal for those who want four-star treatment, a relaxed and friendly atmosphere and excellent food.

**Nearby** Lakes; beaches (5 km); Landes forest (30 km); Sabres (40 km) – railway to Marquèze Ecomuseum.

34 Ave du Lac, Mimizan
40200 Landes
**Tel** 05.58.09.01.55
**Fax** 05.58.09.40.84
**Location** amid forests, 2 km N of Mimizan; on edge of lake, with garden and car parking
**Meals** breakfast, lunch, dinner
**Prices** rooms F-FF; menus FF; reduced rates for children
**Rooms** 5 double, all with bath and shower; 4 suites, all with bath and shower; all rooms have central heating, phone,

TV, radio, minibar
**Facilities** sitting-room, dining-room
**Credit cards** AE, V
**Children** welcome; special meals, baby-listening available
**Disabled** ground-floor bedrooms
**Pets** not accepted
**Closed** Feb; restaurant only, Sun dinner, and Mon out of season
**Proprietor** Jean-Pierre Caule

# The South-West

**Château hotel, Pauillac**

## Château Cordeillan-Bages

This is a château in the Bordeaux manner – not a Loire-style extravagance, but a harmoniously proportioned, single-storey stone mansion dating from the 17th century, with an associated five-acre expanse of vineyard (formerly an important one, and now gradually gaining in stature again). The house was completely restored in 1989 and the decoration is stylish and restful. There is something of the feel of an English country house about the intimate sitting-rooms and elegant dining-room – until you walk out on to the terrace to be confronted by vines. The bedrooms are very comfortable, with the sure hand of the interior designer given full rein.

Chef Thierry Marx, who has taken over the kitchen at Château Cordeillan-Bages, uses his skills to create new dishes based on seasonal produce, as well as traditional regional food, and of course, the wine-list is long. Breakfasts, too, are 'delicious'.

The *Ecole du Bordeaux*, based within Château Cordeillan-Bages, organizes a wide choice of courses for both professional and amateur wine lovers, with visits to other châteaux in this famous wine-growing region.

**Nearby** Château Mouton-Rothschild (museum) (5 km).

Route des Châteaux, 33250 Pauillac
**Tel** 05.56.59.24.24
**Fax** 05.56.59.01.89
**E-mail** cordeillan@relaischateaux.fr
**Location** in wine village on D2, 40 km N of Bordeaux; in own grounds, with ample car parking
**Meals** breakfast, lunch, dinner
**Prices** rooms FF-FFF; junior suite FF-FFF; breakfast FF, menus FF-FFF
**Rooms** 25 double, all with bath; all rooms have central heating, phone, TV, radio, minibar, hairdrier, safe
**Facilities** sitting-rooms, bar, dining-room, breakfast room
**Credit cards** AE, DC, V
**Children** welcome; babysitting available **Disabled** lift/ elevator, access ramp, ground-floor rooms, toilets **Pets** small ones accepted **Closed** 15 Dec to end Jan; restaurant only, Mon and Sat lunch
**Manager** Thierry Marx

# *The South-West*

# Domaine de la Rhue ★

We always had great confidence in the charming young proprietors, Eric and Christine Jooris and reports confirm our faith in this lovely hotel, peacefully set amid rolling countryside out of sight of any other building, yet only a few kilometres away from much-visited Rocamadour. Our visitor describes it as 'magical'.

You might be somewhat disappointed to discover that the hotel does not occupy the magnificent family-owned château, but is set in the adjoining stable block. But your disappointment would be short-lived; this superb 19th-century stone building has been imaginatively converted into a dozen pretty, spacious bedrooms. Several are suitable for families – some with discreet kitchenettes, and their own garden entrance. Breakfast is served in a pleasant salon (stone-flagged, with an open fireplace), and the Joorises are happy to make snack lunches, which can be eaten beside the glorious swimming-pool in front of the hotel.

You might also want to take advantage of Eric's other passion; he is a qualified hot-air balloon pilot and offers his guests the chance to see Rocamadour from the air – 'an experience not to be missed'.

**Nearby** hot-air ballooning; walks; Rocamadour (7 km); Padirac (10 km), Loubressac (20 km); Carennac (20 km).

La Rhue 46500 Rocamadour
**Tel** 05.65.33.71.50
**Fax** 05.65.33.72.48
**E-mail** domainedelarhue@rocamadour.com
**Location** in countryside, 55 km S of Brive La Gaillarde on N20 towards Cressenssac, then N140. Turn right 1 km before crossing with D673 (Racamadour-Padirac); with grounds and ample car parking
**Meals** breakfast
**Prices** rooms F-FF; breakfast F

**Rooms** 13 double, one suite, several suitable for families, all with bath; all rooms have phone
**Facilities** sitting-room; swimming-pool
**Credit cards** MC, V
**Children** accepted
**Disabled** access easy
**Pets** accepted
**Closed** Nov to Easter
**Proprietors** Eric and Christine Jooris

# *The South-West*

**Village hotel, St-Cirq-Lapopie**

## La Pélissaria

Recent reports leave us in no doubt that the Matuchets' distinctive little hotel is as compelling as ever. And the chances of finding a room vacant have increased since they bought an old house next door to the main one, providing three additional large bedrooms (two double beds in each).

The 13th-century house clings to the steep hillside on the edge of the lovely medieval hilltop village of St-Cirq-Lapopie. It was lovingly restored by the Matuchets themselves, and its quirky character is such that you descend the stairs to the bedrooms, which look out on to the tiny garden and enjoy stunning views over the Lot valley. The bedrooms – two of them detached from the house, down the garden – are light, airy and comfortable, with close attention to detail in the furnishings.

Dinner, served in the elegant and intimate beamed dining-room (with roaring log fire on cold nights) is adventurous and delicious; Madame does all the cooking, so the choice of dishes is naturally limited. M. Matuchet is a musician, and tapes of his music provide a background to dinner. Breakfast is served *al fresco* or in your room if you prefer.

**Nearby** Pech-Merle caves and museum; Cahors (35 km).

St-Cirq-Lapopie 46330
Cabrerets
**Tel** 05.65.31.25.14
**Fax** 05.65.30.25.52
**Location** in village, 30 km E of Cahors; with garden; parking difficult
**Meals** breakfast, dinner
**Prices** rooms F-FF; suite FF; breakfast F, dinner from FF
**Rooms** 8 double, 6 with bath, 2 with shower (4 twin); 2 suites with bath; all rooms have phone, TV

**Facilities** dining-room, sitting-room; small swimming-pool
**Credit cards** MC, V
**Children** welcome
**Disabled** one adapted bedroom
**Pets** accepted
**Closed** mid-Nov to Apr; restaurant only, Thu and Fri
**Proprietor** Marie-Françoise Matuchet

# The South-West

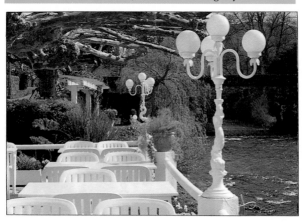

## Arcé ★

Oh dear. 'The car-park was full of GB plates,' commented one reporter, 'so we beat a hasty retreat.' Bad news for those who like to escape while on their travels, but not entirely surprising: we're not the only British guide to list this delightful hotel – now run by the fifth generation of the Arcé family – and it does not face a lot of competition, here in the Basque foothills of the Pyrenees.

The setting – by a river in a typical Basque village – is a magical one, best appreciated from the dining terrace, which juts out over the water and is sheltered by a canopy of chestnut trees. The food is almost as good as the view, featuring plenty of local specialities (game, fish) – though Michelin withdrew its star a few years ago. Inside the shuttered building are spacious public rooms – a beamed sitting-room with assorted furniture and a brick fireplace, a library with books in all languages, and a smart dining-room with picture windows. Some of the bedrooms are impressively large, with an apartment-sized sitting area; others open on to small terraces with mountain views. There is an attractive swimming-pool across the river.

**Nearby** walking, fishing, bicycling; Pyrenees; Spanish border; Atlantic coast – beaches.

64430 St-Etienne-de-Baïgorry
**Tel** 05.59.37.40.14
**Fax** 05.59.37.40.27
**Location** in village 10 km W of St-Jean Pied-de-Port; with garden and car parking
**Meals** breakfast, lunch, dinner, snacks
**Prices** rooms F-FF; suite FF-FFF; breakfast F, menus FF
**Rooms** 22 double, 1 single, 20 with bath, 3 with shower; 6 family rooms with bath; 1 suite; all rooms have central heating, phone, TV, hairdrier
**Facilities** dining-room, sitting-rooms, games room; terraces, swimming-pool, tennis court
**Credit cards** MC, V
**Children** welcome
**Disabled** no special facilities
**Pets** accepted
**Closed** mid-Nov to mid-Mar
**Proprietor** M. Arcé

# The South-West

## Hostellerie St-Jacques

The more we learn about the Babayous' enterprise, the more thoroughly impressed we are by their sure understanding of holiday-makers' needs and priorities.

The front of the creeper-clad 18thC building gives little clue to what lies within – or, more to the point, what lies behind: the Babayou's 'summer sitting-room', which consists of lovely sloping gardens, with masses of colourful flowers, a fair-sized pool, tennis court and plenty of shade and space for children. Inside there is an unusually large dining-room/bar decorated in fresh summery colours, with big windows which open on to the terrace above the garden. All the bedrooms are comfortable, spacious and attractively decorated; several can accommodate families.

The food is rich and varied; even the basic menu is probably enough to satisfy most appetites. A buffet breakfast/brunch is served in the garden or by the pool. Occasionally there are lively evenings with dancing and games, or communal dinners devoted to exploration of regional cuisine. Not your cup of tea? Just give it a try; you might be surprised.

**Nearby** Montbrun (15 km) – fortress; Brantôme (30 km) – monks' garden, château de Richemont; Rochechouart (45 km).

24470 Saint-Saud-Lacoussière
**Tel** 05.53.56.97.21
**Fax** 05.53.56.91.33
**Location** in quiet village, 30 km N of Brantôme; with garden and car parking
**Meals** breakfast/brunch, lunch, dinner
**Prices** rooms F, suites FF; DB&B F; breakfast F, menus F-FF
**Rooms** 22 double (7 twin), 2 suites, all with bath or shower; all rooms have central heating, air-conditioning, phone; 10 have TV and minibar
**Facilities** 2 dining-rooms, bar, TV room; swimming-pool, tennis **Credit cards** MC, V
**Children** very welcome
**Disabled** no special facilities
**Pets** accepted
**Closed** mid-Oct to Mar; restaurant closed to non-residents Sun dinner and Mon
**Proprietor** Babayou-Marcelly family

# The South-West

# Hôtel Arraya

We received several glowing reports on the Arraya, one from a well-travelled couple whose own château features in this guide. Praise indeed.

With its timbered, white-painted houses, Sare can claim to be the prettiest of all the extremely pretty Basque villages. In the heart of the village, this 16th century house was once a hostel for pilgrims on their way across the Pyrenees to Santiago.

Behind the slightly severe frontage on the busy main square lies a country-style hotel of great character, where much 'flair and talent' has gone into the decoration. The sitting-room, bar and dining-room – not to mention every nook and cranny on stairways (no lift) or landings – are filled with glorious old Basque furniture; sofas and chairs are comfortable and inviting, and flowers are everywhere. There are more antiques in the individually decorated bedrooms (not especially spacious, but bright and beautiful); some look out over the fine garden. As if all this is not enough, the cooking is good – 'refined and interesting' was one comment – and there is a particularly well-chosen wine list; and there is even a splendid Gâteau Basque.

**Nearby** Cog railway up La Rhune; Aïnhoa (10 km) – Basque village; Ascain (5 km) – Basque church; St-Jean-de-Luz (14 km).

64310 Sare
**Tel** 05.59.54.20.46
**Fax** 05.59.54.27.04
**E-mail** hotel@arraya.com
**Website** http://www.arraya.com
**Location** in middle of village, 14 km SE of St-Jean-de-Luz; with garden and public car parking (private parking nearby)
**Meals** breakfast, lunch, dinner
**Prices** rooms 395F-595F; breakfast 50F; menus 130F-

190F
**Rooms** 20 double, 17 with bath, 3 with shower (14 twin); one single with shower; all rooms have central heating, phone, TV **Facilities** sitting-room, bar, dining-room
**Credit cards** AE, MC, V
**Children** welcome; special menu available **Disabled** no special facilities **Pets** accepted in restaurant only
**Closed** mid-Nov to end Mar
**Proprietor** Fagoaga family

# *The South-West*

**Village hotel, Trémolat**

## Le Vieux Logis

We continue to list this glorious old hotel, for our money one of the most civilized in a region with many attractive hotels, despite the fact that (to judge by our postbag) precious few readers are inclined to pay its prices. One couple who did stay recently loved their time there so much they have vowed to return.

The Giraudel-Destords have lived in this complex of farm and village houses for nearly 400 years. The part which is now the dining-room once held pigs and wine barrels. Now, all has been designer-decorated to produce comfort of a high degree. The bedrooms are particularly delightful: individually furnished and very cosy in a sophisticated rustic style, with fine materials and furniture; some have four-poster beds. Public rooms are elegant and comfortable, and there are plenty of quiet nooks; the small salon has an open fire, and there are fine antiques throughout. The galleried dining-room is very attractive, and looks out on to the green and flowery garden, where you can have breakfast. The classic and modern cooking of Pierre-Jean Duribreux is excellent (two *toques* from Gault-Millau).

**Nearby** Les Eyzies-de-Tayac (25 km) – National Prehistoric Museum; Monpazier (30 km) *bastide*; Beynac (30 km).

24510 Trémolat
**Tel** 05.53.22.80.06
**Fax** 05.53.22.84.89
**Location** in village 15 km SW of Le Bugue; with garden and private car parking
**Meals** breakfast, lunch, dinner
**Prices** rooms FF-FFFF; breakfast FF, menus FF-FFF, children's F
**Rooms** 24 double (13 twin), all with bath; all rooms have central heating, phone, TV, minibar
**Facilities** 2 dining-rooms, 3 sitting-rooms, bar, conference room, swimming-pool
**Credit cards** AE, DC, MC, V
**Children** welcome
**Disabled** one adapted room; easy access to dining-room
**Pets** welcome
**Closed** never
**Proprietor** M. Bernard Giraudel

# The South-West

---

Village hotel, Carennac

## Hostellerie Fénelon

This jolly-looking Logis – all red roofs and window boxes – in a lovely old village comes strongly recommended for Mme Raynal's warm welcome, the friendly and unobtrusive service of her staff, the 'very good home-style' cooking and the excellent value for money. There is a small pool with tables around it, and another terrace for dining.

■ 46110 Carennac (Lot) **Tel** 05.65.10.96.46 **Fax** 05.65.10.94.86 **Meals** breakfa st, lunch, dinner **Prices** rooms F; breakfast F; DB&B FF; menus FF **Rooms** 16, all with bath or shower, central heating, phone, TV **Credit cards** MC, V **Closed** early Jan to mid-Mar

---

Town hotel, Condom

## Hôtel des Trois Lys

You will receive a warm welcome from Jeannette Manet, and the opening of 'le Dauphin' restaurant, has added to the delight of staying in this lovely 17th-century house, with its sandy stone walls and white shutters, and restrained elegant decoration within. The bedrooms are spacious and smart, with tasteful antique or reproduction furniture and fresh flowers. Swimming-pool.

■ 38 Rue Gambetta, 32100 Condom (Gers) **Tel** 05.62.28.33.33 **Fax** 05.62.28.41.85 **E-mail** hoteltroislys@minitel.net **Website** http://www.gascogne.com/Htroislys **Meals** breakfast **Prices** rooms F; breakfast F **Rooms** 10, all with bath or shower, central heating, phone, TV, hairdrier **Credit cards** AE, MC, V **Closed** Feb

---

Village inn, Dégagnac

## Auberge sans Frontière

The recent proprietors of this simple auberge offer a 'professional but sincere' welcome, says our latest reporter. It is an integral part of sleepy Dégagnac, and not at all touristy – the dining-rooms also serve as a bar and sitting-room. Bedrooms are small-ish but comfortable and inviting. The food offers 'superb' value.

■ Dégagnac, 46340 Salviac (Lot) **Tel** 05.65.41.52.88 **Meals** breakfast, lunch, dinner **Prices** DB&B F; menus F-FF **Rooms** 8, all with central heating **Credit cards** MC, V **Closed** never

---

Village hotel, Domme

## Hôtel de l'Esplanade

In a busy tourist village with splendid views over the Dordogne, this three-fireplace Logis is well furnished with taste and flair. Housekeeping is immaculate, service efficient – and particularly praised by a visitor who needed medical attention. Some bedrooms in annexes. Michelin-starred cuisine. Difficult car parking.

■ 24250 Domme (Dordogne) **Tel** 05.53.28.31.41 **Fax** 05.53.28.49.92 **Meals** breakfast, lunch, dinner **Prices** rooms F-FF; breakfast F, menus FF-FFF **Rooms** 25, all with bath or shower, central heating, phone, TV, hairdrier **Credit cards** AE, MC, V **Closed** Nov to mid-Feb; restaurant only, Mon and Sun dinner out of season

# The South-West

---

## Relais des Voyageurs

This former presbytery – its pretty flower-filled garden used to be the cemetery of the next-door church – has been sympathetically converted. Some of the bedrooms are cramped – but the best are spacious and the dining-room is light and warm. 'We liked the informal atmosphere,' enthuse recent visitors.

■ Place de l'Église, 64270 Escos (Pyrénées-Atlantiques) **Tel** 05.59. 38.42.39 **Meals** breakfast, lunch, dinner **Prices** rooms F; menus F-FF **Rooms** 8, all with bath or shower, central heating, phone **Credit cards** MC, V **Closed** never

---

## Moulin de la Beune

This little mill on the bank of the river Beune is a peaceful place to stay, despite the bustle of the town. Bedrooms are excellent, with bright colour schemes. There's a simple breakfast room and an inviting restaurant ('very good value') in another mill building in the garden.

■ 24620 Les Eyzies-de-Tayac (Dordogne) **Tel** 05.53.06.94.33 **Fax** 05.53.06.98.06 **Meals** breakfast, lunch, dinner **Prices** rooms F-FF, DB&B FF; breakfast 40F, menus 85F-315F **Rooms** 20, all with bath or shower, central heating, phone **Credit cards** AE, MC, V **Closed** Nov to Mar; Tue lunch

---

## Hôtel les Falaises

This good-value Logis enjoys an enviable position – huddled below a fine cliff, on the edge of a tiny medieval village beside the Dordogne – with a restful garden, and a swimmng-pool. Bedrooms are simple, light and well decorated. The hotel has changed hands recently, and the chef gives weekend cooking courses. Reports please.

■ Gluges, 46600 Martel (Lot) **Tel** 05.65.27.18.44 **Fax** 05.65.27.18.45 **Meals** breakfast, lunch, dinner **Prices** rooms F; breakfast F, menus FF **Rooms** 15, all with bath or shower, central heating, phone **Credit cards** AE, MC, V **Closed** Nov to Mar

---

## Les Huitrières du Lac

Primarily a restaurant, specializing (as you might expect) in fish and seafood – though there are alternatives. The large dining-room and the best bedrooms share a view over the adjacent lake. Bedrooms are plain but spacious; some have balconies. Pleasant setting, good value.

■ 1187 Ave du Touring Club, 40150 Hossegor (Landes) **Tel** 05.58. 43.51.48 **Fax** 05.58.41.73.11 **Meals** breakfast, lunch, dinner **Prices** rooms F, DB&B F; menus FF **Rooms** 9, all with bath, central heating, phone **Credit cards** AE, MC, V **Closed** Jan to early Feb

# The South-West

---

Riverside hotel, Lacave

## Hôtel du Pont de l'Ouysse

The *raison d'etre* of this peaceful, small auberge is its stunning dining terrace overlooking the river, shaded by trees . The cooking makes use of local produce, including eel from the Ouysse. Prettily decorated rooms, smart new swimming-pool.

■ Lacave, 46200 Souillac (Lot) **Tel** 05.65.37.87.04 **Fax** 05.65.32.77.41 **E-mail** pont.ouysse@wanadoo.fr **Meals** breakfast, lunch, dinner **Prices** rooms FF; breakfast F, menus from 160F **Rooms** 12, all with bath, phone, TV, air-conditioning **Credit cards** V **Closed** mid-Nov to end Feb

---

Riverside hotel, Lalinde

## Le Château ★

His reputation for cooking established, Guy Gensou has turned to the building – an extraordinary little turreted affair, perched above the Dordogne; bedrooms and bathrooms have been refurbished and a cosy new sitting area designed. 'Service personal, friendly and welcoming' enthused a visitor. Pool.

■ Rue de Verdun, 24150 Lalinde (Dordogne) **Tel** 05.53.61.01.82 **Fax** 05.53.24.74.60 **Meals** breakfast, lunch, dinner **Prices** rooms F-FF, demi-pension obligatory in high season F-FF; breakfast F, menus FF **Rooms** 7, all with bath or shower, phone, TV **Credit cards** AE, DC, MC, V **Closed** 3 weeks in Sep, 20 Dec to 15 Feb

---

Country inn, Lestelle-Bétharram

## Le Vieux Logis

Smart modern additions have taken this thriving hotel in the foothills of the Pyrenees out of our normal size range. But the garden and pool are still very attractive, the cooking is well above average and the rooms are a bargain, even if they do lack character. Accommodation is in the main hotel or in wooden chalets dotted about the garden.

■ Rte des Grottes, 64800 Lestelle-Bétharram (Pyrénées-Atlantiques) **Tel** 05.59.71.94.87 **Meals** breakfast, lunch, dinner **Prices** rooms F; menus FF **Rooms** 40, all with bath or shower, central heating, phone, TV **Credit cards** AE, MC, V **Closed** end Oct, Feb

---

Country hotel, Montfort-en-Chalosse

## Aux Tauzins ★

A reader's firm recommendation brings this three-fireplace Logis into the guide. With white walls, green shutters and low-pitched tiled roof, the building is typical of the area. The large dining-room has excellent country views, and many of the bedrooms have balconies. 'Friendly, efficient service, excellent food.' Pool and mini-golf.

■ 40380 Montfort-en-Chalosse (Landes) **Tel** 05.58.98.60.22 **Fax** 05.58.98.45.79 **Meals** breakfast, lunch, dinner **Prices** rooms F; breakfast F, menus FF **Rooms** 16, all with bath or shower, central heating, phone, TV **Credit cards** MC, V **Closed** first 2 weeks Oct, last 3 weeks Jan

# The South-West

---

Village hotel, Plaisance

## Le Ripa Alta

'Booked for one night, stayed for three,' says a report on this simple hotel. It revolves around the restaurant and the superb cooking of the 'hugely entertaining' Maurice Coscuella. Excellent breakfasts.

■ 3 Place de l'Eglise, 32160 Plaisance (Gers) **Tel** 05.62.69.30.43 **Fax** 05.62.69.36.99 **E-mail** ripaalta@aol.com **Meals** breakfast, lunch, dinner **Prices** rooms F; breakfast F, menus F-FF, children's F **Rooms** 13, all with bath or shower, central heating, phone; most have TV **Credit cards** AE, DC, MC, V **Closed** Nov

---

Converted mill, Poudenas

## Auberge à la Belle Gasconne

A detour to this pretty village to sample Marie-Claude Garcia's splendid cooking is highly recommended. The cosy bedrooms are in the lovingly converted 14th-century watermill next door to her miller's house, jutting out into the Gélise river and there is a romantic terrace and a large garden. Swimming-pool. It earns a rave report from a recent visitor, enthralled by the setting, the building, the rooms and the welcome.

■ 47170 Poudenas (Lot-et-Garonne) **Tel** 05.53.65.71.58 **Fax** 05.53. 65.87.39 **Meals** breakfast, lunch, dinner **Prices** rooms F-FF; breakfast F, menus FF **Rooms** 7, all with bath or shower, central heating, phone **Credit cards** AE, DC, MC, V **Closed** 7 Jan to 10 Feb; Sun evening and Mon except Jul to Aug

---

Village hotel, Puymirol

## Les Loges de l'Aubergade

The Agenais is not noted for its gastronomic highlights; but Michel Trama's cooking – and especially his patisserie – is among the best in France. The 10 spacious bedrooms are highly individual, in a restrained modern Italian style.

■ 52 Rue Royale, 47270 Puymirol (Lot-et-Garonne) **Tel** 05.53.95.31.46 **Fax** 05.53.95.33.80 **Meals** breakfast, lunch, dinner **Prices** rooms FF-FFF; menus from FF **Rooms** 10, all with bath or shower, central heating, air-conditioning, phone, TV **Credit cards** AE, DC, V **Closed** 2 weeks in Feb; restaurant only, Mon out of season.

---

Country hotel, Razac d'Eymet

## La Petite Auberge

Opened by its English owners in 1990, but run in a thoroughly French style, this converted farm – set in tranquil open countryside south of Bergerac – retains an informal 'family' atmosphere and is popular with foreign visitors and locals alike. Comfortable bedrooms. Swimming-pool.

■ 24500 Razac d'Eymet (Dordogne) **Tel** 05.53.24.69.27 **Fax** 05.53. 27.33.55 **E-mail** lparazmet@aol.com **Meals** breakfast, lunch, dinner **Prices** rooms F; breakfast F, menus F-FF **Rooms** 7, all with heating, phone; 2 two-bedroomed apartments **Credit cards** MC, V **Closed** restaurant only Sun and Mon

# The South-West

---

Town hotel, Ribérac

## Hôtel de France

A classic two-fireplace Logis de France – an old flower-decked inn at the heart of a bustling market town, with a pretty and warmly inviting restaurant and modest but spacious bedrooms which can accommodate families, offering excellent value.

■ 3 Rue Marc Dufraisse, 24600 Ribérac (Dordogne) **Tel** 05.53.90.00.61 **Fax** 05.53.91.06.05 **Meals** breakfast, lunch, dinner **Prices** rooms F; breakfast F, menus F-FF **Rooms** 16, all with bath or shower, TV, phone **Credit cards** MC, V **Closed** 15 Nov to 15 Dec

---

Country hotel, Rocamadour

## Les Vielles Tours

A beautifully restored stone building, dating from the 13th and 17th centuries, with its medieval atmosphere largely preserved. The cosy sitting-room occupies the first floor of an interesting circular turret-wing. Spacious, attractively furnished bedrooms. Proprietor Roger Zozzoli's paintings (for sale) are hung throughout the hotel. Madame cooks. Swimming-pool with valley views. A recent reader's report indicates, however, that food, and comfort could be improved. More reports please.

■ Lafage, 46500 Rocamadour (Lot) **Tel** 05.65.33.68.01 **Fax** 05.65. 33.68.59 **Meals** breakfast, lunch by arrangement, dinner **Prices** rooms F; HB F breakfast F, menus FF **Rooms** 18, all with bath or shower, phone, TV on request **Credit cards** MC, V **Closed** mid-Nov to Mar

---

Country hotel, Sabres

## Auberge des Pins

The combined efforts of the Lesclauze family provide an excellent example of unpretentious French hotelkeeping – a three-fireplace Logis in a chalet-style building offering rustic-style accommodation and fine food in well-cared-for surroundings at moderate prices. The rustic restaurant caters as much to locals as to travellers.

■ Route de la Piscine, 40630 Sabres (Landes) **Tel** 05.58.07.50.47 **Fax** 05.58.07.56.74 **Meals** breakfast, lunch, dinner **Prices** rooms F-FF; menus FF-FFF **Rooms** 25, all with bath or shower, central heating, phone, cable TV **Credit cards** AE, V **Closed** Jan

---

Village hotel, St-Cyprien

## L'Abbaye ★

There is a captivating atmosphere about this friendly, constantly improving hotel, situated in the heart of the Périgord region. The dining-room, bedrooms and bathrooms have all been spruced up reently, and there is a new swimming-pool too. In the rustic, stone-flagged sitting-room you can see the old pastry oven and potager, dated 1545.

■ 24220 St-Cyprien (Dordogne) **Tel** 05.53.29.20.48 **Fax** 05.53.29.15.85 **E-mail** hotel@abbaye-dordogne.com **Website** www.abbaye-dordogne.com **Meals** breakfast, dinner **Prices** rooms F-FF; menus F-FF **Rooms** 24, all with bath or shower, phone **Credit cards** AE, MC, V **Closed** mid-Oct to Apr

# The South-West

---

Town hotel, St-Émilion

## Hostellerie de Plaisance

'Delighted to confirm your recommendation,' says a reader of this converted monastery, superbly positioned in the middle of St-Émilion – on top of a small cliff with captivating views, not least from the plush dining-room. Bedrooms are smart and comfortable. Good food, with a 'particularly good-value' three-course menu.

■ Place du Clocher, 33330 St-Émilion (Gironde) **Tel** 05.57.55.07.55 **Fax** 05.57.74.41.11 **Meals** breakfast, lunch, dinner **Prices** rooms F-FF, suites FFFF; breakfast F, menus FF **Rooms** 12, 4 suites. all with bath, central heating, phone; most have air-conditioning **Credit cards** AE, DC, MC, V **Closed** Jan

---

Village inn, St-Félix-Lauragais

## Auberge du Poids Public

This thoroughly well run inn offers impressive views in all directions over the rolling uplands of the Lauragais. The dining-room is rustic and jolly; the bedrooms are rather grander in style. 'Food delicious, staff most helpful,' enthuses a visitor. Garage available.

■ 31540 St-Félix-Lauragais (Haute-Garonne) **Tel** 05.61.83.00.20 **Fax** 05.61.83.86.21 **Meals** breakfast, lunch, dinner **Prices** rooms F; menus FF-FFF **Rooms** 10, all with bath or shower, central heating, phone, TV, minibar **Credit cards** AE, V **Closed** Jan; Sun evening out of season

---

Seaside hotel, St-Jean-de-Luz

## La Fayette

This little family-run hotel occupies a prime spot in the pedestrianised heart of the animated port and resort of St-Jean. The building is in Dutch style, all arches and red brick, and it has a street terrace for outside meals. Small, simple but cheerful bedrooms.

■ 18-20 Rue de la République, 64500 St-Jean-de-Luz (Pyrénées-Atlantiques) **Tel** 05.59.26.17.74 **Fax** 05.59.51.11.78 **Meals** breakfast, lunch, dinner **Prices** rooms F; DB&B F **Rooms** 18, all with central heating, phone, TV **Credit cards** AE, DC, MC, V **Closed** never

---

Country hotel, Sarlat

## Hostellerie de Meysset

'Splendid room, very good food, pleasant owners, good views,' ran the reader's report that introduced this creeper-covered, typically Perigordian country house a couple of years ago. Its style is traditional and unpretentious, though without floral excesses. The 'good' food leans towards traditional regional elements, too.

■ Rte Argentouleau, 24200 Sarlat (Dordogne) **Tel** 05.53.59.08.29 **Fax** 05.53.28.47.61 **Meals** breakfast, lunch, dinner **Prices** rooms F; suites FF breakfast F, menus F-FF **Rooms** 26, all with bath or shower, phone **Credit cards** AE, DC, MC, V **Closed** Mon, Wed lunch

# The South-West

---

Country villa, Soustons

## La Bergerie

Mme Clavier has made her immaculate whitewashed house – built in southern single-storey style – a calm and civilized haven where the slow pace of life is infectious. The (obligatory) set dinner is based on whatever is fresh and good at the time. The bedrooms look on to the neat gardens.

■ Ave du Lac, 40140 Soustons (Landes) **Tel** 05.58.41.11.43 **Meals** breakfast, dinner **Prices** rooms F; DB&B F **Rooms** 12, all with bath, central heating, phone **Credit cards** DC, MC, V **Closed** Nov to Mar

---

Converted mill, Touzac

## La Source Bleue ★

An enthusiastic report praises the good value of this old paper-mill. There is now a fishing lake and a giant bamboo forest, though the beautiful and peaceful position beside the Lot remains a key attraction. The rustic dining-room and the best of the bedrooms are charming. Pool.

■ Moulin de Leygues, Touzac, 46700 Puy-l'Evêque (Lot) **Tel** 05.65.36.52.01 **Fax** 05.65.24.65 .69 **Meals** breakfast, lunch, dinner **Prices** rooms F; breakfast F, menus F-FF **Rooms** 16, all with bath, central heating, phone; some have TV **Credit cards** AE, MC, V **Closed** 15 Dec to 25 Mar; restaurant only, Wed lunch

---

Medieval manor, Vézac

## Manoir de Rochecourbe

This rustic manor-house has been in the Roger family for generations. A round tower housing the staircase gives the house a touch of grandeur, and the great beams and massive fireplaces inside do not disappoint.

■ Vézac, 24220 St-Cyprien (Dordogne) **Tel** 05.53.31.09.84 **Fax** 05.53.28.59.07 **Meals** breakfast **Prices** rooms F; breakfast F **Rooms** 6, all with bath or shower, central heating, phone **Credit cards** AE, DC, MC, V **Closed** 11 Jan to 15 Apr

---

Château hotel, Vieux-Mareuil

## Château de Vieux Mareuil

Behind the thick, ivy-clad stone walls of this 15th-century fortified house lies a stylish little hotel, prettily decorated with plenty of attention to detail. Spacious bedrooms, home-like sitting-room, acres of parkland to explore. Well above-average food and outside dining. Pool. More reports would be welcome.

■ Route Angoulème-Périgueux, 24340 Vieux-Mareuil (Dordogne) **Tel** 05.53.60.77.15 **Fax** 05.53.56.49.33 **E-mail** vieuxmareuil@chateau-hotel-perigord.com **Meals** breakfast, lunch, dinner **Prices** rooms F-FF; breakfast F, menus FF **Rooms** 14, all with bath, central heating, phone, TV, hairdrier **Credit cards** AE, MC, V **Closed** end Oct to Apr; Mon, Sun dinner out of season

# *Massif Central*

For many British visitors, the Massif is 'unknown France' – the high, remote area between Périgord on the west and the Rhône valley on the east. For guidebook purposes, it is a rather problematic region, particularly if (like all our regions) it is defined in terms of *départements*. The points where you might consider the physical Massif to begin and end don't always coincide happily with governmental boundaries (the *département* of Ardèche, for example, falls in our South of France region, but includes territory that is physically very much part of the Massif).

There is also a good case for considering this as 'unspoilt France'. Of course, tourism has had an impact, but it is slight compared with the impact on the much better-known areas to the west, east, north and south. There are bargains to be found as a result.

**Boisset, Auberge de Concasty** 04.71.62.21.16 Jolly little converted farmhouse with pool in grassy garden; country cooking.
**Champagnac, Château de Lavendès** 04.71.69.62.79 Simple but satisfactory Logis in countryside; basic pool.
**Conques, Hostellerie de l'Abbaye** 04.65.72.80.30 Comfortably furnished ancient house with beautiful country views.
**Meyrueis, Château d'Ayres** 04.66.45.60.10 Shuttered medieval house in leafy grounds with pool.

**Reporting to the guide**
We're very keen to hear from readers about their hotel-going experiences. We can't visit every hotel in the guide every year; even if we could, we wouldn't be staying in them all. And it's only when you stay in a place that you find out how the plumbing deals with the demand for hot water, what that much-vaunted 70F breakfast is really like, and what happens when you request something extraordinary like an extra pillow. So please do let us know how you get on next time you're travelling in France.

In particular, please do write when you like a small hotel, whether or not you've chosen it with our help. People are pretty good at letting us know when we've got a place wrong (usually, we hope, because the place has gone downhill). Places that come up to expectations don't always trigger a reaction.

It doesn't have to be a detailed, feature by feature description of the hotel (though highly detailed reports are always very welcome). The key thing is to let us know what you felt about the place, as a customer. We've suggested a structure for readers' reports on page 11, but you certainly don't have to stick to that; if you'd find it easier to dash off a few lines in whatever order they come to mind, please do just that.

# *Massif Central*

**Manor house hotel, Castelpers**

# Château de Castelpers

If our calculations are correct, Yolande Tapié de Celeyran has now been at the helm (and the stove) of this family-home-turned-hotel for more than 30 years – and she shows no sign of weakening. Her house makes a relaxing retreat – a recent visitor longed to spend more time there. It dates from the 17th century and ranges from the purely rustic to the Gothic in style, with a tower, arched windows and rooms of character furnished comfortably with antiques. But it is not a château hotel in the grand manner; families can feel at ease, with swings and spacious lawns (dotted with ancient trees) for children to play on and trout streams to explore, and prices that reflect the modest size of some of the bedrooms. Good food, served in front of an open fire in winter.

**Nearby** Château du Bosc (10 km); Sauveterre-de-Rouergue (20 km).

Castelpers 12170 Requista
**Tel** 05.65.69.22.61
**Fax** 05.65.69.25.31
**Location** in countryside 9 km SE of RN88, 10 km S of Naucelle; in wooded park with private car parking
**Meals** breakfast, lunch, dinner
**Prices** rooms F; menu FF
**Rooms** 6 double (4 twin), 2 family rooms; 3 with bath, 5 with shower; all rooms have phone, 5 have TV

**Facilities** sitting-room, 2 dining-rooms; fishing
**Credit cards** AE, MC, V
**Children** welcome if well behaved
**Disabled** one specially equipped ground-floor bedroom **Pets** accepted, but not in dining-room
**Closed** Oct to Mar; restaurant occasional evening or days only
**Proprietor** Mme de Saint Palais

# *Massif Central*

**Village hotel, Conques**

## Grand-Hôtel Sainte-Foy

Promotion to a full entry was long overdue for this delectable hotel in a lovely old village; as it is, we are somewhat behind the French tourist authorities, who promoted the Sainte-Foy to four-star status in the 1990s – the first hotel in Aveyron to achieve the rating. Marie-France and Alain Garcenot, proprietors since they took over from an aunt in 1987, are justifiably proud of their achievement, but the facilities that are required for star-ratings are not the basis of the hotel's appeal.

Hôtel Sainte-Foy is a lovingly restored, partly timbered old house which takes its name from the great abbey church directly opposite. The house has been beautifully furnished with close attention to detail and to the character of the building. The warm glow of wood is everywhere. The large two-part sitting-room is particularly well furnished with antiques. Bedrooms are highly individual, tasteful and large, with views either over the church or the flowery courtyard garden. You can dine here or in the intimate but pleasantly spacious rooms inside. The increasingly inventive cooking (daily changing menus) gets good reviews.

**Nearby** Church of Ste-Foy (remarkable tympanum and treasury).

Conques 12320 Conques-en-Rouergue
**Tel** 05.65.69.84.03
**Fax** 05.65.72.81.04
**Location** in heart of village, 40 km N of Rodez; with private car parking
**Meals** breakfast, lunch, dinner
**Prices** rooms F-FFF, suites FFF; breakfast F; menus FF; lunch FF
**Rooms** 15 double, 2 suites, all with bath; all rooms have central heating, phone
**Facilities** 3 dining-rooms, sitting-room, bar, interior patio, conference room; 2 terraces
**Credit cards** AE, DC, MC, V
**Children** accepted
**Disabled** 1 special room
**Pets** accepted
**Closed** end Oct to Easter
**Proprietors** Marie-France and Alain Garcenot

# Massif Central

# Le Grand Écuyer

One reporter reckons that the cooking of Yves Thuriès, a pastry-cook, is less impressive than it was a few years ago. But he still gets a star from Michelin and two *toques* from Gault-Millau, and the other attractions of this ancient hunting lodge in the glorious medieval village of Cordes are undiminished.

Le Grand Écuyer is a classified historic monument, transformed into a comfortable, elegant and atmospheric hotel. The dining-room is medieval in style, with old stone walls and tiled floors, dark beamed ceiling, old prints and so on, blending well with the lacy white table-cloths, shining silver, painted plates and tapestry chairs. The sitting-room and 'rather gloomy' bar are more domestic, with deeply upholstered armchairs, low tables and potted plants. Bedrooms (varying in size) are inviting – beamed ceilings, monumental stone fireplaces, rugs on expanses of polished floor – and are beautifully furnished with antiques. Bathrooms are modern. M. Thuriès and his friendly staff ensure that a graciously informal atmosphere prevails.

**Nearby** Rue Droite (14thC houses); Fôret Grésigne (15 km) – marked trails; Albi – *la ville rouge*.

79 Grand Rue Raimond VII
81170 Cordes sur Ciel
**Tel** 05.63.53.79.50
**Fax** 05.63.53.79.51
**Location** in middle of village, 25 km NW of Albi; with public car parking nearby
**Meals** breakfast, lunch, dinner
**Prices** rooms F-FF, suite FFF; menus F-FFF
**Rooms** 10 double, 2 triple, one suite, all with bath; all rooms have central heating,

TV, phone, radio
**Facilities** 2 dining-rooms, breakfast room, sitting-room, bar
**Credit cards** MC, V
**Children** accepted
**Disabled** no special facilities
**Pets** accepted
**Closed** 11 Oct to 1 Apr
**Proprietor** Yves Thuriès

# Massif Central

**Country hotel, Coulandon**

# Le Chalet

We first visited Le Chalet on a summer evening when its secluded, wooded garden (park-like in style and set out some 100 years ago) seemed idyllic. It has a different proprietor now but little else seems to have changed. The big fish pond (where guests may fish) is still perfect for strolling around, drink in hand, before pausing a while on the little raised terrace and then proceeding in to dinner.

It's a modest, traditional place. Rooms (in the chalet-style building itself, and in converted outbuildings) vary in style and size; none is notably stylish, but the best are cheerfully comfortable (with exposed beams and bright wallpaper). Some interesting regional specialities are served in the traditional-style dining-room, and the service is amiable. Saint-Pourçain and Sancerre are special features of the wine list. In fine weather, meals are served outside on the terrace, which has views of the Bourbonnais countryside.

**Nearby** Moulins – timbered houses, cathedral; Souvigny's abbey, Balaine Arboretum; the oak forest of Tronçais; Romanesque churches.

03000 Coulandon
**Tel** 04.70.44.50.08
**Fax** 04.70.44.07.09
**Location** in countryside 6 km W of Moulins, off D945; with large grounds and ample car parking
**Meals** breakfast, lunch, dinner
**Prices** rooms F; breakfast F, menus FF
**Rooms** 15 double, 4 with bath, 11 with shower, 5 twin, 2 with bath, 3 with shower; 7 family rooms, 4 with bath, 3 with shower, 1 triple; all rooms have central heating, phone, TV
**Facilities** dining-room, sitting-room; fishing, swimming-pool
**Credit cards** AE, DC, MC, V
**Children** accepted
**Disabled** 9 ground-floor bedrooms
**Pets** accepted
**Closed** mid-Dec to end Jan
**Proprietor** Heinz Schweizer

# *Massif Central*

**Country hotel, Lacabarede**

# Demeure de Flore

A new shop, *L'Insolite*, selling antiques, has been added to this exceptionally charming hotel, in the foothills of the mountains of Haut-Languedoc. It was opened by Monike and Jean-Marie Tronc in 1992, and they have created something close to our ideal hotel. Their 19th-century *maison de maitre* may be an undistinguished building, but it sits prettily in a mature, wooded *jardin anglais*, far enough from the passing RN112 to feel quite secluded. And within, there is a delightful ambience. None of your traditional French clashes of patterns here: stylish floral prints are set against warm, plain backgrounds. The house has lots of floor-to-ceiling windows, and the general effect is light and fresh. Carefully chosen antiques and ornaments give the feel of a lived-in but cared-for family home. The eleven bedrooms are individually furnished in the same careful way.

In good weather meals, prepared by Jean-Marie using fresh, local ingredients, are served out on the terrace, and 'a bite of lunch' can be had by the smart little pool.

**Nearby** Castres (35 km), Albi (60 km), Toulouse (100 km); Mediterranean beaches within reach.

106 Route Nationale, 81240
Lacabarede
**Tel** 05.63.98.32.32
**Fax** 05.63.98.47.56
**Location** opposite service station on outskirts of village on RN 112 between St-Pons and Mazamet; in gardens with ample car parking
**Meals** breakfast, lunch, dinner
**Prices** rooms F; breakfast F, menus FF
**Rooms** 10 double, one suite, all with bath; all rooms have central heating, phone, TV, hairdrier
**Facilities** sitting-room, dining-room; swimming-pool
**Credit cards** MC, V
**Children** accepted
**Disabled** one adapted room
**Pets** not accepted except by special arrangement
**Closed** Feb
**Proprietor** Monike Flore Tronc

# *Massif Central*

**Farmhouse hotel, Moudeyres**

## Le Pré Bossu

This remote little place prompts a great many reports from readers – and they tell different stories. 'Absolutely delightful', says one; 'over-rated', another. A common reservation is an occasional lack of warmth, physical and metaphorical. But the latest is wholehearted: 'Excellent; comfortable; food outstanding and beautifully served; worth every franc – we will go again.'

Moudeyres is a remote village high (1,200 metres) in the volcanic Mézenc massif, surrounded by fields of wild flowers (in the spring) and mushrooms (in the autumn). The village consists of thatched rough-stone houses, many beautifully restored. The Pré Bossu is no exception, although it was built as recently as 1969, with old materials. The Flemish owners have worked hard to create an attractive and comfortable house. Starting with beams, wood floors and ingle-nook fireplace, they have added fine antique dressers, lace curtains, wild flowers, plants and books. It is all fresh and well-kept. Bedrooms are rustic, too – clean and simple, with good shower rooms; tranquillity is assured. Food is ambitious and reliable (earning a Michelin star), with much emphasis on vegetables and herbs from the garden.

**Nearby** Restored 18thC farm; Le Puy – volcanic rock formations.

43150 Moudeyres
**Tel** 04.71.05.10.70
**Fax** 04.71.05.10.21
**Location** on edge of village, 25 km SE of Le Puy, beyond Laussonne; in garden, with ample car parking
**Meals** breakfast, lunch, dinner
**Prices** rooms F with continental breakfast; buffet breakfast F, menus FF-FFF
**Rooms** 10 double, 5 with bath, 5 with shower (4 twin); one family room; all rooms have central heating, phone
**Facilities** bar, TV room, dining-room (smoking not allowed)
**Credit cards** AE, MC, V
**Children** accepted
**Disabled** no special facilities
**Pets** accepted in bedrooms, but not in dining-room
**Closed** mid-Nov to Easter
**Proprietor** Carlos Grootaert

# *Massif Central*

# Longcol

This 'breath-taking' turreted medieval farmhouse is immersed in woods a few miles from Najac. 'Farming hamlet' might be a more accurate description, since the hotel consists of multiple stone buildings, mostly grouped around the central swimming-pool, with its optical illusion of a sheer drop at one end, and all equipped with distinctive bell-shaped slate roofs and neat small-paned windows.

The *long col* is a loop in the river Aveyron, which meanders through the gorges below. The Luyckx family bought the original farm in 1982, and spent six years restoring it. Since then they have gone from strength to strength, doubling the number of rooms without altering the atmosphere of a polished but welcoming home. They are keen antique collectors, and it shows; the low-beamed rooms are full of beautiful pieces of furniture, tapestries and Asian artefacts. Bedrooms are equally original and comfortable, but vary in size. Meals are served in the light, airy dining-room, or on the little walled terrace in summer – or by the pool, which shares the woody views. Food, under the direction of Francis Cardaillac, is taken seriously; excellent wine list.

**Nearby** Najac – medieval houses and castle.

La Fouillade 12270 Najac
**Tel** 05.65.29.63.36
**Fax** 05.65.29.64.28
**Location** in large wooded grounds NW of village, NE of Najac; with garden and car parking
**Meals** breakfast, lunch, dinner
**Prices** rooms FFF; suite FFF; breakfast F; meals FF
**Rooms** 17 double, 15 with bath, 2 with shower; all rooms have central heating, phone, TV, radio, minibar
**Facilities** dining-room, sitting-room, billiard room, terrace; swimming-pool, tennis court
**Credit cards** DC, MC, V
**Children** welcome; baby-sitting available
**Disabled** no special facilities
**Pets** welcome
**Closed** mid-Nov to Easter; restaurant only, Tue out of season
**Proprietors** Luyckx family

# *Massif Central*

**Riverside hotel, St-Jean-du-Bruel**

## Hôtel du Midi-Papillon

Every year we receive a long, hand-written bulletin conveying the undaunted enthusiasm Jean-Michel Papillon (the fourth generation of Papillons here) has for running this lovable old post inn. And practically every year we receive enthusiastic reports, underlining the fact that the essential appeal of the place is unchanged. Readers say 'wonderful' food, 'faultless' welcome, 'outstanding' value.

The Midi is the rural Logis at its best: a village inn amid grand countryside, offering welcoming rooms (of varying sizes) and excellent food at irresistible prices. It is very much a family-run place, with Mme overseeing the dining-room while Jean-Michel cooks. Vegetables come from the garden, poultry is home-raised, jams and croissants home-made.

The dining-room is divided into three sections, so that although the Papillon family try to accommodate their diners as fairly as possible, some will have the pleasure of dining on the terrace with a splendid river view, while others may find themselves in the intimate *salon* with leather furniture. Perhaps worth expressing a preference.

**Nearby** Gorges de la Dourbie (10 km); Montpellier-le-Vieux.

12230 St-Jean-du-Bruel
**Tel** 05.65.62.26.04
**Fax** 05.65.62.12.97
**Location** by river, in village on D991, 40 km SE of Millau; with garden and garages
**Meals** breakfast, lunch, dinner
**Prices** rooms F; suite F; breakfast F; menus F-FF
**Rooms** 13 double, 8 with bath (5 twin); 1 suite; 1 single; 4 family rooms, 13 with bath, 4 with shower; all rooms have central heating, phone
**Facilities** 3 dining-rooms, bar, sitting-room, TV room; swimming-pool, jacuzzi
**Credit cards** MC, V
**Children** welcome; special menus available
**Disabled** access to dining-room only
**Pets** accepted
**Closed** mid-Nov to Easter
**Proprietors** Papillon familly

# Massif Central

# Hostellerie de la Maronne

This 19th-century country house, set in a beautiful peaceful valley in the Auvergne, has had its critics in the past but these days earns nothing but praise from readers. Or nearly so: our latest reporter notes that the place has quite a formal air, but this is more to do with the elegant style of furnishing than the style of operation – she also commends the owners and staff as 'very welcoming and friendly.'

With its swimming-pool and tennis court surrounded by lovely gardens and sweeping countryside, the *hostellerie* makes a fine retreat whether you are in search of peace or of outdoor exercise. Much has changed during Alain de Cock's tenure: a smart dining-room has been built into the hillside; newly built bedrooms have replaced the least attractive of the old ones, the sitting-room, breakfast room and restaurant have recently received new lighting, carpets and seating.

Food is taken seriously, with 'excellent' results. There is now a range of menus (reaching up to *gastronomique* levels), each offering no choice, as well as a reasonable *carte*. The wine list is quite wide-ranging. Gault-Millau awards a *toque*.

**Nearby** Salers (6 km); Anjony (15 km) – château.

Le Theil 15140 St-Martin-Valmeroux
**Tel** 04.71.69.20.33
**Fax** 04.71.69.28.22
**E-mail** hotelmaronne@cfi15.fr
**Website** www.cfi15.fr/hotelmaronne
**Location** in countryside 3 km E of St-Martin, on D37; with gardens, ample car parking
**Meals** breakfast, lunch, dinner
**Prices** rooms F-FF; DB&B F; breakfast F; menu FF
**Rooms** 21 double, all with bath; all rooms have central heating, phone, satellite TV, minibar; 10 have balcony or terrace **Facilities** dining-room, sitting-room, breakfast room, seminar room; swimming-pool, tennis, *pétanque*, garden
**Credit cards** AE, DC, MC, V
**Children** welcome; baby-sitting by arrangement
**Disabled** lift/elevator
**Pets** accepted but not in dining-room
**Closed** Nov to Mar
**Proprietor** Alain de Cock

# *Massif Central*

### Château hotel, Target

## Château de Boussac

Increased public exposure – now in other British hotel guides as well as this one – has not affected the delicate balancing act conducted by the Marquis and Marquise de Longueil, who continue to welcome guests into their home with captivating charm.

The Château de Boussac lies between Vichy and Moulin, tucked away in the Bourbonnais – quite difficult to find. Solid, turreted and moated, the château could be a tourist sight in its own right; it is built around a courtyard, and the main reception rooms, furnished with Louis XV antiques and chandeliers, open on to a vast terrace with an ornamental lake and formal gardens. But the château is very much lived-in. By day the Marquis dons his overalls and works on the estate, but comes in to cook at least one course of the evening meal and chat to his guests. His wife looks after the rooms with care – there are fresh flowers everywhere, and the antiques are highly polished. Dinner *en famille* can be a rather formal affair, but the food is hard to fault and the Marquis, who speaks English, will make you feel at home. A recent visitor was enchanted and proclaimed it 'one of the highlights of our two-week trip.'

**Nearby** Souvigny (35 km) – Gothic/Romanesque church.

Target 03140 Chantelle
**Tel** 04.70.40.63.20
**Fax** 04.70.40.60.03
**Location** in countryside, off D42, 12 km NW of Chantelle, 50 km W of Vichy; in large park, with enclosed car parking
**Meals** breakfast, dinner
**Prices** rooms FF-FFF; breakfast F, menus FF with wine
**Rooms** 4 double (3 twin), one suite, all with bath; all rooms have central heating
**Facilities** dining-room, sitting-room
**Credit cards** AE, MC, V
**Children** accepted if well behaved
**Disabled** no special facilities
**Pets** accepted if well behaved
**Closed** Nov to Feb (except by reservation in advance)
**Proprietors** Marquis and Marquise de Longueil

# *Massif Central*

# Château de Trancis

We should welcome reports from readers who leave the beaten tourist track to find this impressive place – a classic little Loire-style château on the 500-metre-high fringes of the Auvergne regional park. This unlikely thing is more easily understood when you know that the Italianate architectural flourishes are of 20th-century origin. And its opening as an elegant hotel is due to the former British owners, .

They refurbished it to create the kind of harmonious and stylish ambience that is distinctly rare in and around the Massif Central. Bedrooms are well equipped and individually decorated, with antique furniture and rugs on polished floors. Public rooms embrace an ornate Louis XIV salon, a 'German' dining-room and an 'English' library. The view from the terrace across the smart little pool, where candlelit dinners are served in summer, is pleasant and soothing.

The house is now run by a Dutch couple, the Beymas, who speak English fluently. The house-party atmosphere still prevails, although the five-course dinners are also available to non-residents, so booking in advance is advisable.

**Nearby** Dordogne gorges, Parc Régional des Volcans d'Auvergne.

15210 Ydes
**Tel** 04.71.40.60.40
**Fax** 04.71.40.62.13
**Location** on D15, off D22, 2 km N of village of Saignes, 3 km E of Ydes; in country-side, with parking in grounds
**Meals** breakfast, dinner
**Prices** rooms FF, suite FFFF, including breakfast; DB&B F-F-FFF; menu FF
**Rooms** 6 double (two twin), 1 single, 3 suites, all with bath or shower; all rooms have

central heating, phone, TV, minibar, tea/coffee kit, hairdrier, electric fan
**Facilities** 3 sitting-rooms, 2 dining-rooms; 2 terraces, park, swimming-pool
**Credit cards** AE, MC, V
**Children** accepted
**Disabled** difficult access
**Pets** by arrangement
**Closed** never
**Proprietors** Pieter and Roberta van Beyma

# Massif Central

---

Medieval inn, Cordes

## Hostellerie du Vieux Cordes

A simpler base than the Grand Ecuyer, this stone-built 13thC building is set at the top of the old hill town giving long views, notably from the grassy terrace. Inside, furniture is generally simple and rustic, except in the plush little sitting-room. 'Friendly service, good value,' says a recent report. Mixed views on the food.

■ Rue St-Michel, 81170 Cordes (Tarn) **Tel** 05.63.53.79.20 **Fax** 05.63.56.02.47 **E-mail** www.thuries.fr **Meals** breakfast, lunch, dinner **Prices** rooms 280F-390F; breakfast 40F, menus F **Rooms** 21, all with bath or shower, central heating, phone, TV **Credit cards** AE, DC, MC, V **Closed** Jan to 15 Feb

---

Country hotel, Cuq-Toulza

## Cuq en Terrasses

This old presbytery is in new hands now, but run along the same lines as those of the previous British owners, but with extra emphasis on the dinner menu. It is beautifully and sympathetically done out, with lots of hand-made tiles and natural materials. Reports are positive. 'Beautiful terrace, with breathtaking views stretching as far as the Pyrénées'; 'wonderful dinner and extremely comfortable'; flowery garden, pool.

■ Cuq-le-Château, 81470 Cuq-Toulza (Tarn) **Tel** 05.63.82.54.00 **Fax** 05.63.82.54.11 **E-mail** Cuq-en-Terrasses@wanadoo.fr **Website** www.cuqenterrasses.com **Meals** breakfast, lunch, dinner **Prices** rooms F-FF; breakfast F, menus FF **Rooms** 5, 2 suites, 1 apartment, all with bath or shower; all with central heating, phone, TV; **Credit cards** AE, DC, MC, V **Closed** 3 Jan to 3 Apr

---

Manor house hotel, La Malène

## Manoir de Montesquiou

'Good-sized room, good food, very good views,' says a contented reader of this attractive castle-like 15th-century manor house. Your bedroom may be in one of the turrets; it may have a grand four-poster; it is sure to be comfortable and well looked after. Family run with care and good humour.

■ 48210 La Malène (Lozère) **Tel** 04.66.48.51.12 **Fax** 04.66.48.50.47 **Meals** breakfast, lunch, dinner **Prices** rooms F-FF; breakfast F, menus FF **Rooms** 12, all with bath or shower, central heating, air-conditioning, phone; some have TV **Credit cards** DC, MC, V **Closed** mid-Oct to early Apr

---

Village inn, Montsalvy

## Auberge Fleurie

The two attractive dining-rooms – polished wood dressers, gleaming copper, red-check tablecloths – are the focal point of this delightful creeper-covered auberge. The well-established new regime are continuing to make improvements.

■ Place du Barry, 15120 Montsalvy (Cantal) **Tel** 04.71.49.20.02 **Meals** breakfast, lunch, dinner **Prices** rooms 120F-160F; breakfast 25F, menus 50F-180F **Rooms** 13, all with central heating **Credit cards** AE, DC, MC, V **Closed** restaurant only, mid-Jan to mid-Feb

# *Massif Central*

---

Village hotel, Najac

## L'Oustal del Barry

This spick-and-span little Logis, in the same family for five generations, continues to offer the genuine welcome, excellent food and notably good value for which it is known. Rooms are spacious but simple, with beautiful views.

■ Place du Bourg, 12270 Najac (Aveyron) **Tel** 05.65.29.74.32
**Fax** 05.65.29.75.32 **E-mail** oustal@caramail.com **Meals** breakfast, lunch, dinner **Prices** rooms F with breakfast; menus FF **Rooms** 20, all with central heating, phone, TV, hairdrier; lift/elevator **Credit cards** AE, MC, V
**Closed** Nov to Mar

---

Farmhouse hotel, Pont-de-L'Arn

## La Métairie Neuve

The Metairie is a tastefully renovated old farm with its heritage properly respected – exposed beams, stone walls, polished tiled floors – and with a relaxed atmosphere. Mme Tournier is a charming hostess who keeps the antique-furnished public areas looking immaculate.

■ Pont-de-L'Arn, 81660 Mazamet (Tarn) **Tel** 05.63.97.73.50
**Fax** 05.63.61.94.75 **Meals** breakfast, dinner **Prices** rooms F; menus FF
**Rooms** 14, all with bath, central heating, phone, TV **Credit cards** DC, MC, V **Closed** 15 Dec to 20 Jan; restaurant only, Sun

---

Riverside hotel, St-Sernin-sur-Rance

## Hôtel Carayon ★

Well outside our upper size limit, but perennially a favourite with readers ('excellent' says the latest report). It is a white-painted, shuttered building with café tables in front; most of the rooms are in a smart modern extension. Pierre Carayon's cooking is outstanding. What is more, the menu prices are modest, earning a prized red *repas* rating from Michelin. And the Carayons are an attractive and friendly couple. Two swimming-pools, water-slide, mini-golf, tennis and fitness centre.

■ Place du Fort, 12380 St-Sernin-sur-Rance (Aveyron) **Tel** 05.65.
98.19.19 **Fax** 05.65.99.69.26 **Meals** breakfast, lunch, dinner
**Prices** rooms F; suites FF; menus F-FFF **Rooms** 60, all with bath or shower, central heating, phone, TV, minibar **Credit cards** AE, DC, MC
**Closed** Sun dinner and Mon, out of season

---

Village inn, Vitrac

## La Tomette

'This hotel has all the qualities of peace, welcome, attractive setting and very good food that characterise your selections,' a reader says of the Tomette – a jolly inn, much expanded and improved over the last 20 years or so, evidently without the loss of its essential appeal. Pleasant garden, pool.

■ 15220 Vitrac (Cantal) **Tel** 04.71.64.70.94 **Fax** 04.71.64.77.11
**E-mail** latomette@wanadoo.fr **Meals** breakfast, lunch, dinner **Prices** rooms
230F-440F; breakfast 40F, menus 70F-200F **Rooms** 15, all with bath or shower, central heating, phone, TV **Credit cards** AE, MC, V **Closed** Jan to Mar

# *The South*

Mediterranean France: sea, sun, wine, flowers, fruit, mountains, Roman remains. Heaven on earth – and with more guide entries and potential entries (listed below) than any other region.

**Contenders in the South**

**Aigues-Mortes, Les Arcades** 04.66.53.81.13 Characterful restaurant with individually decorated rooms in ancient building.

**Aix-en-Provence, Hôtel des Augustins** 04.42.27.28.59 Converted monastery in centre of Aix; garden for breakfast.

**Aix-en-Provence, Hôtel des Quatre-Dauphins** 04.42.38.16.39 Prettily designer-decorated little place in Mazarin quarter.

**Avignon, Hôtel de la Mirande** 04.90.85.93.93 Extravagantly elegant town hotel, opened in 1990.

**Montfavet, Les Frênes** 04.90.31.17.93 Elegant mansion, beautiful garden, and superb pool. Good food.

**Les-Baux-de-Provence, Mas de l'Oulivie** 04.90.54.35.78 Newly built, in traditional *mas* style, with attractive pool among olives.

**Les-Baux-de-Provence, La Cabro d'Or** 04.90.54.33.21 Starred restaurant, with lovely pool/gardens and comfortable rooms.

**Bonnieux, Hostellerie Le Prieuré** 04.90.75.80.78 Delightful 17thC abbey in small hillside village.

**Castillon-du-Gard, Le Vieux Castillon** 04.66.37.00.77 Luxurious and stylish conversion of old houses in ancient hilltop village.

**Collias, Hostellerie Le Castellas** 04.66.22.88.88 Stylish, slightly slick little place in centre of old village; small garden, pool.

**Coursegoules, Auberge de l'Escaou** 04.93.59.11.28 Simple, tastefully modernized inn, in quiet, isolated hill village.

**Gordes, Les Romarins** 04.90.72.12.13 Tastefully furnished house overlooking the village; pool.

**Gordes, Les Bories** 04.90.72.00.51 Expensive picturesque restaurant with rooms overlooking valley in medieval village.

**Joucas, Mas des Herbes Blanches** 04.90.05.79.79 Very attractive old *mas* with fine views; well-equipped rooms; pool; good food.

**Joucas, Le Phebus** 04.90.05.78.83 Stylishly decorated, welcoming farmhouse-style place, good food, attractive pool.

**Malemort-du-Comtat, Château Unang** 04.90.69.91.37 18thC house in formal gardens surrounded by vineyards, elegantly furnished but informally run as a B&B.

**Montpellier, Hôtel le Guilhem** 04.67.52.90.90 Tastefully done out old house in old town, with lovely terrace; B&B only.

**Pernes-les-Fontaines, Hôtel l'Hermitage** 04.90.66.51.41 Elegant, patchily furnished Logis in pleasant gardens with pool.

**Le-Puy-Ste-Reparade, Domaine de la Cride** 04.42.61.96.96 Home-like restored farmhouse in a leafy garden with pool.

**Roquebrune-sur-Argens, La Maurette** 04.94.45.46.81 Hilltop farmhouse with views; rooms open on to the garden.

**Russamp-Est, Mas des Aigras** 04.90.34.81.01 Simple but stylish farmhouse B&B in leafy gardens with pool, tennis.

**St-Remy, Mas de la Tour** 04.90.92.61.00 Traditional-style house with rooms opening on to flowery garden and pool.

**Ste-Maxime-sur-Mer, La Croisette** 04.94.96.17.75 Pastel coloured villa with secluded garden and good views; seafood specialities. **Vence, Château du Domaine St Martin** 04.93.58.02.02 Elegantly furnished Relais & Châteaux place, in splendid high setting; terrace, lovely pool, tennis.

# *The South*

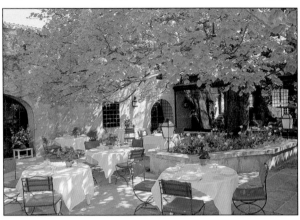

# Mas d'Entremont

This farmhouse-style hotel just outside Aix, continues to receive a blemish-free record of reports from readers (including one who has been going there for over a decade) and impressed one inspector mightily.

The hotel consists of low red-roofed buildings clustered around a courtyard – modern constructions, but using lots of old materials. Within are wooden beams and pillars, rustic furniture, tiled floors and open fireplaces. Bedrooms are also rustic, comfortable and quite stylish. Five (relatively small, but all with terrace or balcony) are in the main building, the rest (bigger) spread around the gardens in bungalows. The setting is peaceful, and the gardens are a delight – with a big swimming-pool shielded by cypresses, plenty of secluded corners, and a pond with fountain, lilies and lazy carp. Overlooking this is a beautiful summer dining-room, with windows that slide away, effectively creating a roofed terrace.

Cuisine is classic in style, with a strong Provençal influence, and excellent in quality, attracting a full house for Sunday lunch. The Marignanes create a relaxed family atmosphere.

**Nearby** Aix-en-Provence; Abbaye de Silvacane (25 km).

Montée d'Avignon 13090
Aix-en-Provence
**Tel** 04.42.17.45.42
**Fax** 04.42.21.15.83
**Location** in countryside just off N7, 2 km NW of Aix; with large grounds and car parking
**Meals** breakfast, lunch, dinner
**Prices** rooms FF-FFF, suite FFF; breakfast F; DB&B FFF-FFFF (for two); menus FF
**Rooms** 17 double (7 twin) all with bath; all rooms have air-conditioning, phone,

satellite TV, minibar, safe, private terrace
**Facilities** dining-room, sitting-areas; swimming-pool, tennis
**Credit cards** MC, V
**Children** accepted; some rooms have side-rooms
**Disabled** lift/elevator
**Pets** accepted
**Closed** Nov to mid-Mar; restaurant only, Sun dinner
**Proprietors** Marignane family

# *The South*

# Villa Gallici

This is certainly one of the most expensive and it is also one of the smallest hotels in Aix; from where we stand it is absolutely the best. We've called it a town villa; though suburban villa might be more accurate, while country villa might convey more of the feel of the place, set in a beautiful garden just north of the centre.

It is a deliciously peaceful, relaxing place, where distinctions between indoors and out seem to blur. A shady terrace is converted to an outdoor sitting-room by deep-cushioned sofas and chairs; breakfast can be had here.

Indoors, bright fabrics and light paintwork bring the sun into the welcoming sitting-rooms. Bedrooms are prettily sumptuous, with extravagant use of draped fabrics; furniture is in elegant 18th-century style throughout, but the decorative themes vary widely.

Light meals can be had by the hotel's pool, surrounded by trees and flowery shrubs. For more serious eating, the hotel's restaurant, which serves Provençal dishes, does not let the side down.

**Nearby** Aix-en-Provence; Abbaye de Silvacane (25 km)

Avenue de la Violette 13100
Aix-en-Provence
**Tel** 04.42.23.29.23
**Fax** 04.42.96.30.45
**E-mail** gallici@relaischateaux.fr
**Website** www.villagallici.com
**Location** just N of city centre, 500m from cathedral; in gardens with secure parking
**Meals** breakfast, lunch, dinner
**Prices** rooms FFF-FFFF; breakfast FF, menu FFF
**Rooms** 22 double with bath; all rooms have central

heating, air-conditioning, phone, TV, radio, minibar, hairdrier
**Facilities** sitting-room, bar, dining-room; terrace, swimming-pool
**Credit cards** AE, DC, MC, V
**Children** not accepted
**Disabled** one ground-floor bedroom
**Pets** accepted (100F charge)
**Closed** never
**Proprietors** M. Dez, M. Montemarco, M. Jouve

# *The South*

**Country hotel, Céret**

## La Terrasse au Soleil

This mainly modern Catalan-style hotel has gradually moved upmarket over its years in the guide, and is now of four-star status, and has now added even its own helicopter landing space. It has expanded, too, and falls outside our usual size limits. But choice in the Pyrenees-Orientales is limited, and an approving reader's report encourages us to stick to the view that this is one of the most appealing places in the region.

A key part of the appeal is the lovely setting, with the splendid Mont Canigou as backdrop on a fine day (320 days of sun per year are claimed, so you should be lucky). As you might expect, it has a terrace, where you can eat out or just observe the view (as Picasso is said to have done); and there are good facilities for the more active. Inside, a relaxed and casual atmosphere prevails despite the modern comforts. The best of the bedrooms – all of which are well equipped – are very spacious and smart.

The restaurant has recently been given a separate identity – La Cerisaie. At lunchtime there is a tempting brunch *carte* as a lighter alternative to the more serious food that for years has merited a Gault-Millau *toque* and other culinary awards.
**Nearby** Perpignan; beaches (30 km); Castelnou (30 km).

Rte de Fontfrède 66400 Céret
**Tel** 04.68.87.01.94
**Fax** 04.68.87.39.24
**E-mail** terrace-au-soleil.hotel@wanadoo.fr
**E-mail** www.la.terrasse-au-soleil.com
**Location** in Pyrenean foothills above town, 26 km SW of Perpignan; with gardens and car parking
**Meals** breakfast, brunch, dinner; room service
**Prices** rooms F-FFF, suites FF-FFF; breakfast F
**Rooms** 14 double, all with bath; 7 suites, with bath; all rooms have air-conditioning, phone, TV, minibar, hairdrier
**Facilities** dining-room, sitting-room, bar; ping-pong, heli-pad, swimming-pool, tennis-court, petanque, golf practice area **Credit cards** AE, DC, MC, V **Children** accepted
**Disabled** facilities **Pets** accepted **Closed** restaurant only, lunch
**Proprietor** M. Leveille-Nizerolle

# *The South*

**Town inn, Château-Arnoux**

## La Bonne Etape

'Exceptional food, impeccable service, beautiful pool and rooms – worth every franc' says a very satisfied visitor to this long-established 'good stopover'. Though service can be slow at breakfast and at peak times, according to a recent report.

The setting (on a busy main road in an unremarkable town) is not auspicious, and the outside gives little hint of what lies within – one of the most satisfactory blends of refinement and hospitality to be found in France. Where to start? Perhaps in the kitchen, where Pierre and Jany Gleize (father and son) make innovative and stylish use of largely home-grown ingredients, earning a star from Michelin and 18/20 from Gault-Millau. Among their specialities is Sisteron lamb (raised on fragrant Provençal pastures). There is a light, warm dining-room – a relaxing place, with well-spaced round tables – as well as a smaller restaurant downstairs.

Bedrooms are more than comfortable – beautifully decorated and furnished with a tasteful mix of modern and antique pieces; bathrooms are 'spacious, with double basins and film star mirrors and lights' reports a delighted guest. The pool is a superb suntrap, with an attractive terrace surround. To cap it all, the Gleize family are welcoming hosts, happily committed to their work.
**Nearby** Les Mées (10 km); Sisteron – citadel; hill-walking.

Chemin du Lac 04160
Château-Arnoux
**Tel** 04.92.64.00.09
**Fax** 04.92.64.37.36
**E-mail** info@bonneetape.com
**Website** www.bonneetape.com
**Location** in country town, on main RN 85 14 km SE of Sisteron (motorway 3 km); car parking, garage and garden
**Meals** breakfast, lunch, dinner
**Prices** rooms FF-FFF, suites FFF-FFFF; breakfast F, menus FF-FFF

**Rooms** 11 double, 7 suites, all with bath; all rooms have air-conditioning, phone, TV, radio, minibar **Facilities** 2 dining-rooms, sitting-room, bar, conference room; heated swimming-pool **Credit cards** AE, DC, MC, V
**Children** accepted
**Disabled** no special facilities
**Pets** accepted **Closed** Jan to mid-Feb, 29 Nov to 10 Dec; Mon, Tue from Nov to Mar
**Proprietors** Gleize family

# *The South*

# La Vieille Fontaine

Built within the walls of the ruined chateau of a medieval fortified village, with cobbled streets and ivy-clad ramparts, this little
hotel is full of charm. *Patron* and chef, M Audibert, is a
Marseillais; his *gratinée de langoustines* and *chou farci à la provençale*,
accompanied by the local Tavel *rosé*, have long been the restaurant's attractions. The hotel is the creation of Mme Audibert, a
native of this once semi-abandoned village. Inspired by the
Louvre pyramid, she has, with great flair, clad the exterior circular staircase to the bedrooms with an elegant glass structure, at
which one can gaze in wonder over breakfast in the courtyard.
Her decorating style is simple and pretty; tiled bathrooms,
Provençal fabrics, furniture from local *antiquaires*. One room
contains a great chunk of the old château wall. Most have terraces; numbers 7 and 8 have views way over the top of the castle
wall to the south. A steep flight of stone steps through terraced
gardens leads to the pool: water gushes down from the hillside,
and it is like bathing in a mountain stream. The welcome is spon-
taneous and warm; dinner on the terrace looking over the hills
and vineyards of the Gard is a delight.
**Nearby** Orange; Avignon; the Gorges of the Ardèche.

30630 Cornillon
**Tel** 04.66.82.20.56
**Fax** 04.66.82.33.64
**Location** well into the
village, with limited
vehicular access
**Meals** breakfast, lunch,
dinner
**Prices** FF; breakfast F
**Rooms** 8 double, all with
bath and shower; all rooms
have TV, phone, electric
heating and entrance
hall; 6 with terraces

**Facilities** sitting-room;
dining-room; courtyard
terrace; terraced garden;
swimming-pool;
**Credit cards** AE, DC, MC, V
**Children** welcome
**Disabled** not suitable
**Pets** accepted: 55F a day
**Closed** mid-Dec to mid-Mar
**Proprietors** M and Mme
Audibert

# *The South*

**Village hotel, Crillon-le-Brave**

# Hostellerie de Crillon le Brave

'Delightful', 'near perfect', enthuse several satisfied visitors to this luxurious hotel occupying the old vicarage in the hilltop village of Crillon-le-Brave. 'Very good restaurant, excellent service, a lovely setting and a charming *patron*.'

The rambling 16thC stone-built house is solid and calm, but most of the credit for the resounding success of the hotel – open only since late 1989 – must go to the aforementioned *patron*, Peter Chittick, a Canadian lawyer with exceptionally clear ideas about hotelkeeping. A considerable share goes also to the perched location, giving uninterrupted views of a heavenly landscape of olive groves and vineyards.

The central trick that Mr Chittick and his collaborator Craig Miller have pulled off is to provide luxury without erasing character. Despite the designer fabrics, fitted carpets and smart bathrooms, the exposed beams, white walls and rustic furniture dominate both in the sitting-rooms and the spacious bedrooms. You eat beneath stone vaults, or out on the pretty terrace. Chef Philippe Monti produces refined Provençale food that is in perfect harmony with this blissful setting.

**Nearby** Mont Ventoux; Orange (35 km); Avignon; Gordes.

Place de l'Eglise, 84410 Crillon-le-Brave
**Tel** 04.90.65.61.61
**Fax** 04.90.65.62.86
**E-mail** crillonbrave@relaischateaux.fr
**Website** www.crillonlebrave.com
**Location** in hilltop village 35km NE of Avignon, on D138 off D974, with garden, private car parking and garages
**Meals** breakfast, lunch (Sat and Sun only), dinner, snacks
**Prices** rooms FF-FFFF, suites FFFF; breakfast F, dinner

about 350F
**Rooms** 17 double (5 twin), 14 with bath, 3 with shower; 5 suites; all rooms have central heating, phone, minibar, hairdrier **Facilities** 3 sitting-rooms, dining-room; swimming-pool **Credit cards** AE, DC, MC, V **Children** welcome; babysitting available **Disabled** access difficult **Pets** accepted **Closed** Jan to Mar; restaurant, lunch, Mon-Fri **Proprietors** Peter Chittick and Craig Miller

# *The South*

**Converted castle, Dieulefit**

# Les Hospitaliers

Readers continue to be impressed by this distinctive hotel, a former stronghold in a dominating position above the perched medieval village of Le Poët-Laval. Apart from the views, especially from the terrace (where meals are served in fine weather) and pool area, the warm welcome and the comfortable top-floor sitting-room are singled out. The restaurant has an interesting collection of paintings; Yvon Morin is a former art dealer. Tables are laid with fine china, white linen or lace, and candles; service is hard to fault, and the food is excellent – the daily changing menu is particularly recommended. Bedrooms are furnished with antiques; size varies along with price.

**Nearby** Montélimar (20 km); Viviers (30 km) – medieval town.

Le Poët-Laval, 26160 La Bégude-de-Mazenc
**Tel** 04.75.46.22.32
**Fax** 04.75.46.49.99
**Location** at top of old village, 5 km W of Dieulefit; with gardens; car parking nearby
**Meals** breakfast, lunch, dinner
**Prices** rooms F-FFF; menus FF
**Rooms** 21 double, 20 with bath, one with shower (8 twin); 3 family rooms, all with bath; all rooms have central heating, phone
**Facilities** 2 dining-rooms, 2 sitting-rooms, bar; swimming- pool
**Credit cards** AE, DC, MC, V
**Children** accepted
**Disabled** no special facilities
**Pets** cats and dogs accepted
**Closed** mid-Nov to Feb
**Proprietors** Morin family

# *The South*

**Country hotel, Les Essareaux**

## La Manescale

The King of Belgium has slept here. No doubt, like so many others, he was charmed by all he found in this remote former shepherd's house up in the hills. The thoughtfulness of owners, M and Mme Warland, permeates what could be described as a pocket-sized hotel with every comfort. The smallest details are attended to here, from towels for the swimming-pool to a small library for serious readers and helpfully labelled light switches. Mme Warland, in her apron, cooks in the kitchen and gathers fresh flowers before meals for the tables; M Warland prints out the menu on his fax machine and delivers her delicious dishes, such as *magret de canard* with apples and bilberries, to diners. Stone steps and pathways connect the main building to garden rooms, each giving privacy and views of the forest and hillsides. Two rooms are named after M Warland's favourite painters – Tiepolo and Dali. A place for lovers of quiet and of nature, there are numerous paths through the woods for long walks. Classical music plays on the terrace at *aperitif* time; the views across vineyards and valleys to Mont Ventoux in the distance are superb. It's a steep walk from parking to hotel: a luggage trolley is provided.
**Nearby** Vaison-la-Romaine 7 km; Côtes du Rhône vineyards.

Route de Faucon
Les Essareaux,
84340 Entrechaux
**Tel** 04.90.46.03.80
**Fax** 04.90.46.03.89
**Location** in the hills
**Meals** breakfast, dinner
**Prices** F-FF; breakfast F;
**Rooms** 5; 2 with bath, 3 with shower; all rooms have phone, TV, central heating, minibar
**Facilities** terrace, gardens; swimming-pool; secure parking
**Credit cards** AE, DC, EC, MC, V
**Children** welcome if well-behaved
**Disabled** not suitable
**Pets** dogs permitted
**Closed** end Oct to Easter
**Proprietors** M and Mme Warland

# The South

**Converted mill, Fayence**

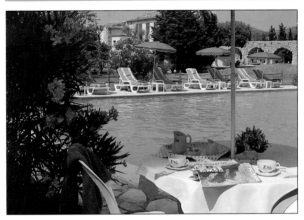

# Moulin de la Camandoule

We stick to this restored olive-mill year after year. As a rule, a minimum stay of three nights is required in the busy season, but this should prove no hardship at the Rillas' deeply relaxing country hotel.

The mill lies in extensive private grounds divided in half by the low Roman aqueduct which used to bring water to the mill. The existing building dates from the 19thC and was rescued from ruin some thirty years ago. Shirley and Wolf Rilla (an English couple) moved here in 1986, and are still making improvements.

Food is a highlight for most visitors. Meals are served outside in summer – on a terrace overlooking the cherry orchard, or by the pool – or in the delightfully rustic dining-room decorated with original mill trappings. Between this and the lofty, beamed sitting-room (with its adjoining 'snuggery') is the ancient water wheel. Bedrooms differ widely in size and style. Books, family paintings, ornaments and fresh flowers add to the welcoming (not at all smart) atmosphere. One reporter was critical of the state of the gardens, and feels that standards may be slipping here generally.

**Nearby** Grasse (23 km) – perfumes; Cannes (30 km).

Chemin Notre-Dame-des-Cyprès 83440 Fayence
**Tel** 04.94.76.00.84
**Fax** 04.94.76.10.40
**Location** at foot of village, 30 km NW of Cannes; in large grounds with ample parking
**Meals** breakfast, lunch, dinner
**Prices** rooms F-FF, DB&B F-FF (obligatory 25 Mar to 15 Oct); breakfast F, menu FF
**Rooms** 9 double, 7 with bath, 2 with shower, (4 twin); 2 suites with bath; all rooms have central heating, phone, TV
**Facilities** dining-room, sitting-room with bar; swimming-pool with bar, barbecue
**Credit cards** MC, V
**Children** accepted
**Disabled** no special facilities
**Pets** accepted (45F)
**Closed** never
**Proprietors** Wolf and Shirley Rilla

# The South

**Converted mill, Fontvieille**

## La Régalido

We continue to be fond of this 19th-century oil mill, a Relais & Chateaux place which manages to remain informal and friendly despite its elegant furnishings and high prices – largely thanks to the presence at all hours of the welcoming and helpful Jean-Pierre Michel, chef-proprietor.

The Régalido has been converted into a fine auberge in a thoroughly Provençal style, decorated with great flair by Madame Michel. There is a charming sitting-room full of flowers, and a log fire lit on chilly days. Tables are beautifully set in the elegant, peaceful, stone-vaulted dining-room, and there is an atmosphere of well-being which suits the excellent cooking of Jean-Pierre. His style is classic, but he has a penchant for Provençal dishes (seafood, olive oil, herbs and garlic) – and terracotta or cast iron pots appear alongside the silver salvers.

Bedrooms are individually decorated, and very comfortable, with lots of extras in the well equipped bathrooms. Friendly staff and a pretty, flowery garden – with a terrace surrounded by mimosa and shaded by fig and olive trees – complete the picture.

**Nearby** Montmajour Abbey; Arles; the Camargue (10 km) – flamingoes, white horses; Tarascon (15 km) – château.

Rue Frederic-Mistral 13990 Fontvieille
**Tel** 04.90.54.60.22
**Fax** 04.90.54.64.29
**Location** in middle of village, 9 km NE of Arles; with gardens and ample car parking
**Meals** breakfast, lunch, dinner
**Prices** rooms FF-FFFF; breakfast F-FF, menus FF-FFF
**Rooms** 15 double, 12 with bath, 2 with shower; all rooms have central heating, air-conditioning, phone, minibar
**Facilities** dining-room, 2 sitting-rooms, bar
**Credit cards** AE, DC, MC, V
**Children** accepted
**Disabled** one specially equipped ground-floor bedroom
**Pets** accepted (60F)
**Closed** Jan; restaurant only, Mon, and Tue lunch
**Proprietor** Jean-Pierre Michel

# *The South*

**Country hotel, Gémenos**

# Relais de la Magdeleine

'If only there were more hotels like this,' begins one enthusiastic reader's report on this lovely old *bastide*. We share the sentiment: for those of us who can't or won't pay the prices (or don't like the style) of Relais & Châteaux places, a gracious country house like this is quite a find. It is a family affair. Daniel Marignane's mother opened the hotel in 1932, he and his wife now run the hotel with great charm and good humour, and their son is now in charge of the kitchen – and achieving great things.

An acid test of a hotel is visitors' reactions to flaws. When they reveal them to us grudgingly, in a favourable light, we know we are on to a winner. 'A touch of shabbiness here and there only adds to the charm,' says one report otherwise full of praise.

The great trick that the Marignanes pull off is that of steering a sensitive middle course. The public rooms are elegant, but lived-in. The bedrooms too are home-like, but the best have posh bathrooms. The hotel pampers grown-ups, but is welcoming to children. Prices have risen here, but many comfortably-off British travellers in France will still find them bearable. If only there were more like this, indeed. Other recent visitors agree.

**Nearby** Cassis (15 km) – coastal inlets; La Ste-Baume massif.

13420 Gémenos
**Tel** 04.42.32.20.16
**Fax** 04.42.32.02.26
**Website** www.relais-magdeleine.com
**Location** on outskirts of town, 23 km E of Marseilles; with garden and ample car parking
**Meals** breakfast, lunch, dinner
**Prices** rooms F-FF; breakfast F; DB&B F-FF; menu FF
**Rooms** 24 double, 20 with bath, 4 with shower (12 twin); 4 family rooms, all with bath; all rooms have central heating, phone, TV
**Facilities** sitting-rooms, dining-rooms; swimming-pool
**Credit cards** MC, V
**Children** accepted
**Disabled** no special facilities
**Pets** not accepted
**Closed** Dec to mid-Mar
**Proprietors** M. and Mme Marignane

# *The South*

**Village hotel, Grimaud**

# Le Coteau Fleuri

Our files contain a pretty solid record of support for this attractive stone house, built into the hillside at the edge of the fashionable perched village of Grimaud, and run by Jacques Minard (previously manager of the Mas de Chatelas) since 1988. Our most recent reporter had not only 'a good time' in general, but 'the best meal of the holiday.'

The house is about a hundred years old and retains a simple Provençal style. There is a rambling garden with olive trees, and a small flowery terrace in front of the hotel. The spotless bedrooms have pretty furnishings and prints, and smart tiled bathrooms; most are rather small, but many have a splendid view of vineyards and the Maures massif (others look out over the garden and the ruins of Grimaud castle and chapel). The public rooms are attractive and relaxing: there is a small bar, a dining-room in two parts (both of which extend on to the terrace and benefit from the view), and a spacious sitting-room with tiled floor and grand piano. Throughout the hotel are masses of fresh flowers. In winter there are log fires.

Food is a highlight; *nouvelle* in style but not in quantity, theatrically presented by attentive staff. The *mousse au chocolat* is acquiring cult status.

**Nearby** St-Tropez (10 km); Pampelonne (15 km).

Place des Pénitents, Grimaud
83310 Cogolin
**Tel** 04.94.43.20.17
**Fax** 04.04.94.43.33.42
**E-mail** coteaufleuri@wanadoo.fr
**Location** in middle of village behind chapel; with car parking in front
**Meals** breakfast, lunch, dinner
**Prices** rooms F; breakfast F, menus from FF
**Rooms** 13 double, 8 with bath, 5 with shower (4 twin); one family room with bath; all rooms have phone
**Facilities** dining-room, sitting-room, bar
**Credit cards** AE, DC, MC, V
**Children** welcome
**Disabled** no special facilities
**Pets** accepted if well behaved
**Closed** 3 weeks Dec, 2 weeks Jan; restaurant only, Tue (except Jul and Aug)
**Proprietors** Jacline and Jacques Minard

# *The South*

# Le Verger ★

'Glad to see Le Verger appearing in your guide,' says a reader, in response to its inclusion for the first time a few years ago. 'I've known this pleasant little spot for some years, and often thought it was your kind of hotel – that is, a very unhotel-like hotel.' Indeed: the Zacharys have kept the scale and feel of the private house they converted in 1987. It is a typical Provençal building – low, with shallow roofs of pale tiles.

'Our friends call this place 'Little Normandy' because it is so green, unlike most of the Côte d'Azur,' says Anne Zachary, highlighting just one attractive aspect of Le Verger. The 'French windows' of harmonious, freshly decorated bedrooms open directly on to the lawn, and so the pool. Meals are served outside in summer, on a partly covered terrace looking across the pool to woods and hills, or before an open fire in a large dining-room in cooler weather. M. Zachary – an experienced chef, with quite a local following – cooks varied and satisfying dishes in the Mediterranean style, with no pretensions. And while you're at dinner your bed will be turned down – one of the little things that Anne insists on, in order to make your stay entirely restful.

**Nearby** Provence countryside; St-Tropez (12 km).

Route de Collobrières 83360 Grimaud
**Tel** 04.94.43.25.93
**Fax** 04.94.43.33.92
**Location** in countryside 1 km W of Grimaud, on D14 off D558, 12 km W of St-Tropez; in spacious gardens with private car parking
**Meals** breakfast, lunch, dinner
**Prices** rooms F-FF; breakfast F, menu FF
**Rooms** 9 double, 7 with bath; 2 with shower; all rooms have central heating, phone, satellite TV
**Facilities** sitting-room, dining-room; swimming-pool
**Credit cards** MC, V
**Children** accepted, but no special facilities
**Disabled** not very suitable
**Pets** welcome
**Closed** Nov to Easter
**Proprietor** Mme Zachary

# *The South*

**Medieval inn, Haut-de-Cagnes**

# Le Cagnard

A reader's report raised some doubts about this lovely hotel, perched along the ramparts of an old hill village – specifically about standards of service in the Michelin-starred restaurant. It is far from the most expensive hotel in the Relais & Châteaux group, but it is pricey enough for expectations in this department to be high. Off went an inspector; happily, all was well.

Le Cagnard has been sensitively converted from a series of medieval houses, most with separate street entrances. In the main house there is a stunning medieval vaulted dining-room where you eat by candlelight. But the real knockout is the upper dining-room, leading out on to the terrace: its elaborate painted ceiling slides away at the touch of a button, opening the room to the sky. The bedrooms vary widely; most retain a medieval feel, thanks to the preservation of features such as stone floors, and are furnished with style, but incongruous exceptions remain. Three rooms in one house have a lovely flowery garden. Access in anything other than a small car is tricky, and getting to some rooms involves a bit of awkward suitcase-lugging.

**Nearby** Château Grimaldi – modern art museum, with Renaissance courtyard; Nice (15 km); Grasse (30 km) – perfumes.

Rue Pontis-Long, Haut-de-Cagnes 06800 Cagnes-sur-Mer
**Tel** 04.93.20.73.21
**Fax** 04.93.22.06.39
**Location** in middle of hill village, 2 km above main town of Cagnes; car parking 300m away at entrance to village
**Meals** breakfast, lunch, dinner
**Prices** rooms F-FFF, suites FFF; breakfast F, menus FF-FFF
**Rooms** 18 double,

10 apartments, all with bath; all rooms have central heating, phone, TV, minibar; most have air-conditioning
**Facilities** dining-room, bar
**Credit cards** AE, DC, MC, V
**Children** accepted
**Disabled** no special facilities
**Pets** accepted
**Closed** restaurant only, Thu lunch and Nov to mid-Dec
**Proprietors** Barel Laroche family

# *The South*

**Village inn, Llo**

# L'Atalaya

The Toussaints' delightful little rustic inn continues to impress. Llo is an attractive village high up in the Pyrenees, and is typical of the Cerdagne – a high sun-drenched plateau of pastures and pine forests, popular for summer and winter sports. The Atalaya, in a prime spot in the village, was expertly converted from an old farmhouse in 1969.

The bedrooms are quiet, comfortable and intimate, with romantic fabrics and soft lighting. Local specialities are served either in the rustic dining-room – gleaming antiques against stone walls – or on a charming flowery terrace.

**Nearby** Odeillo (10 km) – solar furnace; Font-Romeu (15 km).

Llo 66800 Saillagouse
**Tel** 04.68.04.70.04
**Fax** 04.68.04.01.29
**Location** in middle of village, 2 km E of Saillagouse and 10 km E of Bourg-Madame; ample car parking
**Meals** breakfast, lunch, dinner
**Prices** rooms F-FF; breakfast F, DB&B FF-FFF; menus FF
**Rooms** 12 double, 10 with bath, 2 with shower (3 twin); one suite; all rooms have central heating, phone, TV, minibar, safe
**Facilities** sitting-room, bar, dining-room; swimming-pool
**Credit cards** MC, V
**Children** welcome if well behaved
**Disabled** no special facilities
**Pets** accepted in bedrooms only
**Closed** 5 Nov to 20 Dec
**Proprietors** M. and Mme H Toussaint

# *The South*

## Château hotel, Madières

# Château de Madières

This magnificently sited 14th-century fortress, perched above the Vis river gorge, was upgraded a few years ago to four-star status. More importantly, the refurbishments have given the interior a new vitality, shifting the hotel from the 'historic and adequately comfortable' category to the distinctly compelling.

The château was rescued from decay by the Brucys in 1982. They opened for business in 1986, having restored it to its former glory – creating comfortable rooms within the existing framework of medieval walls and arches. No two bedrooms (named after flowers) are alike, though all have modern bathrooms and most have good views. The best are very spacious and delightfully furnished, with bold, colourful fabrics against plain white walls and oriental rugs on tiled floors. Key attractions are the public rooms – a galleried sitting-room with a vast Renaissance fireplace, and the vaulted dining-room, jutting out of the main building, with spectacular valley views. Above it is the main terrace.

Chef, Guy Bonafous, who gained a reputation for fine cooking at l'Oustal del Barry, Najac (page 170), has taken over the cooking from Madame Brucy. The *toque* from Gault Millau remains.
**Nearby** Cirque de Navacelles; Grotte des Demoiselles; Ganges.

Madières 34190 Ganges
**Tel** 04.67.73.84.03
**Fax** 04.67.73.55.71
**E-mail** madières@wanadoo.fr
**Location** on hillside overlooking village, on crossroads of D48 and D25; with shady park and ample car parking
**Meals** breakfast, lunch, dinner
**Prices** rooms FF-FFF; breakfast F, menus FF-FFF, children's FF

**Rooms** 8 double (one twin), 3 apartments, all with bath; all rooms have central heating, phone, TV, minibar
**Facilities** 3 sitting-rooms, bar, 2 dining-rooms, 3 terraces, swimming-pool, fitness room
**Credit cards** AE, MC, V
**Children** accepted
**Disabled** no special facilities
**Pets** accepted
**Closed** Nov to Easter
**Proprietors** Bernard and Françoise Brucy

# *The South*

## Hilltop hotel, Mougins

# Les Muscadins

'It's really delicious!' Our latest reporter doesn't give us any clue as to whether this endorsement is a literal verdict confined to the food, or whether it is a metaphorical verdict on the whole of this lovely place.

Les Muscadins – a white-washed building surrounded by tropical vegetation – is irresistible. The American owner Edward Bianchini has filled it with memorable antiques, many from the lavish homes of 18thC fops called *Muscadins*. .

The luxurious bedrooms are highly individual and beautifully coordinated, and have impeccable bathrooms. The chintzy, floral look in some rooms is giving way to more contemporary geometric designs and colours of black and cream, blue and cream, red and beige, with wrought-iron fittings, as rooms are being redecorated; most also have views of the coast. The pale terracotta and beige dining-room serves simple Mediterranean food and there is an elegantly furnished terrace, with splendid views.

Our inspector was impressed by the changes that have taken place recently.

**Nearby** Cannes; Grasse; Vallauris (10 km) – Picasso museum.

18 Bd Courteline 06250 Mougins
**Tel** 04.92.28.28.28
**Fax** 04.92.92.88.23
**Location** on E road into old village, 2 km N of A8 motorway, 6 km N of Cannes; with car parking
**Meals** breakfast, lunch, dinner
**Prices** rooms FF, suite FFF; breakfast F, menus FF
**Rooms** 7 double, one suite; all with bath, all rooms have central heating, air-conditioning, phone, TV, minibar
**Facilities** sitting-room, dining-room, bar
**Credit cards** AE, DC, MC, V
**Children** welcome
**Disabled** access difficult
**Pets** welcome
**Closed** restaurant only, Nov and Dec
**Proprietor** Edward Bianchini

# *The South*

## Auberge de la Madone

A visitor described the setting of this family-run hotel as 'stunning'. 'Delightful' was the one-word verdict offered by another reader reporting on this top-of-the-range Logis, which happily combines a sense of special hospitality with affordable (though not low) prices. And such is its appeal, that the Millos opened an annexe in the old part of the village – the Auberge du Pourtail. Rooms here are cheaper and you take your meals at the Madone.

You may think that you have taken a wrong turning as you first spy Peillon, perched impossibly above, with little sign of any road leading up. Time stands still here. The medieval village consists of a few dark cobbled alleys leading up to the church, and tall stone houses looking out over rocky crests and distant forests.

The *auberge* is set just outside the walled village itself. Behind, paths lead off into the hills, past the grazing sheep with their tinkling bells; in front is the village car park and *boules* area. Within, the rather small bedrooms (with equally small balconies) are attractive and comfortable with stylish all-white bathrooms. Meals are served on the sunny terrace, under a large awning, or in the welcoming Provençal-style dining-room. Cooking is above average (a *toque* from Gault-Millau), using organic, local ingredients. An all-weather tennis court is another of the hotel's attractions.

**Nearby** Monaco – Palace, museums, exotic gardens.

06440 Peillon-Village
**Tel** 04.93.79.91.17
**Fax** 04.93.79.99.36
**Location** on edge of perched village, 19 km NE of Nice; with ample car parking
**Meals** breakfast, lunch, dinner
**Prices** rooms F-FF; F in annexe; breakfast F; DB&B F-FF; menus FF-FFF
**Rooms** 20 double, 15 with bath, 5 with shower; all rooms have central heating, phone, TV
**Facilities** bar, 2 dining-rooms; tennis court
**Credit cards** MC, V
**Children** very welcome
**Disabled** no special facilities
**Pets** accepted by arrangement
**Closed** mid-Oct to mid-Dec, 7 to 24 Jan; Wed
**Proprietors** Millo family

# *The South*

## Mas des Brugassières ★

'Very relaxed atmosphere – an excellent place to unwind after the long drive south,' is the verdict of one visitor to this modern (1974) 'farmhouse', set in lush gardens surrounded by vineyards. Bedrooms (some non-smoking) have tiled floors and traditional furniture; some open out directly on to the garden and swimming-pool (and are ventilated only by leaving the door open). There is one public room – a sitting-room-cum-bar with simple wooden furniture and vast French windows – but from Easter to October most sitting will be done outside. Mas des Brugassières is basically a breakfast-only place, but in high season light lunches can be had by the pool.

**Nearby** Ste-Maxime – beach resort; Port-Grimaud (15 km)

Plan-de-la-Tour 83120
Ste-Maxime
**Tel** 04.94.55.50.55
**Fax** 04.94.55.50.51
**Location** in countryside
8 km NW of Ste-Maxime; with
gardens and ample car
parking
**Meals** breakfast
**Prices** rooms F-FF, suite FFF;
breakfast F
**Rooms** 14 double, all with
bath and shower (5 twin), 1
family suite; all rooms have
central heating, phone
**Facilities** sitting-room/bar;
swimming-pool, tennis, table
tennis
**Credit cards** MC, V
**Children** accepted
**Disabled** ground-floor
bedrooms
**Pets** dogs accepted at extra
charge (60F)
**Closed** 10 Oct to 20 Mar
**Proprietors** Steve and Annick
Geffine

# *The South*

**Inn, Le Pontet**

## Auberge de Cassagne

Although this Provençal-style *auberge* in a leafy suburb of Avignon rather exceeds our size range (it seems to expand slightly every few years), it is emphatically our kind of hotel.

The mellow 18th-century house sits in lush gardens which are among the main attractions of the hotel. There is ample space for relaxing – a swimming-pool, a plane-shaded terrace for meals, manicured lawns and paved courtyards surrounded by peaceful bungalow-style bedrooms with traditional Provençal furniture and confidently colourful fabrics, as well as all modern conveniences. There are some bedrooms in the main building, along with a cosy sitting-room. The dining-room is a lofty, spacious affair with huge exposed beams, and 'French windows' overlooking the garden.

When chef Philippe Boucher first came to the Auberge de Cassagne he was advertised as an ex-disciple of Paul Bocuse and Georges Blanc; now, he has an established reputation of his own, recognised with a star from Michelin and two *toques* from Gault-Millau. Despite this, we have one negative report: more comments welcome

**Nearby** Avignon – Palais des Papes, Pont St-Bénèzet.

84130 Le Pontet – Avignon
**Tel** 04.90.31.04.18
**Fax** 04.90.32.25.09
**E-mail** cassagne@wanadoo.fr
**Website** http://www.valrugues-cassagne.com
**Location** in rural suburb of Avignon, 4 km NE of middle, 3 km W of A7; with gardens and ample car parking
**Meals** breakfast, lunch, dinner
**Prices** rooms FF-FFF; menus FF (lunch) -FFF, **Rooms** 35 double, all with bath or shower; 5 suites, all with bath; all rooms have central heating, phone, TV, air-conditioning, minibar, safe
**Facilities** dining-room, 2 sitting-rooms, bar; swimming-pool, gym, sauna
**Credit cards** AE, DC, MC, V
**Children** welcome
**Disabled** facilities
**Pets** accepted; 60F charge
**Closed** never **Proprietors** Jean-Michel Gallon, Philippe Boucher and André Trestour

# The South

# Auberge de Reillanne

We don't get many reports on this lovely old *bastide* turned country auberge, but they are always positive, and sometimes verge on the ecstatic. For many years it was admirably run by Maurice Bellaiche. Now Madame Founes, the original owner of Auberge de Reillanne, has repurchased her former home, and is back at the helm, with promises to continue the unpretentious, private-home feel created by M. Bellaiche.

Despite the grandeur of the building – mainly 18th-century, but with parts dating from the 12th – it is not a hotel of four-star sophistication. It's a peaceful place (surrounded by fields, with views towards the Lubéron massif), sparsely furnished with great style and individuality. There are seven very large bedrooms with stone walls and beamed ceilings, and rows of books take the place of the usual mod cons – there are no radios or TVs. In the dining-room, paintings and sculptures are in perfect harmony with the setting.

Simple food, based on fresh local ingredients. We welcome hearing.

**Nearby** Lubéron Park – marked trails; St-Michel observatory (10 km); Aix-en-Provence (70 km); Avignon (80 km).

04110 Reillanne
**Tel** 04.92.76.45.95
**Location** in countryside, 1 km from village, 19 km SW of Forcalquier; in garden, with car parking
**Meals** breakfast, dinner
**Prices** rooms F; DB&B F; breakfast F; menus FF
**Rooms** 5 double, all with bath (2 twin); 2 family rooms, both with bath; all rooms have central heating, phone, minibar

**Facilities** sitting-room, 2 dining-rooms
**Credit cards** MC, V
**Children** welcome
**Disabled** no special facilities
**Pets** welcome if well behaved
**Closed** never
**Proprietor** Marie-Anne Founes

# *The South*

## Auberge du Colombier

Yes, this attractive-looking hotel in Provence really does have rooms at 160F a night – but they are singles, without a garden view, in winter. Whether you'll judge the doubles with garden terraces to be good or bad value at around 600F-700F in summer will probably depend on your luck with the weather; the simple, Provençal-style bedrooms have recently been renovated; the gardens and pool are 'wonderful' (to quote a reporter).

This is an old *mas*, low and white, whose chief attraction is certainly the setting – amid tall, shady trees, with views over wooded hills towards the sea – and the outdoor facilities that go with it. There is an especially attractive terrace for summer eating, a tennis court, and plenty of space around the swimming-pool for lounging. Should the weather let you down, you'll find a pleasant dining-room with rustic furniture indoors.

Food is a source of increasing pride here, and we welcome hearing reports on this. Breakfast is good, with 'some of the best pastries we've had.' This is a useful base for seeing the sights of the Côte d'Azur – though you may be tempted to stay put instead; the Wolffs and their young staff are charming hosts.
**Nearby** St-Paul (10 km); Grasse – perfumeries.

06330 Roquefort-les-Pins
**Tel** 04.92.60.33.00
**Fax** 04.93.77.07.03
**Location** in countryside off D2085, 15 km E of Grasse, 18 km N of Cannes; with large garden and car parking
**Meals** breakfast, lunch, dinner
**Prices** rooms F-FF, apartments F-FF; breakfast F; menus FF, children F
**Rooms** 18 double (7 twin), 2 apartments, all with bath;

all rooms have phone, TV
**Facilities** 2 dining-rooms, sitting-room, bar, conference room; swimming-pool, tennis court, private night-club
**Credit cards** AE, DC, MC, V
**Children** accepted
**Disabled** no special facilities
**Pets** accepted
**Closed** Jan
**Proprietor** M. Wolff

# *The South*

**Country villa, Roussillon**

# Mas de Garrigon

'We arrived without reservation and were willingly accommodated; the Provençal-style room was very comfortable, the bathroom large and well stocked; the pool was heavenly after a long drive, and the surrounding area pleasant for strolling; dinner was wonderful, with a wide selection and large portions.' A reader reports this ideal end to a day's touring, supporting our promotion of this farmhouse-style hotel to a full entry a few years ago.

The ochre-coloured building was purpose-built by the Rech-Druarts in the late 1970s, though you might not guess it: the traditional Provençal farmhouse style has been carefully reproduced, with a multiplicity of rough-tiled roofs facing this way and that, as if built at random over the years. The hotel stands isolated among pines and scrub, facing the Lubéron hills. In front of the house is a neat sheltered pool sharing country views with the sunny private terraces of the bedrooms – done out in restrained modern style, and thoroughly equipped.

The place is run on house-party rather than conventional hotel lines. Guests are encouraged to browse in the well-stocked library or listen to classical music in the comfortable salon – before an open fire in winter. A new chef, Sylvain Bourlet, has taken over the cooking, but Mme Druart continues to be much involved in the menu-planning and daily food shopping.

**Nearby** Gordes (7 km) – château; Village des Bories (5 km).

Rte de St-Saturnin d'Apt,
Roussillon 84220 Gordes
**Tel** 04.90.05.63.22
**Fax** 04.90.05.70.01
**E-mail** mas.de.garrigon@wanadoo.fr
**Location** in countryside, on D2 3 km N of Roussillon, 7 km E of Gordes; in grounds with ample car parking
**Meals** breakfast, lunch, dinner
**Prices** rooms FF; breakfast F, menus FFF
**Rooms** 7 double (2 twin), two family rooms, all with bath; all rooms have phone, TV, minibar, terrace
**Facilities** 3 dining-rooms, bar, library, sitting-room; swimming-pool
**Credit cards** AE, DC, V
**Children** older ones accepted if well behaved **Disabled** ground-floor bedrooms
**Pets** accepted by arrangement
**Closed** restaurant only, Mon; mid-Nov to Mar
**Manager** Mme Christiane Druart

# The South

## La Grande Bastide

The Laloums, who used to run a lakeside hotel in Annecy, fell in love with this 18thC country house just outside St-Paul-de-Vence, in 1993 and set about renovating it. Their use of traditional materials like stone and wood, combined with modern design blends well; and their aim to provide their guests with the welcoming atmosphere of a private home seems to succeed. 'A five star experience at three star prices', according to one contented couple.

The building has solid, stone walls on one side and pale pink washed walls with green shutters on the other, and is set in an oasis-like garden filled with flowers and palm trees. Provençal style bedrooms in soft, pastel shades of blue, pink or apricot with bold fabrics, have prettily painted wooden or stylish wrought-iron furniture; the marble bathrooms are well-equipped. Three rooms have their own terrace leading onto the garden, others have a small balcony; most have lovely views of Saint Paul and the sea. There is a smart swimming-pool and sun terrace. No food as such, except for copious breakfasts and light snacks served on the terrace, but there are plenty of restaurants nearby.

**Nearby** Maeght Foundation – contemporary arts; Cagnes-sur-Mer (5 km); Nice (15 km); Grasse (25 km) – perfumes.

1350 Rte de la Colle, 06570
St-Paul-de-Vence
**Tel** 04.93.32.50.30
**Fax** 04.93.32.50.59
**E-mail** stpaullgb@lemel.fr
**Fax** www.la-grande-bastide.com
**Location** on hillside, 1 km from village centre; with ample car parking
**Meals** breakfast; snacks
**Prices** rooms FF-FFF; suites FFF-FFFF; breakfast F
**Rooms** 10 double, 9 with bath, 1 with shower; 2 suites, all rooms have central heating, air-conditioning, phone, TV, minibar, hairdrier
**Facilities** TV room, library
**Credit cards** AE, V
**Children** welcome
**Disabled** not suitable
**Pets** accepted
**Closed** never
**Proprietors** Brigitte Laloum

# The South

## Country villa, St-Paul-de-Vence

# Le Hameau

It's a standard pattern among readers reporting on Le Hameau that they stay longer than they planned to, which is about as clear a recommendation as you can get. Not only is it a captivating place, but also it offers very good value.

St-Paul-de-Vence is a perfectly preserved hill village. Its ramparts, rising above green terraces of vineyards and bougainvillea, provide panoramic views of the Alpes-Maritimes, and its old streets are lined by galleries, workshops and chic boutiques. Of the few hotels in and around the village, Le Hameau is one of the most desirable – an unusually stylish and notably relaxed place, overseen now by.Lisa Burlando and her husband, Carmine.

It consists of a cluster of red-roofed Provençal villas, surrounded by orange, and other fruit trees. Bedrooms are rustic in style, with beams, dark-wood furniture and rugs on red-tiled floors; they vary in size and price considerably – many have their own terrace or balcony. There is a cool, neat breakfast room, but you will be hoping to have no need of it – one of Le Hameau's great delights is breakfast (with home-made jam) taken in the large terraced garden, which accommodates a small but smart pool. Reports are welcome.

**Nearby** Maeght Foundation – contemporary arts; Cagnes-sur-Mer (5 km); Nice (15 km); Grasse (25 km) – perfumes.

---

528 Rte de la Colle 06570 St-Paul-de-Vence
**Tel** 04.93.32.80.24
**Fax** 04.93.32.55.75
**Location** one km outside village, 20 km from Nice; with gardens and ample car parking
**Meals** breakfast
**Prices** rooms FF, suites FF; breakfast F
**Rooms** 14 double; 3 suites; 11 with bath, 3 with shower; all rooms have central heating,
air-conditioning, phone, minibar, safe; some with hairdrier, satellite TV
**Facilities** sitting-room, dining-room; swimming-pool
**Credit cards** AE, MC, V
**Children** accepted if well behaved
**Disabled** no special facilities
**Pets** accepted if well behaved
**Closed** mid-Nov to 24 Dec, Jan to mid-Feb
**Managers** Lisa Burlando and Carmine Cherchi

# *The South*

## Town hotel, St-Tropez

## La Ponche

You might not think St-Tropez would be our kind of town, but La Ponche is our kind of hotel, at least when we're feeling like a treat. Tucked away in a tiny square overlooking the small fishing port and tiny beach of La Ponche (where Vadim's *And God Created Woman* was filmed, starring Brigitte Bardot), this cluster of 17thC houses offers a compelling combination of sophistication and warmth. Margerite Barbier started her fishermen's bar in 1937; later her daughter, Simone Duckstein, steadily transformed it into a stylish, arty 4-star hotel, full of personal touches. Paintings by Mme Duckstein's first husband cover the walls.

You can eat on a terrace, looking across a square to the sea, or in one of several areas indoors, including the main dining-room – unpretentious but sophisticated. The food is memorable, particularly the seafood. Bedrooms are captivating and very comfortable. Many have recently been smartly re-vamped, with stylish colour schemes and slick bathrooms. A couple of noisier bedrooms facing the street may induce you to sleep with the double-glazed windows closed and the air-conditioning on.

**Nearby** Beaches: Les Graniers (100m); La Bouillabaisse (1 km); Tahiti (4 km).

3 Rue des Remparts 83990 St-Tropez
**Tel** 04.94.97.02.53
**Fax** 04.94.97.78.61
**E-mail** hotel@laponche.com
**Location** in heart of old town, overlooking Port des Pêcheurs; with private garage and valet parking (90F)
**Meals** breakfast, lunch, dinner
**Prices** rooms FF-FFFF, suites FFF-FFFF; breakfast FF lunch FF, dinner FF-FFF

**Rooms** 11 double with bath; 2 family rooms with bath; 2 apartments; 3 suites; all have air-conditioning, central heating, phone, satellite TV, minibar, safe
**Facilities** TV room, bar, 2 dining-rooms
**Credit cards** AE, MC, V
**Children** accepted
**Disabled** access difficult
**Pets** accepted
**Closed** end Oct to end Mar
**Proprietor** Mme Barbier

# *The South*

**Seaside hotel, Les Stes-Maries-de-la-Mer**

# Mas de la Fouque ★

Prices at this casual but exclusive retreat in a lagoonside setting near the main resort of the Camargue are about as high as any in this guide. But the hotel 'provides every luxury and was well worth the money,' according to a recent visitor and his wife, who could find no fault. Its appeal lies in the peaceful, away-from-it-all atmosphere – 'from the room we could watch egrets wading and the famous white horses of the Camargue grazing'. Rooms throughout are tastefully decorated – white walls, tiled floors, timbered ceilings – and the bedrooms are the epitome of comfort, with private terraces built over the lagoon. Despite the four-star luxuries, this is very much a family-run hotel with a friendly, relaxed atmosphere. Food is excellent, with regional dishes elegantly presented; many vegetables and herbs are home-grown.
**Nearby** The Camargue; Aigues-Mortes (25 km); Arles (38 km).

Rte du Petit Rhône 13460 Les Stes-Maries-de-la-Mer
**Tel** 04.90.97.81.02
**Fax** 04.90.97.96.84
**Location** in the Camargue, 4 km NW of Les Stes-Maries-de-la-Mer; with ample car parking
**Meals** breakfast, lunch, dinner
**Prices** rooms FFFF; dinner FF-FFF
**Rooms** 10 double, all with bath and terrace (4 twin);1 family room and 2 suites, with

whirlpool bath and shower; all rooms have phone, TV, air-conditioning, minibar, fans
**Facilities** 2 sitting-rooms, bar, dining-room; tennis, swimming-pool, putting
**Credit cards** AE, DC, MC, V
**Children** welcome if well supervised
**Disabled** access easy; all on ground floor
**Pets** dogs accepted
**Closed** 2 Nov to 25 Mar
**Proprietor** Jean-Paul Cochat

# The South

## Village mansion, Seillans

## Hôtel des Deux Rocs

A captivating hotel in a captivating hill village, the hotel's setting (it is an 18th-century mansion, just outside the medieval walls) remains one of its main attractions. The streets may be very steep and cobbled, and parking may be awkward, but for most visitors that counts for little compared to the pleasure of breakfast or an evening drink beside the fountain on the shady little square in front, looking across the green valley.

Inside there are two inviting little *salons*, one serving as a bar, and a long wood-and-stone dining-room. The food is traditional and excellent. Bedrooms vary in size and standard. Those at the back of the house are rather cramped, while some of those at the front are marvellously spacious and light, with vigorous colour schemes. Mme Hirsch has retired now, but she has passed on her housekeeping skills to Marie Perks, who worked with her for four years, and now runs Deux Rocs with her husband, Graham. Food is plentiful, with some regional-based dishes, and served in the light, Provençal-style dining-room. An elderly couple, who visited were delighted by the considerate and efficient staff.

**Nearby** Lac de Saint Cassien (15 km); Gorges du Verdon (40 km); Grasse (32 km); Cannes (47 km).

Place Font d'Amont 83440 Seillans
**Tel** 04.94.76.87.32
**Fax** 04.94.76.88.68
**Location** at top of small village, 30 km W of Grasse; with terrace
**Meals** breakfast, lunch, dinner
**Prices** rooms F; breakfast F; DB&B F menus F-FF
**Rooms** 14 double (4 twin), all with bath or shower; all rooms have central heating, phone
**Facilities** dining-room, bar, sitting-room
**Credit cards** MC, V
**Children** accepted
**Disabled** no special facilities
**Pets** welcome
**Closed** never
**Proprietor** Marie and Graham Perks

# *The South*

## Château de Trigance ★

For well over 30 years now, Jean-Claude Thomas and his wife have run this characterful and comfortable hotel in the remote limestone hills that surround the dramatic Gorges du Verdon, but they show no sign of flagging. Trigance remains a welcoming port of call in a region of few villages and even fewer hotels, and the cooking by young chef Philippe Joffroy is an added bonus.

On arrival, you might be taken aback. Is this fortress perched high on a rocky hilltop really your hotel? (Yes.) And if it is, how are you going to penetrate its defences? (By climbing a steep flight of rocky stairs – don't worry, your bags will be carried up.)

Once inside, you are in the Middle Ages. Stone by stone, M. Thomas has painstakingly rebuilt his 11thC castle (for many years it served as a quarry for the local villagers); he will be delighted to show you before-and-after photographs to prove it. The impressive stone-vaulted, candle-lit dining-room, and the sitting-room below, are windowless and highly atmospheric, furnished in medieval style. Most of the bedrooms (cut into the hill) are similar, with canopied beds, antique furniture, tapestries and banners – and fine views from their windows.

**Nearby** Verdon gorge – Europe's 'Grand Canyon'.

83840 Trigance
**Tel** 04.94.76.91.18
**Fax** 04.94.85.68.99
**E-mail** trigance@relaischateaux.fr
**Location** overlooking tiny village, 10 km NW of Comps-sur-Artuby; with terrace, and private car parking
**Meals** breakfast, lunch, dinner
**Prices** rooms FF, suites FF; menus 210F-300F
**Rooms** 8 double, all with bath; 2 suites; all rooms have central heating, phone, TV
**Facilities** dining-room, sitting-room
**Credit cards** AE, DC, MC, V
**Children** welcome
**Disabled** access very difficult
**Pets** accepted
**Closed** Nov to mid-Mar
**Proprietor** Thomas family

# *The South*

## Village inn, Vallon-Pont-d'Arc

## Le Manoir du Raveyron

It sounds grand, but is nothing of the sort: this is the sort of rustic village inn that is the bedrock of French hotelkeeping – a two-fireplace Logis offering simple but satisfactory accommodation, modest prices, a warm welcome and excellent wholesome food (visit the place on a Sunday and you'll find it bursting at the seams with lunching families.) The hotel faces an ugly modern building; but the surroundings do not intrude, because the old stone building is set well back from the street, behind gates and a large and leafy courtyard-cum-garden. We get occasional reports confirming our recommendation of the Manoir, but there are new owners here, so we would welcome more.

**Nearby** Gorges de l'Ardèche; Pont d'Arc (5 km); Marzal (20 km).

Rue Henri Barbusse 07150
Vallon-Pont-d'Arc
**Tel** 04.75.88.03.59
**Fax** 04.75.37.11.12
**Location** in village on D579, 33 km S of Aubenas, 51 km NE of Alés; with garden and car parking
**Meals** breakfast, lunch, dinner
**Prices** rooms F; menus FF, children's F
**Rooms** 14 double, one single, all with shower; all rooms

have central heating
**Facilities** dining-room, sitting-room/bar
**Credit cards** MC, V
**Children** welcome
**Disabled** no special facilities
**Pets** accepted
**Closed** mid-Oct to mid-Mar
**Proprietors** Dierckx family

# *The South*

---

Converted castle, Les Arcs

# Le Logis du Guetteur ★

This 11thC fort still looks more or less as it must have done nine centuries ago. The modernised bedrooms are quiet, with lovely views, and there is a pleasant pool. But the main emphasis is on the medieval cellar restaurant and terrace, where satisfying classic dishes are served.

■ Place du Château, 83460 Les Arcs (Var) **Tel** 04.94.99.51.10 **Fax** 04.94.99.51.29 **E-mail** callegari.marion@wanadoo.fr **Meals** breakfast, lunch, dinner **Prices** rooms FF; breakfast F, menus FF **Rooms** 12, all with bath or shower, central heating, air-conditioning **Credit cards** AE, DC, MC, V **Closed** mid-Jan to mid-Feb

---

Seaside hotel, Argelès-sur-Mer

# Le Cottage

An enthusiastic readers' report restores the entry of this three-fireplace Logis, evidently much improved since its last appearance: 'We'd be pleased to go back. Bright, simple room; elegant, innovative and delicious dinner.' Pleasant garden, with pool.

■ 21 Rue Arthur-Rimbaud, 66700 Argelès-sur-Mer (Pyrénées-Orientales) **Tel** 04.68.81.07.33 **Fax** 04.68.81.59.69 **Meals** breakfast, lunch, dinner **Prices** rooms F-FF; breakfast F, lunch F, menus FF **Rooms** 32 (2 suites), all with central heating, phone, satellite TV, hairdrier, safe; some with air-conditioning **Credit cards** MC, V **Closed** 15 Oct to Apr

---

Country hotel, Auribeau

# Auberge de la Vignette Haute

This extraordinary place has been virtually rebuilt since the disastrous fire of 1986, but has the feel of a medieval farmhouse. It is filled with gleaming rustic antiques, and bedrooms are spacious, and highly individual. Pool. There is a farm menagerie nearby. Caters for parties, so you might want to avoid weekends.

■ 06810 Auribeau (Alpes-Maritimes) **Tel** 04.93.42.20.01 **Fax** 04.93.42.31.16 **Meals** breakfast, lunch, dinner **Prices** rooms FF-FFFF; breakfast FF, lunch FF-FFF, menus FFF (drinks included) **Rooms** 15, all with bath, central heating, phone, TV, minibar **Credit cards** AE, MC, V **Closed** never; restaurant only, mid-Nov to mid-Dec

---

Village hotel, Le Barroux

# Les Géraniums

Well off the beaten track, this is the sort of simple and peaceful *auberge* that is becoming increasingly hard to find. Comfortable rustic-style bedrooms and smart, modern bathrooms (some separating walls are rather thin). Attractive beamed dining-room. Cooking is uncomplicated but 'excellent'. 'Bustling', 'friendly', 'good value for money' comment several satisfied customers.

■ Le Barroux, 84330 (Vaucluse) **Tel** 04.90.62.41.08 **Fax** 04.90. 62.56.48 **Meals** breakfast, lunch, dinner **Prices** rooms F; breakfast F; DB&B F; menus F (except Sun) -FF **Rooms** 22, all with bath or shower, central heating, phone **Credit cards** AE, DC, MC, V **Closed** 15 Nov to 15 Mar

# The South

---

## Auberge de la Benvengudo

The Beaupied family's creeper-clad hotel remains compelling – and more affordable than most places in the area. Rooms have the style of a private country house: a cosy sitting-room with beams, an intimate dining-room and bedrooms with pretty curtains. Light lunches are served by the pool in the summer. Tennis and boules.

■ Vallon de l'Arcoule, 13520 Les Baux-de-Provence (Bouches-du-Rhône) **Tel** 04.90.54.32.54 **Fax** 04.90.54.42.58 **E-mail** benvengudo@aol.com **Meals** breakfast, lunch, dinner **Prices** rooms FF, suites F-FF (reductions in Mar and Oct); menus FF **Rooms** 22, all with bath or shower, central heating, air-conditioning, phone, TV **Credit cards** AE, MC, V **Closed** end Oct to early Mar; restaurant only, Sun

---

## La Gardiole

We have conflicting reports on this pink-washed hotel – one of the more modest places in this 'exclusive' area. It is furnished simply – dark-wood chairs and rugs on polished tiled floors. The regional cooking is 'not cheap but very good'. Pool. More reports, please.

■ Chemin de la Garoupe, 06160 Cap d'Antibes (Alpes-Maritimes) **Tel** 04.93.61.35.03 **Fax** 04.93.67.61.87 **Meals** breakfast, lunch, dinner **Prices** rooms FF; menus FF **Rooms** 17, all with bath or shower, central heating, air-conditioning, phone, TV, minibar, safe; **Credit cards** AE, MC, V **Closed** 31 Oct to Apr

---

## La Garoupe

New to the guide this year and in the same hands as La Gardiole (above), but a more expensive option, La Garoupe has a swimming-pool, and is situated in the middle of a pine wood, just a short distance from the beaches and the town centre.

■ Boulevard Francis Meilland, 06160 Cap d'Antibes (Alpes-Maritimes) **Tel** 04.92.93.33.33 **Fax** 04.93.67.61.87 **Meals** breakfast, lunch, dinner **Prices** rooms FF; menus FF **Rooms** 20, all with bath or shower, central heating, air-conditioning, phone, TV, minibar, safe **Credit cards** AE, MC, V **Closed** 31 Oct to Apr

---

## Domaine d'Auriac

A relaxing country house of which the primary attractions are outdoors: golf and tennis on the doorstep, a pool surrounded by beautifully manicured gardens and a dining terrace with a blissfully verdant view. But conditions indoors are comfortable too.

■ Route de Saint-Hilaire, 11009 Carcassonne (Aude) **Tel** 04.68.25.72.22 **Fax** 04.68.47.35.54 **E-mail** auriac@relaischateaux.fr **Meals** breakfast, lunch, dinner **Prices** rooms FF-FFFF; breakfast FF; menus FFF **Rooms** 26, all with bath or shower, central heating, air conditioning, phone, TV, minibar **Credit cards** AE, DC, MC, V **Closed** 15 Feb-2 Mar, 15 Nov-7 Dec; hotel & rest, Sun eve, Mon (7 Mar-31 May), Sun, Mon (17 Oct-29 May); rest only, Sat, Sun lunch (5 Jun-11 Oct), except bank holidays

# *The South*

---

Country hotel, Céret

# Le Mas Trilles

Two separate reports force this charming 17thC farmhouse to our attention – 'the hotel we enjoyed most in two very enjoyable weeks,' says one; 'like staying with friends, in a beautiful setting,' says the other. Simple, stylish furnishings in spacious rooms. Lush garden with a fair-sized heated pool. Enclosed car park.

■ Le Pont de Reynès, 66400 Céret (Pyrénées-Orientales) **Tel** 04.68. 87. 38. 37 **Fax** 04.68.87.42.62 **Meals** breakfast, dinner **Prices** rooms F-FFF; DB&B F-FF; breakfast F, menus FF **Rooms** 10, all with bath, terrace, central heating, phone, TV **Credit cards** MC, V **Closed** mid-Oct to Easter

---

Village hotel, Cotignac

# Lou Calen

The shady garden, dining terrace and pool are the key attractions of this shuttered house on the occasionally noisy village square of Cotignac. Furnished in a home-like blend of antique and rustic styles; bedrooms vary considerably in size, style and price. Cooking is simple but hearty.

■ 1 Cours Gambetta, 83850 Cotignac (Var) **Tel** 04.94.04.60.40 **Fax** 04. 94.04.76.64 **Meals** breakfast, lunch, dinner **Prices** F; DB&B F-FF; FB FF; menus FF **Rooms** 16, all with bath or shower, central heating, phone, TV **Credit cards** AE, DC, MC, V **Closed** Jan to late Mar; Wed except Jul and Aug; restaurant only Wed

---

Château hotel, Eygalières

# Mas de la Brune

A typical Provençal *mas* – a superb Renaissance mansion, now a listed historic monument, and part of the *Châteaux et Hôtels de France* group, but disappointingly lacking in atmosphere, according to a recent reporter. The breakfast-room and salon are both stone-vaulted; the bedrooms are furnished with colourful, harmonious fabrics. No restaurant or bar.

■ 13810 Eygalières-en-Provence (Bouches-du-Rhône) **Tel** 04.90.95. 90.77 **Fax** 04.90.95.99.21 **Meals** breakfast **Prices** FF; suite FFFF; breakfast F **Rooms** 10, all with bath, central heating, air-conditioning, phone, hairdrier, TV, minibar, safe **Credit cards** MC, V **Closed** Jan-Mar

---

Seaside hotel, Eze

# Château Eza

Stunning views are only one attraction of this luxury hotel perched at the top of the precipitous medieval village of Eze. Bedrooms and suites are magnificent, with priceless antiques and marble bathrooms. Dishes, which have a Provençal and Italian influence, are served in the glass dining-room or outdoor terraces.

■ Rue de la Pise, 06360 Eze (Alpes-Maritimes) **Tel** 04.93.41.12.24 **Fax** 04.93.41.16.64 **Meals** breakfast, lunch, dinner **Prices** rooms FFFF, suites FFFF; lunch FF (including wine and coffee), menus FFF **Rooms** 10, all with bath, central heating, air-conditioning, phone, TV, radio, hairdrer, video recorders **Credit cards** AE, DC, MC, V **Closed** Nov to early Apr

# *The South*

---

Country hotel, La Favède

# A l'Auberge Cévenole

Set in a circle of hills, it is peaceful and alluring. The building is a much-expanded 1950s villa in an exceptional garden with secluded corners, plus a fair-sized (unheated) swimming-pool. A rash of shepherds and shepherdesses covers many of the walls; bedrooms and bathrooms range from adequate to very comfortable.

■ La Favède, 30110 Les Salles-du-Gardon (Gard) **Tel** 04.66.34.12.13 **Fax** 04.66.34.50.50 **Meals** breakfast, lunch, dinner **Prices** rooms F-FF; breakfast F; menus FF **Rooms** 19, all with bath or shower, central heating, phone **Credit cards** MC, V **Closed** mid-Oct to Mar

---

Country inn, Gigondas

# Les Florets

This small, family-run hotel is appropriately named: floral bed-rooms, flowers on the tables and (at the right time of year) sur-rounded by a riot of blossom on the nearby hills. Food is excellent, and the patron is a winemaker.

■ Route des Dentelles, 84190 Gigondas (Vaucluse) **Tel** 04.90.65.85.01 **Fax** 04.90.65.83.80 **Meals** breakfast, lunch, dinner **Prices** rooms F; breakfast F, lunch FF, menus FF **Rooms** 15, all with central heating, phone; some have TV **Credit cards** AE, DC, MC, V **Closed** Jan, Feb; restaurant only, Wed

---

Farm guest-house, Gordes

# La Ferme de la Huppe

'Very comfortable room in a converted stable. Beautiful pool and a lovely courtyard garden. Well run by a Dutch/Swiss family. Food very good.' So ran the reader's report that earned a place for this huddle of farm buildings. Furnishings are stylishly rustic, with some antiques and tasteful fabrics. More reports, please.

■ Les Pourquiers, 84220 Gordes (Vaucluse) **Tel** 04.90.72.12.25 **Fax** 04.90.72.01.83 **Meals** breakfast, lunch (Sun only), dinner **Prices** rooms F-FF with breakfast; menus FF, children's FF **Rooms** 9, 4 with air-conditioning, all with bath, central heating, phone, TV, minibar, hairdrier **Credit cards** MC, V **Closed** early Nov to late Mar

---

Country hotel, Gordes

# Le Gordos

No restaurant, but few other drawbacks to this *mas de pierre seche*, just outside Gordes – especially if the Provençal sun shines. Most of the rooms are in outbuildings opening directly on to some part of the garden, where breakfast is served. There is tennis, as well as an attractive pool. 'Very good' service. A grander sister hotel set in Romanesque cloisters, La Bastide de Gordes, has just been opened and makes a tempting alternative. Reports welcome.

■ Rte de Cavaillon, 84220 Gordes (Vaucluse) **Tel** 04.90.72.00.75 **Fax** 04.90.72.07.00 **E-mail** hotellegordes@.pacwam.fr **Website** http://www.ProvenceGuide.com **Meals** breakfast, snacks **Prices** rooms F-FF; continental breakfast F **Rooms** 19, all with bath or shower, phone, TV; some with terrace **Credit cards** AE, V **Closed** Nov to mid-Mar

# *The South*

---

Château hotel, Lamastre

## Château d'Urbilhac

This fairy-tale château – 19thC but in Renaissance style, with round tower and steep roof – has a peaceful, elevated setting in a large park, with a good pool. The interior is rather ponderous but does not lack character or comfort. 'Good food' but 'atmosphere a little stilted' comments a visitor.

■ 07270 Lamastre (Ardèche) **Tel** 04.75.06.42.11 **Fax** 04.75.06.52.75 **Meals** breakfast, lunch, dinner **Prices** rooms F-FF; menus from FF; DB&B (obligatory in season) FF **Rooms** 12, all with bath or shower, phone **Credit cards** AE, DC, MC, V **Closed** Oct to May

---

Town hotel, Lamastre

## Hôtel du Midi

The restaurant is the heart of this hotel, serving a very successful blend of traditional and nouvelle dishes. The dining-rooms are rather plain but intimate, service helpful and friendly. Bedrooms, in a separate building a minute's walk away, are comfortably spacious and tastefully furnished.

■ Place Seignobos, 07270 Lamastre (Ardèche) **Tel** 04.75.06.41.50 **Fax** 04.75.06.49.75 **Meals** breakfast, lunch, dinner **Prices** rooms F; menus FF-FFF **Rooms** 12, all with bath or shower, central heating, phone; some have TV **Credit cards** AE, DC, MC, V **Closed** Sun evening, Mon; mid-Dec to Feb

---

Seaside hotel, Le Lavandou

## Auberge de la Calanque

This arcaded hotel overlooking the marina of Le Lavandou has no right to be here, but it comes strongly recommended by a reader – not only for the 'fantastic' view but also the 'very comfortable, airy' rooms and 'very helpful' manager. Restaurant 'L'Algue Bleue' in the hotel, but also lots of others nearby.

■ 62 Avenue du Général de Gaulle, 83980 Le Lavandou (Var) **Tel** 04.94.71.05.96 **Fax** 04.94.71.20.12 **Meals** breakfast, lunch, dinner **Prices** rooms FF-FFF; breakfast F, menu FF **Rooms** 38, all with bath/shower, central heating, phone, TV **Credit cards** AE, DC, MC, V **Closed** mid Oct to mid-Apr; restaurant only, end Oct, Wed out of season

---

Village inn, Maussane-les-Alpilles

## L'Oustaloun

This village hostellerie – a cheaper alternative to staying in nearby Les Baux – has abundant old-world charm and character. The restaurant occupies three 16thC stone-vaulted rooms, with a terrace for summer dining; food is 'simple regional fare done to perfection' says a reporter. Bedrooms are simple in style but furnished with handsome antiques.

■ Place de l'Église, 13520 Maussane-les-Alpilles (Bouches-du-Rhône) **Tel** 04.90.54.32.19 **Fax** 04.90.54.45.57 **Meals** breakfast, lunch, dinner **Prices** rooms F; breakfast F, menus FF **Rooms** 9, all with bath or shower, phone, TV **Credit cards** AE, MC, V **Closed** 1 Dec to 15 Dec, Jan to mid-Feb; restaurant only, Wed dinner, Thu lunch

# *The South*

---

Village hotel, Mirmande

# La Capitelle

A rough-stone building in a backwater setting in a walled medieval village, yet only a few minutes' drive from the autoroute – La Capitelle makes an excellent stopover. It has an air of confident good taste, with a stylishly traditional feel to the individually and boldly decorated bedrooms, and the vaulted dining-room.

■ Le Rempart, 26270 Mirmande (Drôme) **Tel** 04.75.63.02.72 **Fax** 04.75.63.02.50 **Meals** breakfast, lunch, dinner **Prices** DB&B only F (two people sharing); menus FF, children's 55F **Rooms** 11, all with bath or shower, central heating, phone **Credit cards** AE, DC, MC, V **Closed** Dec to Mar; Tue and Wed lunch

---

Country hotel, Montferrat

# La Calanco

The proprietor of one of our Burgundian entries suggests this new hotel in a 400-year-old house, tucked away from the crowds. Six 'lovely' bedrooms, tastefully decorated and thoughtfully equipped, and 'unobtrusive and considerate hospitality'.

■ Rue du docteur Rayol, 83131 Montferrat (Var) **Tel** 04.94.70.93.10 **Fax** 04.94.70.91.49 **Meals** breakfast, dinner on request **Prices** rooms F with breakfast; dinner from FF **Rooms** 6, all with bath, central heating, hairdrier **Credit cards** MC, V **Closed** never

---

Château hotel, Nans-les-Pins

# Domaine de Chateauneuf

For golfing bon viveurs, this takes some beating – a polished little hotel beside the golf course of Sainte-Baume. The four-square 17thC house, white-painted and red-roofed, stands surrounded by pines. Inside, the style of the public rooms is grandly traditional; bedrooms have a fresh, designer style. If golf is not for you, there are tennis courts and a swimming-pool.

■ R4560, 83860 Nans-les-Pins (Var) **Tel** 04.94.78.90.06 **Fax** 04.94.78.63.30 **Meals** breakfast, lunch, dinner **Prices** rooms FF-FFFF; breakfast F, menus FF **Rooms** 30, all with bath or shower, phone, satellite TV, minibar, hairdrier, air-conditioning **Credit cards** AE, DC, MC, V **Closed** mid Jan to end Feb

---

Manor house hotel, Noves

# Auberge de Noves

Luxurious and pricey (nothing like an *auberge*) isolated in the Provençal countryside. The bedrooms are beautiful and highly individual, the cooking exquisite (Michelin starred). The charming M. Lalleman displays a genuine interest in his guests despite what they are paying him.

■ 13550 Noves (Bouches-du-Rhône)**Tel** 04.90.24.28.28 **Fax** 04.90.24.28.00 **E-mail** noves@relaischateaux.fr **Website** www.aubergedenoves. com **Meals** breakfast, lunch, dinner **Prices** rooms FF-FFFF; breakfast FF, menus FF-FFF **Rooms** 19, 4 suites, all with bath, central heating, air-conditioning, phone,TV **Credit cards** AE, DC, V **Closed** mid Nov to mid Dec; restaurant only, Mon, and Tue (except public holidays) dinner

# The South

---

Country hotel, Olargues

## Domaine de Rieumegé

A reader alerted us to this rustic 17thC house in the foothills of the Haut-Languedoc national park. Good food in the barn-like restaurant, antique furnishings in the cosy sitting-room and simple bedrooms. Pool and tennis in the lush grounds.

■ Rte de St-Pons, 34390 Olargues (Hérault) **Tel** 04.67.97.73.99 **Fax** 04.67.97.78.52 **Meals** breakfast, lunch, dinner, snacks **Prices** rooms F-FF; breakfast F; menus FF (children 60F) **Rooms** 13, all with bath or shower, central heating, phone; TV on request **Credit cards** AE, DC, MC, V **Closed** Nov to Easter

---

Converted mill, Ornaisons

## Relais du Val d'Orbieu

A carefully converted old mill encircled by trees, with simply but neatly furnished rooms, mostly at ground level and opening on to a grassy courtyard. The fixed-price menu is 'excellent', the carte 'fabulous', the welcome warm. Pool and tennis. More reports, please.

■ 11200 Ornaisons (Aude) **Tel** 04.68.27.10.27 **Fax** 04.68.27.52.44 **Meals** breakfast, lunch, dinner **Prices** rooms F-FF, suites FF-FFF; breakfast F, menus FF, children's F **Rooms** 20, all with bath, central heating, phone, TV, radio, minibar, hairdrier **Credit cards** AE, DC, MC, V **Closed** 28 Nov to 5 Jan; restaurant only, lunch Nov to Feb

---

Country hotel, Pégomas

## Le Bosquet

This modern hotel with a spacious garden but no restaurant has a special place in the affections of many British and other foreign visitors – probably due to the relaxed atmosphere, coupled with the very un-Provençal prices. Pool, tennis. Our most recent reporter was 'very happy' here.

■ 74 Chemin des Perissols, 06580 Pégomas (Alpes-Maritimes) **Tel** 04.92.60.21.20 **Fax** 04.92.60.21.49 **Meals** breakfast **Prices** rooms F, studios F; breakfast F **Rooms** 24, all with bath or shower, central heating, phone **Credit cards** MC, V **Closed** Feb

---

Seaside hotel, Ile de Port-Cros

## Le Manoir

This large green-shuttered 19thC manor house stands on a lush, secluded island (a nature reserve) a few km off the south coast and is run along house-party lines. White-walled bedrooms are furnished with 19thC pieces – simple but stylish and comfortable. Good seafood. Terraces overlook the sea and surrounding fields. Swimming-pool.

■ Ile de Port-Cros, 83400 Hyères (Var) **Tel** 04.94.05.90.52 **Fax** 04.94.05.90.89 **Meals** breakfast, lunch, dinner **Prices** DB&B FF-FFF **Rooms** 23, all with bath or shower, central heating, phone **Credit cards** MC, V **Closed** Oct to Apr

# *The South*

---

Château hotel, Rochegude

## Château de Rochegude

Despite the high cost of rooms here, we cannot resist including this sumptuous château because of its wonderful setting – overlooking the vineyards of the Rhône plain – and its equally wonderful food (one Michelin star). Bedrooms are palatial. Relais & Châteaux.

■ 26790 Rochegude (Drôme) **Tel** 04.75.97.21.10 **Fax** 04.75.04.89.87 **Meals** breakfast, lunch, dinner **Prices** rooms FF-FFFF; breakfast FF, menus FF-FFF **Rooms** 29, all with bath, central heating, air-conditioning, phone, TV, most have minibar **Credit cards** AE, DC, MC, V **Closed** Mid-Jan to mid-Mar

---

Seaside hotel, St-Clair

## Hôtel Belle-Vue

This informal seaside hotel in lush, colourful gardens lives up to its name, with a wonderful view across the bay. It offers unpretentious but comfortable accommodation; bedrooms vary – the best are bright and spacious, with big new bathrooms; some have sea views. More reports welcome.

■ Blvd du Four des Maures, St-Clair, 83980 Le Lavandou (Var) **Tel** 04.94.00.45.00 **Fax** 04.94.00.45.25 **Meals** breakfast, lunch, dinner **Prices** rooms F-FF; menus FF **Rooms** 19, all with bath or shower, central heating, phone, TV **Credit cards** AE, DC, MC, V **Closed** Nov to Mar

---

Villa guest-house, St-Jean-Cap-Ferrat

## Clair Logis

It is not easy to find such a reasonably priced hotel in such an exclusive area, let alone one which has the charm of a private villa and is set in lush, secluded gardens. Bedrooms are simple (those in the annexe are not particularly spacious) and four can accommodate families. No restaurant.

■ 12 Ave Centrale, 06230 St-Jean-Cap-Ferrat (Alpes-Maritimes) **Tel** 04.93.76.04.57 **Fax** 04.93.76.11.85 **Meals** breakfast **Prices** rooms F-FF; breakfast F **Rooms** 18, all with bath, central heating, phone; most have TV, minibar **Credit cards** AE, DC, MC, V **Closed** 15 Jan to end May, mid-Nov to mid-Dec

---

Village hotel, St-Paul-de-Vence

## La Colombe d'Or

A famous, chic small hotel, distinguished by a vast collection of modern art, but also a delightfully idiosyncratic place to stay. All is simple and in exquisite 'country' taste; outside, there is a creeper-surrounded terrace, almost unchanged since Picasso and his friends were regulars. The food is unsophisticated, but that hardly matters.

■ Place de Gaulle, 06570 St-Paul-de-Vence (Alpes-Maritimes) **Tel** 04.93.32.80.02 **Fax** 04.93 .32.77.78 **Website** www.La-Colombe-dor.com **Meals** breakfast, lunch, dinner **Prices** rooms FFF-FFFF; HB from FF-FFF; breakfast F, menus FF-FFF **Rooms** 26, all with bath, some with spa baths, central heating, air-conditioning, phone, TV, radio **Credit cards** AE, DC, MC, V **Closed** early Nov to 20 Dec

# *The South*

---

Country villa, St-Paul-de-Vence

## Les Orangers

A traditional Provençal house in a fine hillside setting (good views), furnished with simple good taste and immaculately kept. In the sitting-room there are exposed beams, solid antiques, fresh flowers; most of the bedrooms have balconies or terraces. 'A lovely hotel despite the busy street,' enthuses a visitor.

■ Chemin des Fumerates, 06570 St-Paul-de-Vence (Alpes-Maritimes) **Tel** 04.93.32.80.95 **Fax** 04.93.32.00.32 **Meals** breakfast **Prices** rooms F-FF; breakfast F **Rooms** 10, all with bath, central heating, phone **Credit cards** MC, V **Closed** never

---

Country hotel, St-Pierre-dels-Forcats

## Mouli del Riu

St-Pierre is in one of the Pyrenees' major ski areas, around Font-Romeu. The Mouli – a modern and undistinguished house, despite the traditional-sounding name – is a simple and rather quirky place. It has been in the guide since 1989, but we welcome more reports.

■ St-Pierre-dels-Forcats, 66210 Mont-Louis (Pyrénées-Orientales) **Tel** 04.68.04.20.36 **Fax** 04.68.04.20.25 **Meals** breakfast, lunch, dinner **Prices** rooms F; menus F-FF **Rooms** 15, all with bath, central heating **Credit cards** AE, MC, V **Closed** Wed; Nov to mid-Dec

---

Town hotel, St-Rémy-de-Provence

## Hôtel des Arts

The shady pavement tables of this unpretentious place have long been a happy spot to sit and watch the Provençal world go by. The restaurant serves well cooked, reasonably priced, simple food (liberally laced with the region's herbs). Bedrooms seem secondary but are neatly done out in rustic style.

■ 30 Blvd Victor-Hugo, 13210 St-Rémy-de-Provence (Bouches-du- Rhône) **Tel** 04.90.92.08.50 **Fax** 04.90.92.55.09 **Meals** breakfast, lunch, dinner **Prices** rooms F; menus FF **Rooms** 17, all with central heating, phone **Credit cards** AE, MC, V **Closed** Feb; restaurant, Tue

---

Château hotel, St-Rémy-de-Provence

## Château des Alpilles

An elegant, upright 19thC manor house offering an atmosphere of gracious living combined with the facilities of a modern luxury hotel. Bedrooms are spacious and furnished with antiques, the bathrooms marble and modern. Food is served by the swimming-pool in summer.

■ Route Départementale 31, 13210 St-Rémy-de-Provence (Bouches-du Rhône) **Tel** 04.90.92.03.33 **Fax** 04.90.92.45.17 **E-mail** chateau.alpilles@wanadoo.fr **Meals** breakfast, dinner **Prices** rooms FF-FFF, suites FFFF; breakfast F, menu FF **Rooms** 20, all with bath, central heating, air-conditioning, phone, satellite TV, radio, minibar **Credit cards** AE, DC, MC, V **Closed** 7 Jan to 17 Feb

# *The South*

---

Country hotel, St-Rémy-de-Provence

## Domaine de Valmouriane

The McHugos offer an indulgent experience at their own charming farmhouse, stylishly converted into a hotel in the late 1980s. It is beautifully furnished in rustic style, and the flowery gardens contain a smart pool. Good, inventive food.

■ Petite Route des Baux, 13210 St-Rémy-de-Provence (Bouches-du-Rhône) **Tel** 04.90.92.44.62 **Fax** 04.90.92.37.32 **E-mail** domdeval@wanadoo.fr **Website** www.valmouriane.com **Meals** breakfast, lunch, dinner **Prices** rooms FF-FFF; breakfast F, menus FF **Rooms** 14, all with bath, central heating, air-conditioning, phone, TV, minibar, hairdrier **Credit cards** AE, DC, MC, V **Closed** never

---

Farm guest-house, St-Rémy-de-Provence

## Mas des Carassins

One of the few hotels occupying an authentic mas: a farmhouse built in 1854, mellow and peaceful, set in large and rambling gardens. Almost all the bedrooms have views of the rocky Alpilles and there is a cosy sitting-room with books and plenty of local information, with advice from the friendly Ripert family.

■ 1 Chemin Gaulois, 13210 St-Rémy-de-Provence (Bouches-du-Rhône) **Tel** 04.90.92.15.48 **Fax** 04.90.92.63.47 **Meals** breakfast; simple evening meal on request **Prices** rooms F; breakfast F **Rooms** 15, all with bath, central heating, phone **Credit cards** MC, V **Closed** Nov to Apr

---

Village inn, St-Restitut

## Auberge des Quatres Saisons

The vine-clad auberge is a fascinating conversion of ancient houses in a backwater perched village, preserving many of the old stone walls. Bedrooms are quiet, rather dark and cosy – with heavy patterns and furniture, in Provençal style. Good regional fare.

■ Place de l'Eglise, 26130 St-Restitut (Drôme) **Tel** 04.75.04.71.88 **Fax** 04.75.04.70.88 **Meals** breakfast, lunch, dinner **Prices** rooms F; menus FF **Rooms** 10, all with bath or shower, phone **Credit cards** AE, DC, MC, V **Closed** Jan; Sat lunch

---

Seaside villa, St-Tropez

## Le Yaca

This smart little hotel has been cleverly converted from three 200-year-old buildings, using a confusing mix of styles, but with 'rustic-chic' predominating. Bedrooms are furnished with antiques, simply decorated in a typical southern style, but with all the comforts.

■ 1 Blvd d'Aumale, 83990 St-Tropez (Var) **Tel** 04.94.97.11.79 **Fax** 04.94.97.58.50 **Meals** breakfast **Prices** rooms FFFF, suite FFFF; breakfast F **Rooms** 23, all with bath, central heating, air-conditioning, phone, TV, radio, minibar **Credit cards** AE, DC, MC, V **Closed** mid-Oct to Easter

# *The South*

---

Converted abbey, Salon-de-Provence

# L'Abbaye de Sainte-Croix

A former monastery rescued from ruin in 1969 by the Bossard family. Superb views; cosy vaulted sitting-room with huge open fireplace; restrained solid furnishings. Bedrooms, some former monks' cells, vary in size. Food is a highlight – Michelin star.

■ Route du Val de Cuech, 13300 Salon-de-Provence (Bouches-du-Rhône) **Tel** 04.90.56.24.55 **Fax** 04.90.56.31.12 **Meals** breakfast, lunch, dinner **Prices** rooms FF-FFFF; breakfast FF; menus FFF **Rooms** 25, all with bath or shower, central heating, phone, TV, minibar **Credit cards** AE, DC, MC, V **Closed** Nov to mid-Mar; restaurant only, Mon, Thu lunch

---

Village hotel, Séguret

# Table du Comtat

Built against the hillside above a tiny, unspoilt medieval village, this hotel enjoys wonderful views. The much modernized interior is light, airy and spacious, with attractive fabrics and furniture. Excellent, eclectic food, meriting a *toque* from Gaullt-Millau. Pool.

■ Séguret, 84110 Vaison-la-Romaine (Vaucluse) **Tel** 04.90.46.91.49 **Fax** 04.90.46.94.27 **Meals** breakfast, lunch, dinner **Prices** rooms F-FF; menus FF-FFF **Rooms** 8, all with bath, central heating, phone, TV **Credit cards** AE, DC, MC, V **Closed** Feb, 23 Nov to 11 Dec; restaurant only, Tue eve, Wed (except Apr to end Dec)

---

Country hotel, Tourtour

# La Bastide de Tourtour

This modern but traditional-style hotel offers comfort and attentive service (it is in the Châteaux et Hôtels de France group), and the food is excellent, if not in the first rank. For many, the key attraction is the secluded setting, high up amid pine forests. Swimming-pool.

■ Rte de Draguignan, Tourtour, 83690 Salernes (Var) **Tel** 04.94.70.57.20 **Fax** 04.94.70.54.90 **Meals** breakfast, lunch, dinner **Prices** rooms F-FFF; lunch FF, menus FF-FFF **Rooms** 25, all with bath, phone, TV, minibar, safe **Credit cards** AE, DC, V **Closed** never

---

Manor house hotel, Tourtour

# L'Auberge Saint-Pierre

This 16thC manor house is a peaceful, unpretentious retreat run as a welcoming hotel by the helpful Marcellins. The public rooms preserve something of a medieval feel; the spacious bedrooms have been refurbished. Food relies heavily on produce of the home farm, and is served on the terrace in good weather. There is tennis, archery, cycling and fishing, as well as a pool and sauna.

■ Tourtour, 83690 Salernes (Var) **Tel** 04.94.70.57.17 **Fax** 04.94.70. 59. 04 **Meals** breakfast, lunch, dinner **Prices** rooms F-FF; breakfast F; DB&B F; menus FF **Rooms** 16, all with bath or shower, central heating, phone **Credit cards** V **Closed** Oct to end Mar; restaurant only, Wed

# *The South*

---

Restaurant with rooms, Valence

## Pic

Despite the death in 1992 of Jacques Pic, this remains, under daughter Anne, one of the best restaurants in the country – yet it is delightfully free of any snobby atmosphere. The good news is that the Pic family have added another small restaurant, the Auberge du Pin, and 10 more comfortable bedrooms. Pool; garage; free shuttle from Valence station.

■ 285 Ave Victor-Hugo, 26001 Valence (Drôme) **Tel** 04.75.44.15.32. **Fax** 04.75.40.96.03 **E-mail** pic@relaischateaux.fr **Website** www.pic-valence.com **Meals** breakfast, lunch, dinner **Prices** rooms FF-FFFF; breakfast FF, menus FF-FFF **Rooms** 15, all with bath, central heating, air-conditioning, phone, TV, safe **Credit cards** AE, DC, MC, V **Closed** restaurant only, Sun eve, Mon and Tue lunch Nov to Mar ; 2 weeks Jan

---

Village hotel, Vénasque

## Auberge la Fontaine

First an excellent restaurant, then five lovely suites, then in 1993 an alternative 'bistro' – the Soelkes show no sign of flagging. The rooms in this 18thC village house are decorated in rustic style – stone-flagged floors, wooden furniture, dried flowers.

■ Place de la Fontaine, Vénasque, 84210 Carpentras (Vaucluse) **Tel** 04.90.66.02.96 **Fax** 04.90.66.13.14 **E-mail** fontvenasq@aol.com **Meals** breakfast, lunch (in bistro), dinner **Prices** rooms FF; breakfast F, lunch FF, dinner FF **Rooms** 5, all with bath, central heating, air-conditioning, kitchen, phone, TV, radio, hairdrier, terrace **Credit cards** MC, V **Closed** restaurant only, Wed eve; bistro only, Sun eve, Mon

---

Town villa, Vence

## La Roseraie

This 'belle époque' villa has undergone considerable refurbishment, including most recently an orangery-style reception area. The decorative wrought-iron, made by local craftsmen, is a particular favourite. Bedrooms, decorated in Provençal style, are 'rather small but comfortable'. Splendid views, and the place itelf is 'an oasis of peace'. Sculpture displays round the pretty pool; art exhibits in the house. There is a new proprietor, so reports please.

■ Ave Henri Giraud, 06140 Vence (Alpes-Maritimes) **Tel** 04.93.58.02.20 **Fax** 04.93.58.99.31 **Meals** breakfast **Prices** rooms F-FF; breakfast F **Rooms** 14, all with bath, central heating, phone, TV, radio, minibar, hairdrier **Credit cards** AE, MC, V **Closed** never

---

Town hotel, Villeneuve-lès-Avignon

## Hôtel de l'Atelier

This old town house has been sympathetically restored – original stone walls much in evidence – with careful attention to detail. There is a picturesque courtyard at the back, enclosed by a jumble of old buildings – an ideal place in which to sit and drink muscat.

■ 5 Rue de la Foire, 30400 Villeneuve-lès-Avignon (Gard) **Tel** 04.90.25. 01.84 **Fax** 04.90.25 .80.06 **Meals** breakfast **Prices** rooms F; breakfast F **Rooms** 19, all with bath or shower, central heating, phone; some have TV **Credit cards** AE, DC, MC, V **Closed** Nov to Dec

# The South

---

Village hotel, Villeneuve-lès-Avignon

# Hostellerie la Magnaneraie

Much up-graded in recent years, the Magnaneraie is a mellow stone house in a well-heeled residential corner of Villeneuve-lès-Avignon. The Prayals pride themselves on the place's easy-going elegance, but we don't rate this very high on personal approach.

■ Rue du Camp-de-Bataille, 30400 Villeneuve-lès-Avignon (Gard)
**Tel** 04.90.25.11.11 **Fax** 04.90.25.46.37 **Meals** breakfast, lunch, dinner
**Prices** rooms F-FFF; suites FFF-FFFF; breakfast F; menus FF **Rooms** 25,
all with bath, central heating, air-conditioning phone, cable TV, minibar;
some rooms have private terrace **Credit cards** AE, DE, MC, V
**Closed** never

# Corsica

Corsica isn't our strong point. The reports we get from readers on Corsican hotels can be counted on the fingers of one hand.

**Contenders in Corsica**
**Pioggiola, Auberge de l'Aghjola** 04.95.61.90.48 Family-run creeper-clad inn; beams and painted furniture.
**Porticcio, Le Maquis** 04.95.25.05.55 Sophisticated fairly pricey (but special) hotel by water's edge.
**St-Florent, Hôtel Bellevue** 04.95.37.00.06 Chic, freshly decorated modern hotel with sea views and ambitious food.

---

Seaside hotel, Barcaggio

# La Giraglia

The rooms in this simple creeper-covered stone building are no more than adequate, but the position overlooking the sea is superb and the atmosphere is relaxed and welcoming. This is a lovely and wild part of Corsica, well off the beaten tourist track. We would welcome more reports.

■ Barcaggio, 20275 Essa (Corse) **Tel** 04.95.35.60.54 **Fax** 04.95.35.65.92 **Meals** breakfast **Prices** rooms F including breakfast **Rooms** 14, all with central heating, phone; most with shower **Credit cards** not accepted **Closed** 30 Sep to 1 Apr

---

Country hotel, Calvi

# La Signoria

A very welcome addition to our thin Corsica section – a 17thC country house in lush grounds, furnished and decorated with stylish simplicity. Inventive and excellent food is served in a beamed, ochre-washed room or beneath palms on the terrace overlooking the smart pool. There is also tennis and a steam room.

■ Route de la Forêt de Bonifato, 20260 Calvi (Corse) **Tel** 04.95.65.93.00 **Fax** 04.95.65.38.77 **Meals** breakfast, lunch (except Jul/Aug), dinner **Prices** rooms FF-FFFF; breakfast FF; meals FF-FFF **Rooms** 10, all with bath, air-conditioning, phone, hairdrier, TV, minibar, safe **Credit cards** AE, MC, V **Closed** Nov to Mar

---

Village inn, Monticell

# A Pasturella

Recent reports confirm the attractions of this modest little 'gem' on the square of a sleepy hill village, its bar at the very heart of local life. Bedrooms are pretty and mostly spacious, with terraces and balconies giving views. Food is wholesome and generous.

■ Monticello, 20220 l'Ile-Rousse (Corse) **Tel** 04.95.60.05.65 **Fax** 04.95.60.21.78 **Meals** breakfast, lunch, dinner **Prices** rooms F; menu FF **Rooms** 12, all with bath or shower, phone **Credit cards** DC , MC, V **Closed** Nov; restaurant only, Sun dinner Dec to Mar

# Index of hotel names

In this index, hotels are arranged in order of the most distinctive part of their name; very common prefixes such as 'Auberge', 'Hôtel', 'Hostellerie' and 'Le/La/Les' are omitted, but more significant elements such as 'Château' are retained.

# Index of hotel names

# Index of hotel names

# Index of hotel names

# *Index of hotel locations*

In this index, hotels are arranged by the name of the city, town or village they are in or near. Hotels located in a very small village may be indexed under the name of a larger place nearby.

# Index of hotel locations

# Index of hotel locations